2nd Workshop on Information Extraction from Scientific Publications (WIESP 2023)

Nusa Dua, Indonesia
1 November 2023

ISBN: 978-1-7138-9007-2

Printed from e-media with permission by:

Curran Associates, Inc.
57 Morehouse Lane
Red Hook, NY 12571

Some format issues inherent in the e-media version may also appear in this print version.

Printed with permission by Curran Associates, Inc. (2024)

For permission requests, please contact the Association for Computational Linguistics at the address below.

Association for Computational Linguistics
209 N. Eighth Street
Stroudsburg, Pennsylvania 18360

Phone: 1-570-476-8006
Fax: 1-570-476-0860

acl@aclweb.org

Additional copies of this publication are available from:

Curran Associates, Inc.
57 Morehouse Lane
Red Hook, NY 12571 USA
Phone: 845-758-0400
Fax: 845-758-2633
Email: curran@proceedings.com
Web: www.proceedings.com

IJCNLP-AACL 2023

The 2nd Workshop on Information Extraction from Scientific Publications

Proceedings of WIESP 2023

November 1, 2023

The IJCNLP-AACL organizers gratefully acknowledge the support from the following sponsors.

Platinum

Gold

Silver

Order copies of this and other ACL proceedings from:

Association for Computational Linguistics (ACL)
209 N. Eighth Street
Stroudsburg, PA 18360
USA
Tel: +1-570-476-8006
Fax: +1-570-476-0860
acl@aclweb.org

2nd WIESP at IJCNLP-AACL 2023

Building on the success of the First WIESP at AACL-IJCNLP 2022, the Second Workshop on Information Extraction from Scientific Publications (WIESP) provided a platform for researchers to foster discussion and research on information extraction, mining, generation, and knowledge discovery from scientific publications using Natural Language Processing and Machine Learning techniques. Much technological change happened in one year (since the 1st WIESP), especially with Generative Artificial Intelligence research. We incorporated a few additional topics to stay abreast with the latest developments and research in the community.

The Workshop on Information Extraction from Scientific Publications (WIESP) is a forum to foster discussion and research using Natural Language Processing and Machine Learning. In this space, leading professionals, organizations, early career researchers and students can cooperate towards building the algorithms, models, and tools that will pave the way for machine comprehension of science in the future.

WIESP 2023 received 22 submissions, of which 17 were accepted (15 papers and 2 shared task system papers).

WIESP 2023 was held on November 1st 2023.

Organizing Committee

Tirthankar Ghosal, Oak Ridge National Laboratory, USA
Felix Grezes, Center for Astrophysics | Harvard & Smithsonian, USA
Thomas Allen, Center for Astrophysics | Harvard & Smithsonian, USA
Sergi Blanco-Cuaresma, Center for Astrophysics | Harvard & Smithsonian, USA; and Laboratoire de Recherche en Neuroimagerie, University Hospital (CHUV) and University of Lausanne (UNIL), Lausanne, Switzerland
Alberto Accomazzi, Center for Astrophysics | Harvard & Smithsonian, USA
Kelly Lockhart, Center for Astrophysics | Harvard & Smithsonian, USA

Program Committee

Daniel Acuna
Akiko Aizawa
Thomas Allen
Akhil Pandey Akella
Hamed Alhoori
Atilla Kaan Alkan
Hardik Arora
Premjith B
Arne Binder
Sergi Blanco-Cuaresma
Elena Callegari
Jennifer D'Souza
Vignesh Edithal
Sergey Feldman
Madhusudan Ghosh
Felix Grezes
Hen-Hsen Huang
Daisuke Ikeda
Sarvnaz Karimi
Harksoo Kim
Sandeep Kumar
Asheesh Kumar
Xiangci Li
Kelly Lockhart
Faith Mutinda
Sujit Pal
Ted Pedersen
Rajesh Piryani
Trinita Roy
Atriya Sen
Grishma Sharma
Neil Smalheiser
Wojtek Sylwestrzak
Rohan Tondulkar

Shuntaro Yada
Pierre Zweigenbaum

We thank our program committee members for their critical evaluation and contribution to shape the WIESP 2023 program.

Table of Contents

Investigating the Impact of Syntax-Enriched Transformers on Quantity Extraction in Scientific Texts

Necva Bölücü, Maciej Rybinski, Stephen Wan
CSIRO Data61
{necva.bolucu;maciek.rybinski;stephen.wan}@csiro.au

Abstract

Measurement extraction is an information extraction subtask focused on extracting quantities and their dependent entities within a given scientific text. Quantity extraction is the first and most important step in measurement extraction. Most existing approaches model the problem as a sequence-labeling task using pre-trained language models (PLMs). However, none of the existing systems have utilised explicit syntactic knowledge to extend the PLM-based modeling. We propose a syntax-enriched extension by integrating dependency tree representations as syntactic knowledge into transformer-based language models to address the task of quantity extraction. We apply our approach to a range of established transformer-based models to evaluate our approach and analyze its impact in experiments on scientific literature datasets. Our experimental results and in-depth analysis show that our approach, syntax-enriched RoBERTa, outperforms the other models, even in situations with scarce training data in the scientific domain. The results demonstrate the adaptability of the proposed model to the tasks, especially useful in low-resource scenarios.[1]

1 Introduction

Current growth rates in scientific publishing increase the interest in extracting information from scientific documents to provide scientists with improved methods for organising, indexing, and querying the vast existing literature (Nasar et al., 2018; Weston et al., 2019; Hong et al., 2021). *Information extraction* (IE) is a task enabling extracting and organising information from large amounts of data from unstructured sources. IE includes several subtasks, such as *named entity recognition* (NER), *relation extraction* (RE), and *relation classification* (RC). Properties specific to scientific documents result in IE subtasks tailored for IE in the scientific literature and applied in various domains, e.g., biomedical (Lewis et al., 2020; Zhang, 2021; Gérardin et al., 2023) or chemistry (Rocktäschel et al., 2012; Luo et al., 2018; He et al., 2020).

One such example is the subtask of extracting measurements and their contexts, as scientific research often relies on precise measurements for the reproducibility of experimental methods. The reproducibility supports extending and building on top of others' work, thus promoting scientific progress. The automatic detection of the measurements and their contexts in scientific texts is a key enabling factor for producing high-quality quantity-centric search systems for scientific literature (Liu et al., 2017; Kang et al., 2017; Kononova et al., 2019).

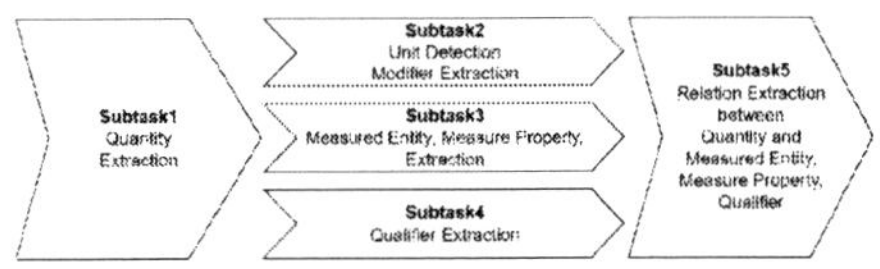

Figure 1: Subtasks of MeasEval shared task (Harper et al., 2021).

Measurement extraction (ME) is a type of IE subtask for scientific documents focused on the identification of quantities and related information and classification of relations between identified quantities and related entities (Göpfert et al., 2022). A large body of research in ME is centered around MeasEval (Harper et al., 2021), a shared task that also introduced a new annotated ME dataset consisting of scientific articles from different scholarly domains. MeasEval decomposes the ME into five finer subtasks, presented in Figure 1.

- *Subtask 1: Quantity Extraction* is the task of identifying quantities—numeric values with corresponding (optional) units of measurement and modifiers[2]. For example, in an expression 'over 5 tonnes', 5 is the numeric

[1]The code is publicly available at `https://github.com/adalin16/syntax_NER`.

[2]Modifiers are tokens in the quantity span that modify the

Proceedings of the 2nd Workshop on Information Extraction from Scientific Publications, pages 1–13
Nov 1, 2023. ©2023 Association for Computational Linguistics

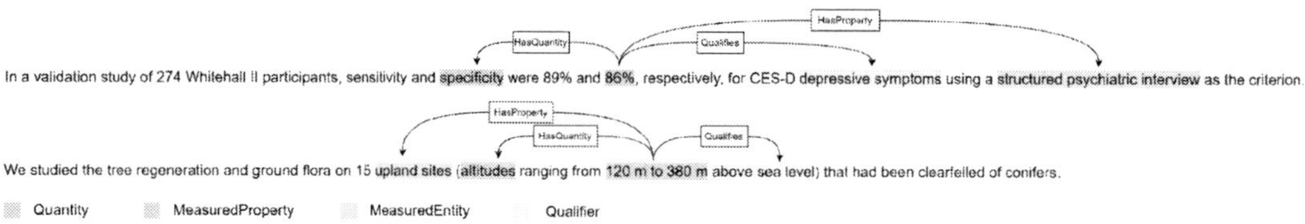

Figure 2: Sample sentences with annotation of quantity and dependent entities.

value, 'tonnes' is the unit of measurement, and 'over' is the modifier.

- *Subtask 2: Unit Detection & Modifier Extraction* has two sub-problems. Unit detection is the task of extraction of units from extracted quantities and Modifier Extraction is the task of classifying quantities into different modifiers (e.g., 'count', 'range', 'mean', etc.).

- *Subtask 3: Measured Entity (ME) & Measured Property (MP) Extraction* is the task of extracting dependent entities that elaborate the extracted quantity (e.g., ME: 'GHQ symptom caseness', 'response categories', etc., MP: 'sensitive', 'scores', 'transit depths', etc.).

- *Subtask 4: Qualifier (QUAL) Extraction* is the task of extracting dependent entities which qualify the extracted quantity (e.g., 'after 13 passages', 'orbits the planet' etc.).

- *Subtask 5: Relation Extraction* is the task of extracting relations ('has quantity', 'has property', 'qualifies') between extracted quantities and dependent entities ('measured properties', 'measured entities', 'qualifiers') and their relations to the extracted quantities.

Here, we focus on the first subtask—quantity extraction—which is required for the other subtasks: its results are directly used for subtasks 2, 3, and 4. Finally, the results of subtask 1 and 4 are used for subtask 5. This highlights the importance of quantity extraction to the overall success of the ME models, as errors incurred at this stage are propagated downstream (Göpfert et al., 2022). Sample sentences for quantities and dependent entities are given in Figure 2.

Existing methods for quantity extraction model the problem as a sequence labeling task and usually fine-tune pre-trained language models (PLMs) (Davletov et al., 2021a; Gangwar et al., 2021b). However, such models do not capture some of the syntactic relations and long-range word dependencies, which have been proven to have a positive impact on natural language understanding (Du et al., 2021). So far, the integration of linguistic knowledge and graph structures into transformer-based PLMs has been proposed for various natural language processing (NLP) problems (e.g., *Machine Translation* (MT) (Bugliarello and Okazaki, 2019; Akoury et al., 2019), *Semantic Textual Similarity* (STS) (Peng et al., 2021)), but not for quantity extraction.

Here, we propose to improve the self-attention mechanism of PLMs to incorporate syntactic information for quantity extraction – Syntax-Enriched Quantity Extraction (SEQE) (§3.2)[3]. Similar to previous studies that used dependency tree representation as syntactic information (Bugliarello and Okazaki, 2019; Guo et al., 2021), we use the dependency tree representation of the input sentence to generate syntax-enriched local attention of the PLM encoder, which provides structural information representing human understanding of the text. Since there are numerous PLMs pre-trained on different NLP data and the size of these models varies in terms of the number of parameters, we test our proposed model SEQE with different PLMs: BERT (Devlin et al., 2019), RoBERTa (Liu et al., 2019), and LUKE (Yamada et al., 2020) (see §4). Our method is simple yet effective, improves the task of quantity extraction, and achieves performance gains over baseline PLMs.

Overall, we provide a detailed analysis with prediction interpretation and error analysis pointing to future research directions in measurement extraction (see §5).

2 Related Work

Quantity Extraction In the literature, quantity extraction is often solved as a sequence label-

meaning of the quantity, for example, 'greater than', 'over', 'fewer than'.

[3] "Syntax-enriched" and "syntax-aware" are used interchangeably in the literature implying integration of syntactic information into the systems.

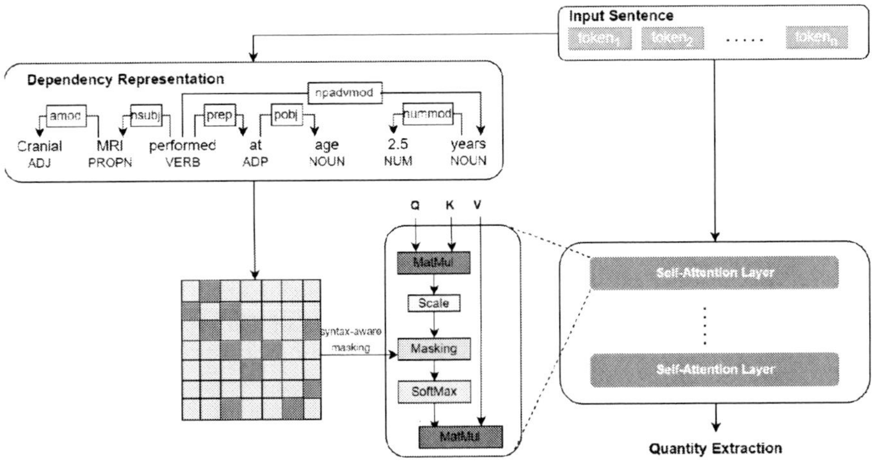

Figure 3: The overall Architecture of SEQE. Note that the syntax mask is generated from the dependency tree representation of the input, where m=1 is used for the sample sentence and the dark green color in the mask represents the value '1' and the light-green color represents the value '0'.)

ing problem using several methods, such as Conditional Random Field (CRF) (Foppiano et al., 2019), Bidirectional Long Short-Term Memory (BiLSTM) (Huang et al., 2015), transformer-based pre-trained language models (PLMs) with fine-tuning (Davletov et al., 2021b; Cao et al., 2021). Most of the systems submitted to the MeasEval shared task use PLMs for the problem. Davletov et al. (2021b) fine-tune LUKE NER model (Yamada et al., 2020) for quantity extraction as sequence labeling problem. Cao et al. (2021) apply a cascaded approach, extracting quantities via RoBERTa (Liu et al., 2019) encoder with an ensembling of PointerNet (Vinyals et al., 2015) and a CRF layers on top of the encoder. Gangwar et al. (2021a) extract quantities using SciBERT with a CRF layer for the sequence labeling problem (SciBERT (Beltagy et al., 2019) is another BERT variant pre-trained on papers from the scientific corpus (semanticscholar.org)). Karia et al. (2021) use a similar approach with BioBERT (Lee et al., 2020)—a BERT variant pre-trained on a biomedical corpus from a BERT checkpoint.

Syntax-Enriched Models Recently, models that integrate syntactic information—so-called syntax-enriched models—have been applied to various NLP problems, such as machine translation (Bastings et al., 2017; Nguyen et al., 2020), semantic role labeling (Wang et al., 2019; Marcheggiani and Titov, 2019), and question answering (Schlichtkrull et al., 2020). These models have gained attention due to their enhanced ability to capture information over long distances, especially between discontinuous constituents (Wang and Li, 2022). In contrast to these models, we incorporate the syntactic information using a distance-based masking approach and use it to alter the activation propagation in the attention heads of PLMs to improve the quantity extraction task. There are also studies that integrate syntactic information into the attention mechanisms of transformer-based models such as LISA (Linguistically-Informed Self-Attention) (Strubell et al., 2018) and Syntax-BERT (Bai et al., 2021). These models inject syntactic information by using only syntactic parents of tokens as masks to the one attention head (Strubell et al., 2018), or by generating 3 masks (parent, child, and sibling masks) from the syntax tree and injecting them into the attention mechanism of PLMS by utilising topical attention layer to aggregate task-oriented representations. Both of these approaches are different from the method proposed in this paper.

Although there is no attempt in the literature to extract quantities using syntactic information, there are studies that show promise in using syntactic information for RE (Tian et al., 2021, 2022; Sun and Grishman, 2022) and NER (Aguilar and Solorio, 2019; Nie et al., 2020; Xiong et al., 2022). However, these approaches do not integrate syntactic information in the attention-level of transformer-based PLMs.

3 Method

In this section, we present the proposed model that exploits syntactic information for quantity extraction. We base our model on the architecture of Transformer (Vaswani et al., 2017) and integrate syntactic information into the encoder with a syntax-enriched local attention mechanism for quantity extraction task. This method allows to incorporate syntactical constraints and long-range syntactic word dependencies into the sentence with syntactic representation without external information for the problem.

First, we describe the self-attention mechanism in Section 3.1. Then, we introduce the syntax-enriched quantity extraction model (SEQE) in Section 3.2.

3.1 Preliminaries

Self-Attention Transformer architecture introduced by Vaswani et al. (2017), has become ubiquitous in modern NLP, as it offers significant effectiveness improvements on many problems. The transformer consists of encoder-decoder blocks and uses stacked self-attention to encode contextual information for input tokens in which three components of queries $\mathbf{Q}$, keys $\mathbf{K}$, and values $\mathbf{V}$ are learned during training.

Attention is described as a mapping between $\mathbf{Q}$, and ($\mathbf{K}$, $\mathbf{V}$) pairs to obtain an output vector. We describe the simplest form, single-head attention $\mathbf{A}$ which is computed using the *scalar-dot product* between a query and the keys, followed by its softmax to obtain the weights of values:

$$\mathbf{A}(\mathbf{Q},\mathbf{K},\mathbf{V}) = softmax(\frac{\mathbf{Q}\mathbf{K}^T}{\sqrt{d}})\mathbf{V}, \quad (1)$$

where d is the dimension of keys which is used as a scaling factor in the equation. We note that, in practice, the attention matrix is a series of such attention heads, called multi-head attention, given by $MultiHead(Q,K,V) = concat(head_1,\cdots,head_h)W^O$.

3.2 Syntax-Enriched Quantity Extraction

As mentioned earlier, one limitation of PLMs is that they take a sequence of tokens as input without explicitly incorporating structural information. Some previous works have tried to induce syntactic structure into the self-attention layer (Strubell et al., 2018; Bai et al., 2021). Syntax-Enriched Quantity Extraction (SEQE) is designed to incorporate syntactic information in the self-attention layer of transformer-based PLM for quantity extraction task. The overall architecture of the proposed model is illustrated in Figure 3. As shown in the figure, we generate a syntax mask for the input sentence in a preprocessing step: (1) the dependency tree representation of the input sentence is generated by an external parser, (2) the dependency matrix is extracted from the dependency tree representation given as a graph $G = (V, E, X)$, where V is the set of nodes (skipping ROOT node), E is the set of labeled edges representing dependency relations (without labels), and X is the set of tokens of the sentence. Each token x_i is mapped to a node v_i and the distance, from node v_i to v_j is denoted by $dis(v_i, v_j)$) and $D(i,j) = min\ dis(v_k, v_j),\ k \in [i-1, i+2]$. (3) syntax mask is generated using a dependency matrix as follows:

$$\mathbf{M}_{ij} = \begin{cases} 0 & D(i,j) \leq m \\ -\infty & otherwise, \end{cases} \quad (2)$$

where m is a distance threshold hyperparameter for syntax mask that needs to be fine-tuned.

Next, the sentence is embedded similarly to a standard PLM and given as input to the self-attention layer with a syntax-enriched local attention mechanism. Syntax-enriched local attention, where tokens can attend to other tokens if they are close in the dependency tree representation (m), is computed as follows for a given query $\mathbf{Q}$ and key $\mathbf{K}$:

$$softmax(\frac{\mathbf{Q}\mathbf{K}^T}{\sqrt{d}} + \mathbf{M})\mathbf{V} \quad (3)$$

4 Experiments

4.1 Task

Quantity Extraction task is based on the extraction of quantities $q_1, \cdots, q_m$ from a given sentence $s = w_1, \cdots, w_n$ where a quantity q_i is a sequence of words. The problem can be formulated as a token-level classification task in which the model takes a set of input-output pairs $Z = \{(w_1, y_1), \cdots (w_n, y_n)\}$ and try to classify using a function $f : X \rightarrow R$ that maps given words into a set of labels $y \in Y$ (B-Quantity, I-Quantity, O), BIO tags for NER problem.

4.2 Datasets

We use two English datasets for the quantity extraction task:

- **MeasEval**[4] (Harper et al., 2021) dataset contains 110 articles from 10 different subject areas.
- **Grobid (GeneRation Of BIbliographic Data)**[5] (Foppiano et al., 2019) dataset is composed of 32 scientific publications and 3 patents, a total 35 documents, collected across different domains and annotated for quantity and unit extraction.

Table 1 reports the statistics of the datasets.

Dataset	Train	Valid	Test	Avg l
MeasEval	1,284	427	755	8.37
Grobid	5,669	-	1,285	8.68

Table 1: Number of sentences in each dataset with avg l which denotes the average length of quantities

4.3 Evaluations

Our method, SEQE, is an extension of PLMs. For this reason, we use base versions of the PLMs and LISA (Strubell et al., 2018)[6] as the baselines to compare our model against. Conceptually, LISA (also an 'add-on' to other PLMs) is the closest method to SEQE. In LISA syntactic information is injected into only a single attention head, where each token is attending only to its syntactic parent. We run experiments on both datasets, with all models fine-tuned on training subsets. We use the following PLMs in the experiments: BERT (Devlin et al., 2019), RoBERTa (Liu et al., 2019), and LUKE (Yamada et al., 2020). We use two variants of each PLM, where the '-base' variant consists of 12 layers, 12 attention heads, and 768 hidden dimensions, while the '-large' variant has 24 layers, 16 attention heads, and 1024 hidden dimensions.

For both experiments, in addition to the baseline PLMs (baseline models), we also compare our results with state-of-the-art models: LIORI (Davletov et al., 2021a) and Grobid (Foppiano et al., 2019).

Evaluation Metric As an evaluation metric, in addition to the token-level macro F_1 score, we also used the macro F_1 score from Seqeval (Nakayama, 2018), span-level evaluation metric, since we try to solve quantity extraction problem as a sequence labeling problem and the important label is only quantity.

[4]https://github.com/harperco/MeasEval

[5]https://github.com/kermitt2/grobid-quantities

[6]https://github.com/strubell/LISA

4.4 Experimental setup

We utilise Hugging Face[7] library for the baseline experiments which are fine-tuning PLMs. We fine-tune the baseline BERT model using Optuna (Akiba et al., 2019), a hyperparameter optimization framework, and apply the same hyperparameters for other PLMs (batch size of 32, max length of 128, the learning rate of 1e-5 and 10 epoch of training). For the proposed model experiments, we extract dependency tree representations from the texts utilising an external deep biaffine dependency parser (Dozat and Manning, 2016)[8] integrated into the SpaCy library[9] (Honnibal and Montani, 2017). We use the English model `en_core_web_sm` of SpaCy in the experiments. Since the nodes in the dependency tree representation are words, in the attention mechanism of SEQE we apply the same masking value (that would have corresponded to the full word) to the sub-word tokens produced by specific tokenisers (WordPiece, byte-level BPE). We finetune the syntax-enriched BERT model using Optuna and apply the same hyperparameters for other syntax-enriched PLMs (distance threshold of 3, batch size of 8, learning rate of 5e-5 and 5 epoch of training). We train all experiments on a single NVIDIA Quadro RTX 5000 GPU.

We train each model five times with different random seeds and report the mean and standard deviation of the results to account for the training variance of the models.

Statistical significance The statistical significance of the differences in macro F_1 score is evaluated with an approximate randomization test (Chinchor, 1992) with $99,999$ iterations and significance level $\alpha = 0.05$ for each baseline PLM and its syntax-enriched version (e.g., BERT $\rightarrow$ Syntax-enriched BERT). For significance testing, we used outputs yielding the 3rd-best results for each of the models (so, a median from the 5 runs reported to account for variance).

5 Results and Discussion

5.1 Main Results

Experimental results are shown in Table 2 and 3 for the base and large models, respectively. We report the results on the test sets of MeasEval and

[7]https://huggingface.co/

[8]The parser achieves 95.7% UAS and 94.1% LAS on the most popular English PTB dataset (Marcus et al., 1993).

[9]https://spacy.io/

		MeasEval		Grobid	
Models	**Params**	**Macro F_1**	**Seq F_1**	**Macro F_1**	**Seq F_1**
Base Models					
BERT (Devlin et al., 2019)	110M	87.26±1.66	57.15±7.24	89.45±1.42	72.28± 6.45
+ LISA		89.45±1.15	68.41± 5.89	89.51±1.31	73.47± 6.18
+ SEQE (Ours)	+ 0.01M	92.38†±1.42	74.17†±6.45	93.45†±1.54	78.36†±6.58
SciBERT (Beltagy et al., 2019)	110M	88.78±1.43	60.41±4.86	90.32±1.25	74.57±5.14
+ LISA		90.18±1.52	67.11±3.52	89.47±1.51	76.25±4.18
+ SEQE (Ours)	+ 0.01M	92.32†±1.30	73.98†±2.36	83.38±1.26	79.22†±3.14
RoBERTa (Liu et al., 2019)	125M	89.63±1.33	65.62±5.54	91.24±1.32	75.42±6.21
+ LISA		90.17±1.25	66.54±5.10	90.89±1.42	75.10±5.89
+ SEQE (Ours)	+ 0.01M	90.58†±1.42	69.05†±4.41	91.25±1.48	75.61±4.48
LUKE (Yamada et al., 2020)	253M	91.22±0.79	72.66±5.06	92.22±0.88	77.68± 4.02
+ LISA		90.23±1.11	73.56±4.99	91.17±1.05	77.15±4.45
+ SEQE (Ours)	+ 0.01M	90.89±1.02	74.57±5.03	91.77±1.11	79.55±5.18

Table 2: Base PLM results on quantity extraction datasets. † means statistically significant improvement over the corresponding baseline PLM. Reported results are averaged over 5 runs.

		MeasEval		Grobid	
Models	**Params**	**Macro F_1**	**Seq F_1**	**Macro F_1**	**Seq F_1**
State-of-the-art Models					
LIORI (Davletov et al., 2021b)	-	90.85	75.13	92.46	76.19
Grobid (Foppiano et al., 2019)	-	86.13	65.16	80.14	54.92
Large Models					
BERT (Devlin et al., 2019)	340M	87.07±1.68	57.75±4.78	88.95±1.54	72.36±5.04
+ LISA		90.45±1.51	68.48±4.15	90.36±1.51	74.47±4.25
+ SEQE (Ours)	+ 0.02M	91.88†±1.42	72.762†±3.78	92.982†±1.50	76.95†±4.11
RoBERTa (Liu et al., 2019)	355M	91.74±0.39	77.01±3.33	93.57±1.32	78.63±4.15
+ LISA		91.18±0.56	76.43±3.14	94.01±1.17	78.44±4.16
+ SEQE (Ours)	+ 0.02M	**92.49†±0.78**	77.75†±2.85	**94.28†±0.82**	78.52±3.03
LUKE (Yamada et al., 2020)	483M	91.16±0.40	76.22±0.71	93.55±0.52	77.87±1.18
+ LISA		90.89±0.51	76.48±0.69	93.10±0.71	78.15±1.11
+ SEQE (Ours)	+ 0.02M	91.14±0.67	**77.89**±0.73	93.48±0.72	**79.83†±1.21**

Table 3: Large PLM results on quantity extraction datasets. † means statistically significant improvement over the corresponding baseline PLM. Reported results are averaged over 5 runs.

Grobid datasets. The results show that the proposed SEQE method achieves consistent gains over the baseline PLMs and LISA for the quantity extraction task, especially for BERT. Even though the baseline RoBERTa performs best among all the baseline models, it shows that the quantity extraction task benefits from injecting syntactic information into the PLMs. The proposed approach outperforms LISA and among the experiments of syntax-enriched PLMs, syntax-enriched RoBERTa achieves the highest score and outperforms baseline RoBERTa with an increase of 0.75 and 0.71 in the Macro F_1 score for the MeasEval and Grobid datasets, respectively. Syntactic information does not result in a notable improvement for LUKE, which is a word- and entity-level model (pre-trained with a large amount of entity-annotated corpus) using entity-aware attention mechanism. SEQE decreased the Macro F_1 score for LUKE-large. However, we obtain the highest span-level Macro F_1 with the syntax-enriched LUKE-large, which mainly shows the weakness of word-level models for this evaluation metric. Importantly, syntax-enriched PLMs with fewer parameters (BERT, SciBERT) outperform their large baseline counterpart PLMs (Wang and Wang, 2020; Yang et al., 2020), showing the importance of syntactic information to the small models.

		Target	
		MeasEval	**Grobid**
Source	**MeasEval**	92.49±0.78	90.45±1.45
	Grobid	90.17±0.95	94.28±0.82

Table 4: Token-level Macro F_1 scores of RoBERTa (large) + SEQE for cross-domain experiments.

5.2 Cross-Domain Results

Cross-domain NER focuses on transferring from a source domain to a target domain. We run

		Predicted		
		B-Q	I-Q	O
True	B-Q	476	31	59
	I-Q	43	889	78
	O	24	42	8403

(a) MeasEval dataset

		Predicted		
		B-Q	I-Q	O
True	B-Q	390	53	99
	I-Q	12	912	49
	O	40	123	7340

(b) Grobid dataset

Table 5: Confusion matrix for the syntax-enriched RoBERTa (large) for quantity extraction task. (B-Quantity (B-Q), I-Quantity (I-Q))

cross-domain experiments with syntax-enriched RoBERTa (large) yielding the best token-level Macro F_1 scores on MeasEval and Grobid datasets. Cross-domain experimental results are shown in Table 4.

When we compare the within-domain and cross-domain results, we observe a slight decrease for both datasets. The macro F_1 scores for the within-domain experiments for MeasEval and Grobid are 92.49% (MeasEval $\rightarrow$ MeasEval)and 94.28% (Grobid $\rightarrow$ Grobid), respectively, while for the cross-domain experiments they are 90.17% (Grobid $\rightarrow$ MeasEval) and 90.45% (MeasEval $\rightarrow$ Grobid). Despite the effectiveness decrease, the results are still comparable to those of the baseline models.

5.3 Error Analysis

In Table 5, we show the confusion matrices for the predictions of the model with the best results (syntax-enriched RoBERTa) for the MeasEval (Table 5a) and Grobid (Table 5b) datasets. Typically, the model does not confuse the Quantity tags (B-Quantity, I-Quantity), but instead makes errors in deciding whether a token is a quantity or not. This makes sense, since the number of O tags is higher than the number of Quantity tags. We perform a comprehensive analysis of the errors made by the models to understand which quantity formats the model performs well on, and which it performs poorly on.

We categorise the prediction errors made by the model by exploring the properties of individual tokens for which the model made incorrect predictions for each of the datasets. For MeasEval, of the 24 tags for which the model confused an O tag for a B-Quantity, 7 are punctuation characters and 7 are numbers written as numeric or alphabetic, and the others are modifiers for quantities that occur frequently in the datasets, such as *approximately, low*, etc. Out of the 42 tags where the model confused an O tag for an I-Quantity, 10 are units, and 6 are numbers written as numeric or alphabetic.

For the Grobid dataset, of the 40 tags where the model confused a O tag for a B-Quantity, 7 are numbers written as numeric or alphabetic, and 10 are punctuations. Interestingly, 10 of the mislabeled tokens are units, such as *m, %*. Out of the 123 tags where the model confused a O tag for an I-Quantity, 16 are units, 24 are numbers written as numeric or alphabetic and 33 are punctuations.

After analyzing all the errors made by the models, we found that the syntax-enriched model tends to find longer quantity spans compared to the baseline PLMs. The common errors made by both models can be divided into 3 categories: (1) labeling modifier words as O (e.g., range, between), (2) labeling numbers written as numeric or alphabetic as B-Quantity, (3) labeling stop words in quantities as O (e.g., a, the).

5.4 Discussion

Based on the results, we analyse the impact of the syntax-enriched attention mechanism on the problem by visualising the model's decision. For this purpose, we used the transformers-interpret[10], a post-hoc explanation tool compatible with models from the transformers package designed for the sequence labeling problem. Tokens are assigned an importance score indicating how their presence contributes to the prediction of a particular positive token (Attribution Label) with the cumulative importance scores (Attribution score) for that token. Tokens highlighted in green have a positive contribution to the model's decision, while tokens highlighted in red have a negative contribution.

We randomly select a few sentences from the test set and analyze the predictions of the best-performing model (syntax-enriched RoBERTa-large) and its baseline version (RoBERTa-large)[11]. Figure 4 shows the visualisation of the models for the sentence *"In addition, the number of emerged Striga plants for each plot was recorded at 67, 101 and 121 das."* with the quantity *"67, 101 and 121 das"*. While the baseline model correctly predicts

[10] `https://github.com/cdpierse/transformers-interpret`

[11] Dependency tree representations of the sentences are given in Figure 6.

Legend: ■ Negative □ Neutral ■ Positive

True Label	Predicted Label	Attribution Label	Attribution Score	Word Importance
B-Quantity	B-Quantity (0.99)	67	2.92	#s In addition , the number of emerged Str iga plants for each plot was recorded at 67 , 101 and 121 d as . #/s
I-Quantity	I-Quantity (0.99)	,	1.53	#s In addition , the number of emerged Str iga plants for each plot was recorded at 67 , 101 and 121 d as . #/s
I-Quantity	I-Quantity (1.00)	101	2.34	#s In addition , the number of emerged Str iga plants for each plot was recorded at 67 , 101 and 121 d as . #/s
I-Quantity	I-Quantity (0.99)	and	2.13	#s In addition , the number of emerged Str iga plants for each plot was recorded at 67 , 101 and 121 d as . #/s
I-Quantity	I-Quantity (0.99)	121	1.45	#s In addition , the number of emerged Str iga plants for each plot was recorded at 67 , 101 and 121 d as . #/s
I-Quantity	I-Quantity (0.99)	d	1.64	#s In addition , the number of emerged Str iga plants for each plot was recorded at 67 , 101 and 121 d as . #/s
I-Quantity	I-Quantity (0.98)	as	1.26	#s In addition , the number of emerged Str iga plants for each plot was recorded at 67 , 101 and 121 d as . #/s

(a) RoBERTa-large

Legend: ■ Negative □ Neutral ■ Positive

True Label	Predicted Label	Attribution Label	Attribution Score	Word Importance
B-Quantity	B-Quantity (0.94)	67	1.97	#s In addition , the number of emerged Str iga plants for each plot was recorded at 67 , 101 and 121 d as . #/s
I-Quantity	I-Quantity (0.77)	,	1.42	#s In addition , the number of emerged Str iga plants for each plot was recorded at 67 , 101 and 121 d as . #/s
I-Quantity	B-Quantity (0.79)	101	0.82	#s In addition , the number of emerged Str iga plants for each plot was recorded at 67 , 101 and 121 d as . #/s
I-Quantity	I-Quantity (0.75)	and	1.77	#s In addition , the number of emerged Str iga plants for each plot was recorded at 67 , 101 and 121 d as . #/s
I-Quantity	B-Quantity (0.69)	121	1.06	#s In addition , the number of emerged Str iga plants for each plot was recorded at 67 , 101 and 121 d as . #/s
I-Quantity	I-Quantity (0.87)	d	2.13	#s In addition , the number of emerged Str iga plants for each plot was recorded at 67 , 101 and 121 d as . #/s
I-Quantity	I-Quantity (0.56)	as	0.84	#s In addition , the number of emerged Str iga plants for each plot was recorded at 67 , 101 and 121 d as . #/s

(b) Syntax-enriched RoBERTa-large

Figure 4: Visualisation of the sentence *"In addition, the number of emerged Striga plants for each plot was recorded at 67, 101 and 121 das."*

Legend: ■ Negative □ Neutral ■ Positive

True Label	Predicted Label	Attribution Label	Attribution Score	Word Importance
B-Quantity	B-Quantity (0.99)	>	1.63	#s The colored letters indicate a comparatively high expression level of the M HC - I allele , comprising > 10 % of c DNA sequence reads . #/s
I-Quantity	B-Quantity (0.96)	10	3.24	#s The colored letters indicate a comparatively high expression level of the M HC - I allele , comprising > 10 % of c DNA sequence reads . #/s
I-Quantity	I-Quantity (0.48)	%	1.80	#s The colored letters indicate a comparatively high expression level of the M HC - I allele , comprising > 10 % of c DNA sequence reads . #/s

(a) RoBERTa-large

Legend: ■ Negative □ Neutral ■ Positive

True Label	Predicted Label	Attribution Label	Attribution Score	Word Importance
B-Quantity	B-Quantity (0.92)	>	2.49	#s The colored letters indicate a comparatively high expression level of the M HC - I allele , comprising > 10 % of c DNA sequence reads . #/s
I-Quantity	B-Quantity (0.87)	10	1.41	#s The colored letters indicate a comparatively high expression level of the M HC - I allele , comprising > 10 % of c DNA sequence reads . #/s
I-Quantity	I-Quantity (0.75)	%	2.40	#s The colored letters indicate a comparatively high expression level of the M HC - I allele , comprising > 10 % of c DNA sequence reads . #/s

(b) Syntax-enriched RoBERTa-large

Figure 5: Visualisation of the sentence *"The colored letters indicate a comparatively high expression level of the MHC-I allele, comprising >10% of cDNA sequence reads."*

the quantity, lots of tokens have positive and negative effects on the prediction of token labels, especially some distant tokens (e.g., the word 'addition'). In the syntax-enriched model, on the other hand, the contributing tokens are closer together, due to dependency relations extracted from the sentence's dependency tree and incorporated in the attention mechanism. In particular, the syntax-enriched model appears to base its decision on the positive contribution of a predicate syntactically close the quantity span (here, 'recorded').

We observe similar results in Figure 5 for the sentence *"The colored letters indicate a comparatively high expression level of the MHC-I allele, comprising >10% of cDNA sequence reads."* with the quantity *">10%"*. Since numbers written as numeric or alphabetic are usually placed at the beginning of quantities, both models tend to label 10 as B-Quantity. Apart from this result, we see that close tokens have a positive effect in predicting token labels for the syntax-enriched model.

6 Conclusion

We introduce the SEQE model that integrates syntactic information into the Transformer attention mechanism to provide a complementary structure for the quantity extraction modeled as a sequence labeling problem. We demonstrate the effectiveness of the proposed SEQE model, which uses syntactic information, by comparing it to baseline

PLMs on the quantity extraction task. We find that the proposed method outperforms the baseline PLMs and SOTA models and the syntax-enriched RoBERTa achieves the best effectiveness among all evaluated methods. We also find that syntactic information added at the attention-level of the PLMs contributes to more accurate entity span extraction, which is also very important for other (downstream) subtasks of ME, as these other subtasks depend directly on the quality of quantity extraction. Finally, the SEQE model is versatile in a sense that it can be easily integrated into all tasks that use pre-trained transformer models.

In future work, we will explore the performance of the transformer models extended using semantic representations such as AMR (Banarescu et al., 2013), UMR (Van Gysel et al., 2021), and UCCA (Abend and Rappoport, 2013).

Our work aims to explicitly extract quantity extraction using linguistic knowledge as syntactic information integrated into the attention mechanism of the PLMs encoder. We focus on autoencoding models (BERT, RoBERTa, LUKE) that rely on the encoder part of the original transformer. However, autoregressive models (e.g., GPT (Radford et al., 2018), GPT-2 (Radford et al., 2019)) and seq2seq models (e.g., BART (Lewis et al., 2019), T5 (Raffel et al., 2020)) are widely used in the literature for the token classification problem. In addition, non-autoregressive models (Gu et al., 2017) have become popular due to their fast inference speed, as they omit the sequential dependencies in inference. We hope to extend our study on syntax-enriched masking for quantity extraction to these models.

Finally, we will investigate the impact of our approach on downstream subtasks of ME defined in the MeasEval shared task (Harper et al., 2021).

Limitations

Even though our proposed model outperforms the baselines, there are still limitations, mainly based on the syntax-enriched mask integrated into PLMs. We utilised dependency tree representations in the syntax-enriched attention mechanism. Although the labels of the dependency arcs give the syntax type of the relation between the connected words, we ignore the arc labels to keep the masking simple. In addition, our model depends on the effectiveness of the dependency parser model used 'off-the-self' in our method.

Ethical Statement

The datasets used in our experiments are publicly available. Both these datasets are focused on processing (publicly available) scientific literature, thus constituting a low-risk setting.

References

Omri Abend and Ari Rappoport. 2013. UCCA: A Semantics-based Grammatical Annotation Scheme. In *Proceedings of the 10th International Conference on Computational Semantics (IWCS 2013)–Long Papers*, pages 1–12.

Gustavo Aguilar and Thamar Solorio. 2019. Dependency-aware named entity recognition with relative and global attentions. *arXiv preprint arXiv:1909.05166.*

Takuya Akiba, Shotaro Sano, Toshihiko Yanase, Takeru Ohta, and Masanori Koyama. 2019. Optuna: A next-generation hyperparameter optimization framework. In *Proceedings of the 25th ACM SIGKDD international conference on knowledge discovery & data mining*, pages 2623–2631.

Nader Akoury, Kalpesh Krishna, and Mohit Iyyer. 2019. Syntactically supervised transformers for faster neural machine translation. *arXiv preprint arXiv:1906.02780.*

Jiangang Bai, Yujing Wang, Yiren Chen, Yaming Yang, Jing Bai, Jing Yu, and Yunhai Tong. 2021. Syntax-BERT: Improving pre-trained transformers with syntax trees. *arXiv preprint arXiv:2103.04350.*

Laura Banarescu, Claire Bonial, Shu Cai, Madalina Georgescu, Kira Griffitt, Ulf Hermjakob, Kevin Knight, Philipp Koehn, Martha Palmer, and Nathan Schneider. 2013. Abstract meaning representation for sembanking. In *Proceedings of the 7th linguistic annotation workshop and interoperability with discourse*, pages 178–186.

Jasmijn Bastings, Ivan Titov, Wilker Aziz, Diego Marcheggiani, and Khalil Sima'an. 2017. Graph Convolutional Encoders for Syntax-aware Neural Machine Translation. *CoRR*, abs/1704.04675.

Iz Beltagy, Kyle Lo, and Arman Cohan. 2019. SciBERT: A pretrained language model for scientific text. *arXiv preprint arXiv:1903.10676.*

Emanuele Bugliarello and Naoaki Okazaki. 2019. Enhancing machine translation with dependency-aware self-attention. *arXiv preprint arXiv:1909.03149.*

Jiarun Cao, Yuejia Xiang, Yunyan Zhang, Zhiyuan Qi, Xi Chen, and Yefeng Zheng. 2021. CONNER: a cascade count and measurement extraction tool for scientific discourse. In *Proceedings of the 15th International Workshop on Semantic Evaluation (SemEval-2021)*, pages 1239–1244.

Nancy Chinchor. 1992. The statistical significance of the muc-4 results. In *Proceedings of the 4th Conference on Message Understanding, MUC 1992*, pages 30–50.

Adis Davletov, Nikolay Arefyev, Denis Gordeev, and Alexey Rey. 2021a. LIORI at SemEval-2021 task 2: Span prediction and binary classification approaches to word-in-context disambiguation. In *Proceedings of the 15th International Workshop on Semantic Evaluation (SemEval-2021)*, pages 780–786, Online. Association for Computational Linguistics.

Adis Davletov, Denis Gordeev, Nikolay Arefyev, and Emil Davletov. 2021b. LIORI at SemEval-2021 task 8: Ask transformer for measurements. In *Proceedings of the 15th International Workshop on Semantic Evaluation (SemEval-2021)*, pages 1249–1254.

Jacob Devlin, Ming-Wei Chang, Kenton Lee, and Kristina Toutanova. 2019. BERT: Pre-training of Deep Bidirectional Transformers for Language Understanding. In *Proceedings of the 2019 Conference of the North American Chapter of the Association for Computational Linguistics: Human Language Technologies, Volume 1 (Long and Short Papers)*, pages 4171–4186, Minneapolis, Minnesota.

Timothy Dozat and Christopher D Manning. 2016. Deep biaffine attention for neural dependency parsing. *arXiv preprint arXiv:1611.01734*.

Chunning Du, Jingyu Wang, Haifeng Sun, Qi Qi, and Jianxin Liao. 2021. Syntax-type-aware graph convolutional networks for natural language understanding. *Applied Soft Computing*, 102:107080.

Luca Foppiano, Laurent Romary, Masashi Ishii, and Mikiko Tanifuji. 2019. Automatic identification and normalisation of physical measurements in scientific literature. In *Proceedings of the ACM Symposium on Document Engineering 2019*, pages 1–4.

Akash Gangwar, Sabhay Jain, Shubham Sourav, and Ashutosh Modi. 2021a. Counts@ iitk at semeval-2021 task 8: Scibert based entity and semantic relation extraction for scientific data. *arXiv preprint arXiv:2104.01364*.

Akash Gangwar, Sabhay Jain, Shubham Sourav, and Ashutosh Modi. 2021b. Counts@IITK at SemEval-2021 task 8: SciBERT based entity and semantic relation extraction for scientific data. In *Proceedings of the 15th International Workshop on Semantic Evaluation (SemEval-2021)*, pages 1232–1238, Online. Association for Computational Linguistics.

Christel Gérardin, Yuhan Xiong, Perceval Wajsbürt, Fabrice Carrat, and Xavier Tannier. 2023. Impact of translation on biomedical information extraction from real-life clinical notes.

Jan Göpfert, Patrick Kuckertz, Jann Weinand, Leander Kotzur, and Detlef Stolten. 2022. Measurement Extraction with Natural Language Processing: A Review. *Findings of the Association for Computational Linguistics: EMNLP 2022*, pages 2191–2215.

Jiatao Gu, James Bradbury, Caiming Xiong, Victor OK Li, and Richard Socher. 2017. Non-autoregressive neural machine translation. *arXiv preprint arXiv:1711.02281*.

Qipeng Guo, Xipeng Qiu, Xiangyang Xue, and Zheng Zhang. 2021. Syntax-guided text generation via graph neural network. *Science China Information Sciences*, 64(5):1–10.

Corey Harper, Jessica Cox, Curt Kohler, Antony Scerri, Ron Daniel Jr, and Paul Groth. 2021. Semeval-2021 task 8: Measeval–extracting counts and measurements and their related contexts. In *Proceedings of the 15th International Workshop on Semantic Evaluation (SemEval-2021)*, pages 306–316.

Jiayuan He, Dat Quoc Nguyen, Saber A Akhondi, Christian Druckenbrodt, Camilo Thorne, Ralph Hoessel, Zubair Afzal, Zenan Zhai, Biaoyan Fang, Hiyori Yoshikawa, et al. 2020. Overview of ChEMU 2020: named entity recognition and event extraction of chemical reactions from patents. In *Experimental IR Meets Multilinguality, Multimodality, and Interaction: 11th International Conference of the CLEF Association, CLEF 2020, Thessaloniki, Greece, September 22–25, 2020, Proceedings 11*, pages 237–254. Springer.

Zhi Hong, Logan Ward, Kyle Chard, Ben Blaiszik, and Ian Foster. 2021. Challenges and advances in information extraction from scientific literature: a review. *JOM*, 73(11):3383–3400.

Matthew Honnibal and Ines Montani. 2017. spaCy 2: Natural language understanding with Bloom embeddings, convolutional neural networks and incremental parsing. *To appear*, 7(1):411–420.

Zhiheng Huang, Wei Xu, and Kai Yu. 2015. Bidirectional LSTM-CRF models for sequence tagging. *arXiv preprint arXiv:1508.01991*.

Tian Kang, Shaodian Zhang, Youlan Tang, Gregory W Hruby, Alexander Rusanov, Noémie Elhadad, and Chunhua Weng. 2017. EliIE: An open-source information extraction system for clinical trial eligibility criteria. *Journal of the American Medical Informatics Association*, 24(6):1062–1071.

Neel Karia, Ayush Kaushal, and Faraaz Mallick. 2021. KGP at SemEval-2021 Task 8: Leveraging Multi-Staged Language Models for Extracting Measurements, their Attributes and Relations. In *Proceedings of the 15th International Workshop on Semantic Evaluation (SemEval-2021)*, pages 387–396.

Olga Kononova, Haoyan Huo, Tanjin He, Ziqin Rong, Tiago Botari, Wenhao Sun, Vahe Tshitoyan, and Gerbrand Ceder. 2019. Text-mined dataset of inorganic materials synthesis recipes. *Scientific data*, 6(1):203.

Jinhyuk Lee, Wonjin Yoon, Sungdong Kim, Donghyeon Kim, Sunkyu Kim, Chan Ho So, and Jaewoo Kang. 2020. BioBERT: a pre-trained biomedical language representation model for biomedical text mining. *Bioinformatics*, 36(4):1234–1240.

Mike Lewis, Yinhan Liu, Naman Goyal, Marjan Ghazvininejad, Abdelrahman Mohamed, Omer Levy, Ves Stoyanov, and Luke Zettlemoyer. 2019. Bart: Denoising sequence-to-sequence pre-training for natural language generation, translation, and comprehension. *arXiv preprint arXiv:1910.13461*.

Patrick Lewis, Myle Ott, Jingfei Du, and Veselin Stoyanov. 2020. Pretrained language models for biomedical and clinical tasks: understanding and extending the state-of-the-art. In *Proceedings of the 3rd Clinical Natural Language Processing Workshop*, pages 146–157.

Sijia Liu, Liwei Wang, Donna Ihrke, Vipin Chaudhary, Cui Tao, Chunhua Weng, and Hongfang Liu. 2017. Correlating lab test results in clinical notes with structured lab data: a case study in HbA1c and glucose. *AMIA Summits on Translational Science Proceedings*, 2017:221.

Yinhan Liu, Myle Ott, Naman Goyal, Jingfei Du, Mandar Joshi, Danqi Chen, Omer Levy, Mike Lewis, Luke Zettlemoyer, and Veselin Stoyanov. 2019. RoBERTa: A Robustly Optimized BERT Pretraining Approach. *arXiv preprint arXiv:1907.11692*.

Ling Luo, Zhihao Yang, Pei Yang, Yin Zhang, Lei Wang, Hongfei Lin, and Jian Wang. 2018. An attention-based BiLSTM-CRF approach to document-level chemical named entity recognition. *Bioinformatics*, 34(8):1381–1388.

Diego Marcheggiani and Ivan Titov. 2019. Graph Convolutions over Constituent Trees for Syntax-Aware Semantic Role Labeling. *CoRR*, abs/1909.09814.

Mitchell Marcus, Beatrice Santorini, and Mary Ann Marcinkiewicz. 1993. Building a large annotated corpus of English: The Penn Treebank.

Hiroki Nakayama. 2018. seqeval: A python framework for sequence labeling evaluation. Software available from https://github.com/chakki-works/seqeval.

Zara Nasar, Syed Waqar Jaffry, and Muhammad Kamran Malik. 2018. Information extraction from scientific articles: a survey. *Scientometrics*, 117:1931–1990.

Thanh-Tung Nguyen, Xuan-Phi Nguyen, Shafiq Joty, and Xiaoli Li. 2020. Differentiable Window for Dynamic Local Attention. In *Proceedings of the 58th Annual Meeting of the Association for Computational Linguistics*, pages 6589–6599.

Yuyang Nie, Yuanhe Tian, Yan Song, Xiang Ao, and Xiang Wan. 2020. Improving named entity recognition with attentive ensemble of syntactic information. *arXiv preprint arXiv:2010.15466*.

Qiwei Peng, David Weir, and Julie Weeds. 2021. Structure-aware sentence encoder in bert-based Siamese network. In *Proceedings of the 6th Workshop on Representation Learning for NLP (RepL4NLP-2021)*, pages 57–63.

Alec Radford, Karthik Narasimhan, Tim Salimans, Ilya Sutskever, et al. 2018. Improving language understanding by generative pre-training.

Alec Radford, Jeffrey Wu, Rewon Child, David Luan, Dario Amodei, Ilya Sutskever, et al. 2019. Language Models are Unsupervised Multitask Learners. *OpenAI blog*, 1(8):9.

Colin Raffel, Noam Shazeer, Adam Roberts, Katherine Lee, Sharan Narang, Michael Matena, Yanqi Zhou, Wei Li, and Peter J Liu. 2020. Exploring the limits of transfer learning with a unified text-to-text transformer. *The Journal of Machine Learning Research*, 21(1):5485–5551.

Ryokan Ri, Ikuya Yamada, and Yoshimasa Tsuruoka. 2022. mLUKE: The power of entity representations in multilingual pretrained language models. In *Proceedings of the 60th Annual Meeting of the Association for Computational Linguistics (Volume 1: Long Papers)*, pages 7316–7330, Dublin, Ireland. Association for Computational Linguistics.

Tim Rocktäschel, Michael Weidlich, and Ulf Leser. 2012. ChemSpot: a hybrid system for chemical named entity recognition. *Bioinformatics*, 28(12):1633–1640.

Michael Sejr Schlichtkrull, Nicola De Cao, and Ivan Titov. 2020. Interpreting Graph Neural Networks for NLP With Differentiable Edge Masking. *CoRR*, abs/2010.00577.

Emma Strubell, Patrick Verga, Daniel Andor, David Weiss, and Andrew McCallum. 2018. Linguistically-informed self-attention for semantic role labeling. *arXiv preprint arXiv:1804.08199*.

Huiyu Sun and Ralph Grishman. 2022. Employing Lexicalized Dependency Paths for Active Learning of Relation Extraction. *Intelligent Automation & Soft Computing*, 34(3).

Yuanhe Tian, Guimin Chen, Yan Song, and Xiang Wan. 2021. Dependency-driven relation extraction with attentive graph convolutional networks. In *Proceedings of the 59th Annual Meeting of the Association for Computational Linguistics and the 11th International Joint Conference on Natural Language Processing (Volume 1: Long Papers)*, pages 4458–4471.

Yuanhe Tian, Yan Song, and Fei Xia. 2022. Improving Relation Extraction through Syntax-induced Pre-training with Dependency Masking. In *Findings of the Association for Computational Linguistics: ACL 2022*, pages 1875–1886.

Jens EL Van Gysel, Meagan Vigus, Jayeol Chun, Kenneth Lai, Sarah Moeller, Jiarui Yao, Tim O'Gorman, Andrew Cowell, William Croft, Chu-Ren Huang, et al. 2021. Designing a uniform meaning representation for natural language processing. *KI-Künstliche Intelligenz*, 35(3-4):343–360.

Ashish Vaswani, Noam Shazeer, Niki Parmar, Jakob Uszkoreit, Llion Jones, Aidan N Gomez, Łukasz Kaiser, and Illia Polosukhin. 2017. Attention is all you need. *Advances in neural information processing systems*, 30.

Oriol Vinyals, Meire Fortunato, and Navdeep Jaitly. 2015. Pointer networks. *Advances in neural information processing systems*, 28.

Chang Wang and Bang Wang. 2020. Encoding sentences with a syntax-aware self-attention neural network for emotion distribution prediction. In *Natural Language Processing and Chinese Computing: 9th CCF International Conference, NLPCC 2020, Zhengzhou, China, October 14–18, 2020, Proceedings, Part II 9*, pages 256–266. Springer.

Haitao Wang and Fangbing Li. 2022. A text classification method based on LSTM and graph attention network. *Connection Science*, 34(1):2466–2480.

Yufei Wang, Mark Johnson, Stephen Wan, Yifang Sun, and Wei Wang. 2019. How to best use syntax in semantic role labelling. *arXiv preprint arXiv:1906.00266*.

Leigh Weston, Vahe Tshitoyan, John Dagdelen, Olga Kononova, Amalie Trewartha, Kristin A Persson, Gerbrand Ceder, and Anubhav Jain. 2019. Named entity recognition and normalization applied to large-scale information extraction from the materials science literature. *Journal of chemical information and modeling*, 59(9):3692–3702.

Ying Xiong, Hao Peng, Yang Xiang, Ka-Chun Wong, Qingcai Chen, Jun Yan, and Buzhou Tang. 2022. Leveraging Multi-source knowledge for Chinese clinical named entity recognition via relational graph convolutional network. *Journal of Biomedical Informatics*, 128:104035.

Ikuya Yamada, Akari Asai, Hiroyuki Shindo, Hideaki Takeda, and Yuji Matsumoto. 2020. LUKE: Deep contextualized entity representations with entity-aware self-attention. *arXiv preprint arXiv:2010.01057*.

Baosong Yang, Derek F Wong, Lidia S Chao, and Min Zhang. 2020. Improving tree-based neural machine translation with dynamic lexicalized dependency encoding. *Knowledge-Based Systems*, 188:105042.

Linlin Zhang. 2021. ZJU's IWSLT 2021 speech translation system. In *Proceedings of the 18th International Conference on Spoken Language Translation (IWSLT 2021)*, pages 144–148, Bangkok, Thailand (online). Association for Computational Linguistics.

A Multilingual PLMs

We primarily use monolingual PLMs for our experiments. However, syntax-enriched multilingual PLMs are applied to various tasks. Therefore, we perform experiments with multilingual PLMs: XLM (Cao et al., 2021) and the multilingual version of LUKE (Ri et al., 2022). The results are given in Table 6. We observe that the improvements of quantity extraction with multilingual PLMs are relatively smaller than with monolingual PLMs.

B Syntactic Representation

Figure 6 shows the dependency tree visualisation of sentences given in Section 5.4.

		MeasEval		Grobid	
Base-size Baseline Models					
XLM	125M	88.58±0.82	61.34±5.18	89.57±0.97	73.18±5.89
mLUKE	585M	88.98±0.72	62.59±3.21	88.75±0.75	73.61±3.18
Large-size Baseline Models					
XLM	355M	89.37±0.79	67.22±2.96	90.20±0.75	75.69± 3.47
mLUKE	868M	88.83±0.66	63.81±3.68	87.94±0.44	74.15±3.08
Syntax-Enriched Base-size Models					
XLM	125M + 0.01M	89.45±1.15	68.32±4.25	90.03±0.98	74.66±4.67
MLUKE	585M + 0.01M	87.55±0.82	62.05±2.36	87.16±0.78	73.18 ±1.94
Syntax-Enriched Large-size Models					
XLM	355M + 0.02M	90.22±0.56	76.21±0.92	91.36±0.61	78.35±1.45
MLUKE	868M + 0.02M	88.62±0.65	64.56±2.45	88.03±0.66	74.31±2.51

Table 6: Multilingual PLM results on quantity extraction datasets. Reported results are averaged over 5 runs.

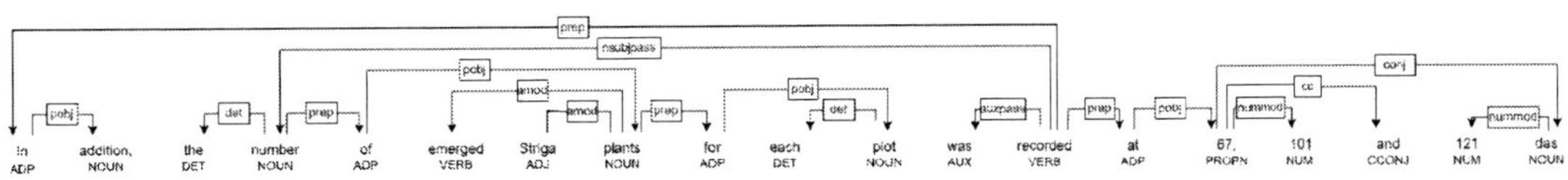

(a) In addition, the number of emerged Striga plants for each plot was recorded at 67, 101 and 121 das.

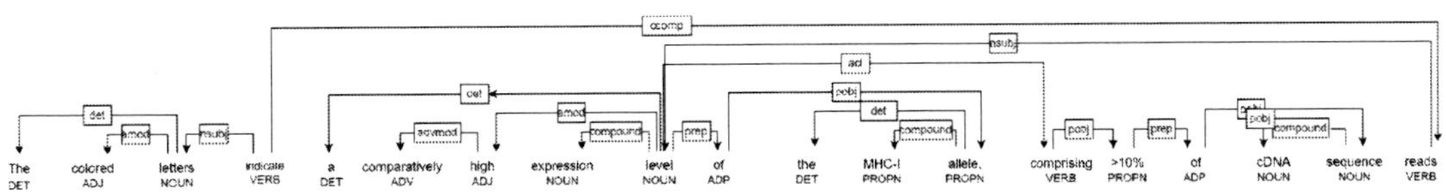

(b) The colored letters indicate a comparatively high expression level of the MHC-I allele, comprising >10% of cDNA sequence reads.

Figure 6: Dependency tree visualisation of sentences given in Section 5.4

NanoNER: Named Entity Recognition for nanobiology using experts' knowledge and distant supervision

Ran Cheng, Martin Lentschat, Cyril Labbé
Univ. Grenoble Alpes, CNRS, Grenoble INP, LIG, 38000 Grenoble, France
{martin.lentschat,cyril.labbe}@univ-grenoble-alpes.fr

Abstract

Here we present the training and evaluation of NanoNER, a Named Entity Recognition (NER) model for Nanobiology. NER consists in the identification of specific entities in spans of unstructured texts and is often a primary task in Natural Language Processing (NLP) and Information Extraction. The aim of our model is to recognise entities previously identified by domain experts as constituting the essential knowledge of the domain. Relying on ontologies, which provide us with a domain vocabulary and taxonomy, we implemented an iterative process enabling experts to determine the entities relevant to the domain at hand. We then delve into the potential of distant supervision learning in NER, supporting how this method can increase the quantity of annotated data with minimal additional manpower. On our full corpus of 728 full-text nanobiology articles, containing more than 120k entity occurrences, NanoNER obtained a F1-score of 0.98 on the recognition of previously known entities. Our model also demonstrated its ability to discover new entities in the text, with precision scores ranging from 0.77 to 0.81. Ablation experiments further confirmed this and allowed us to assess the dependency of our approach on the external resources. It highlighted the dependency of the approach to the resource, while also confirming its ability to rediscover up to 30% of the ablated terms. This paper details the methodology employed, experimental design, and key findings, providing valuable insights and directions for future related researches on NER in specialized domain. Furthermore, since our approach require minimal man-power, we believe that it can be generalized to other specialized fields.

1 Introduction

As the volume of the scientific literature increases, the demand for NLP models able to deal with domain vocabulary and specific knowledge is becoming increasingly apparent. The NanoBubbles [1] project, from which the work presented here originates, aims at studying *how, when and why science fails to correct itself*. It focuses on the nanobiology domain and combines approaches from the natural sciences, natural language processing and social sciences. The field of nanobiology being characterized by both its multidisciplinarity and its high degree of specialization is a perfect example of the need for specialized tools. Thus, we must leverage methods from Natural Language Processing (NLP) to assist in the extraction of important information from a large number of articles. The main task of this paper is to train a Named Entity Recognition (NER) model in the field of nanobiology.

The primary task of Named Entity Recognition is to identify and classify specific entities (i.e. named entities) in a text. Compared to other fields, Biomedical NER (BMNER) is a particularly challenging problem, mainly due to the high cost of obtaining quality annotated data and the complexity of domain terminology. A famous example of a model able to perform BMNER is bioBERT (Lee et al., 2020), which is pre-trained on a large-scale corpus of biomedical text. It performs well on a standard set of biomedical benchmarks in several downstream tasks (e.g., NER, Relations Extraction, Q&A). To our knowledge, NER in the nanobiology domain remains an uncharted territory, as existing BMNER models are not trained to recognize entities of interest in this specific field.

Training an efficient NER model requires a large amount of annotated data, which is not easy to come by in specialized domains as the manual work it requires need to be carried out by fields experts. In our work for NER in the nanobiology field, we use distant supervision to alleviate for the lack of annotated data and thus allow the creation of a corpus of articles from a specialized domain large enough to train a NER model. Using BioBERT

[1] https://nanobubbles.hypotheses.org/

Proceedings of the 2nd Workshop on Information Extraction from Scientific Publications, pages 14–24
Nov 1, 2023.

(Lee et al., 2020) as base model, this approach requires minimal human work. We believe that the approach we implemented, and describe here, is adapted to other scientific domain.

First, we harnessed existing nanobiology ontologies (i.e., the Nanoparticle ontology (Thomas et al., 2011) and eNanoMapper (Hastings et al., 2015)) for their concept hierarchy and vocabulary. Then, an iterative process took place with a team of domain experts, who determined the essential labels for our NER model and curated the vocabulary. A round of vocabulary extension, with expert curation, took place before the automatic annotation of the corpus. Ablation experiments were also implemented to measure the influence of the vocabulary coverage in our distant supervision setting.

In summary, the main contributions of this paper are as follows:

1. We have implemented a method to create annotated data for NER. It consists in an iterative process, involving ontology and corpus analysis followed by use of expert knowledge and their validation. This lead us to identify five labels, with vocabularies covering 1438 terms, that are highly relevant to nanobiology.

2. We created NanoNER, a NER model for nanobiology using a distant supervision learning approach and trained on automatically annotated entities in a corpus of 728 unlabelled full-text nanobiology articles. Detailed ablation experiments were conducted to evaluate the influence of the vocabulary coverage.

3. Finally, ablation experiments allowed us to estimate the dependency of our model to the annotation resource. We can effectively measure how well NanoNER is capable to generalize, i.e. its ability to (re)find entities not present in the training set, as well as the essential and minimal terms needed to obtain satisfactory results.

2 Related work

Existing BMNER solutions encompass early NER methods, such as dictionary matching or rule-based approaches, as well as supervised machine learning methods such as Markov models (Ponomareva et al., 2007a). Conditional Random Fields (CRFs) were then employed to perform BMNER (Ponomareva et al., 2007b; Friedrich et al., 2006). Unlike Markov models, CRFs can consider the characteristics of the entire input sequence, not just the current state. And Support Vector Machine (SVM) can be used in binary classification problems for NER tasks, such as determining whether a word is a named entity of a particular type (Ju et al., 2011).

Recently, deep learning approaches using large amounts of labeled data, such as models built on BioBERT (Lee et al., 2020), have achieved state-of-the-art results on BMNER. For instance, on the jnlpba (Huang et al., 2020) dataset, the KeBioLM model (Yuan et al., 2021) obtained a F1 score of 0.82 on recognizing entities relating to proteins, genes and cells. In the bc5cdr (Li et al., 2016) dataset, the BINDER (Zhang et al., 2022) model using a contrastive learning approach, achieved a F1 score of 0.91 on chemical and disease entities. However, BMNER presents specific difficulties. For instance, Dong et al. (2016) conducted an extensive study on electronic medical records and identified that such technical texts often contain a substantial amount of specialized terminology and knowledge, and frequently present issues such as spelling errors, abbreviations, and idiosyncratic terms, all of which add to the difficulty of the NER task. In this difficult setting, they proposed a method based on CNN (Convolutional Neural Networks) and Word2Vec for performing BMNER and managed to achieve a F1 score of 0.73.

To address the scarcity of annotated data in deep learning models, some weak supervision and distant supervision solutions have been proposed. Mintz et al. (2009) were among the pioneers of distant supervision learning, introducing this method in information and relation extraction tasks. Their goal was to extract relations between entities from a large amount of unlabeled text, using existing knowledge bases as distant supervision signals. Distant supervision was initially widely applied to relation extraction tasks and later extensively used in NER tasks. Distant supervision methods for NER have been validated in previous studies. Shang et al. (2018) revised the LSTM-CRF NER model of Lample et al. (2016) and utilized the MeSH database for chemical and disease entity research. Since the automatic annotation of a corpus tend to introduce noise in the training data, some methods have been proposed to reduce this effect (Meng et al., 2021), such as using early stopping or introducing the concept of pseudo-labels (Liang et al., 2020). Early stopping prevent over-fitting the model on the training data and fosters the learning of important features of the corpus. Pseudo-labeling data expand the training set by generating new labeled data that can then be used alongside existing datasets.

BMNER using ontologies and distant supervision have already been performed in the biomedical domain (Fries et al., 2017; Wang et al., 2021) and this type of approach could be generalized to any domain for which a semantic and lexical resource exists. These works used different technics to minimize the risk of noise propagation, e.g. filtering candidate annotations through heuristics based on part-of-speech analysis (Fries et al., 2017) or disambiguating ambiguous entities based on other entities present in the same context (Wang et al., 2021). In our work, we rely on domain experts at crucial steps: (1) determining the labels and then (2) filtering and validating the vocabulary of our annotation resource.

To the best of our knowledge, no one has yet proposed a BMNER model that meets the information mining needs of the nanobiology field. We thus aim at training a NER model, using minimal manpower, but which still meets experts requirements regarding the entities of interest of the domain.

3 Data preparation

Here we describe the essential resources for our work, the corpus and ontologies used, the expert work on selecting labels relevant to the domain at hand as well as the vocabulary associated, and the automatic annotation on the scientific articles. All codes necessary to replicate this study are available online[2].

3.1 Corpus

The corpus used in this study comprises 728 research articles focused on the field of nanobiology. The vast majority of these articles are written in English. In total, the corpus contains 158,283 sentences and 3,762,791 tokens. On average, each paper in the corpus consists of 217 sentences, and each sentence contains approximately 24 tokens. This extensive dataset provides a rich foundation for in-depth analysis and research in the field of nanobiology. The articles were first obtained in PDF format and the abstract and full text of each article was extracted using Grobid (Lopez, 2008-2023). Parts of the documents that are not considered as the core of the articles were excluded (e.g. References, Acknowledgment, Appendix).

3.2 Ontology

As resources, we used the NanoParticle Ontology for cancer nanotechnology research (NPO) (Thomas et al., 2011) and eNanoMapper (ENM) (Hastings et al., 2015), which are the two main ontology in the field of nanobiology. As described in the ENM official documentation, ENM is an automatic extension of NPO and reuses several other ontologies including NPO, CHEMINF (Hastings et al., 2011), CHEBI (Degtyarenko et al., 2007) and ENVO (Buttigieg et al., 2013). The NPO possesses 1904 classes and 81 properties, while ENM contains over 25k classes, 697 individuals and 55 properties (August 2023). Since ENM is built automatically we used it as a secondary source to NPO, in order to minimize the risk of noise propagation. The ontologies were used in CSV format, where each concept in the ontology had a unique key, definition, synonyms, and parent key. These resources will be used for their subsumption relations and vocabularies, providing us with a taxonomy and lexical database.

3.3 Labels and vocabulary

To determine the labels our model will be trained to recognize, and their vocabulary, we used an iterative process of reducing the ontologies, expanding the obtained vocabulary and having every steps validated by domain experts. Because of the large number of concepts in the NPO and ENM ontologies, the difficulty of finding a focus to start with and the fact that our aim is to create an automatically labeled corpus, we first retained only the concepts that presented at least one occurrence in our corpus (i.e. $\approx 30\%$ of NPO's and $\approx 10\%$ of ENM's). Concepts that have never appeared in the corpus were discarded, and subsumption relations within the ontology were reconstructed to obtain a reduced ontology.

Using these reduced ontologies, three domain experts (cf. Acknowledgements) examined their structures and the remaining concepts. Together, they identified five labels as being the core concepts of interest to the field of nanobiology, namely `Nanoparticle`, `Property`, `Material`, `Event` and `Technology`. Table 1 presents a short description of each label, along

[2]https://gricad-gitlab.univ-grenoble-alpes.fr/nanobubbles/nano-ner-wiesp-2023.git

with the core concepts combined under them (the number of their respective sub-concepts before expert selection is indicated between parenthesis) and a vocabulary extract in the last column.

The concepts corresponding to each label are taken as the root concept of ontology sub-trees. We then amalgamated all the terms under the root concepts with all of the terms of all of its respective sub-concepts to built the labels vocabulary. In any conflict between the NPO and ENM structure, NPO was prefered. The labels were subsequently subjected to a first detailed verification by the domain experts, who selected sub-concepts with relevant vocabulary only, which drastically downsized the number (). In addition to verifying each label's vocabulary, they encountered six specific cases of terms under `Material` that they thought should be moved under `Nanoparticle`: *buckyball, carbon dot, surface group, dendrimer, liposome* and *fullerene*.

Table 2 presents the characteristics of the labels vocabulary. Terms designates the vocabulary size for the label based on the ontologies lexicon. Vocabulary indicates the size of the extended vocabulary based on terminological variations retrieval (cf. below), which includes the original terms. Occurrences gives the raw frequency of all label's terms in our corpus. Also, since this was obtained by reducing ontologies, the Depth and Width columns give an insight of the shape of each sub-tree.

After the expert determined the labels and corresponding terms, we recorded the variants of all the terms using FASTR (Jacquemin et al., 1997). Given a list of terms and a corpus of texts, FASTR is able to extract the terminological variations using solely lexical, syntactical and meta-grammatical rules. This tool is also able to account for variations in word order and part-of-speech changes. It can deals with multi-word terms and is able to recognise variations in an expression (e.g. *'molecular function'* $\rightarrow$ *'functional roles of molecular'*). Although the results of FASTR seemed rather accurate at first, a second round of expert validation of the vocabulary took place. Out of 2,211 unique variations, experts reduced the number to 1,438 terms (i.e. 65%) and thereby preserved the quality of the training data.

3.4 Automatic corpus annotation

We annotated the data for our distant supervision approach using Prodigy (Montani and team, 2023) under a research licence. The annotation follows the CoNLL2003 (Sang and Meulder, 2003) standard, which uses the BIO annotation format. The Occurrences column in Table 2 displays the number of annotation under each label in our corpus.

4 Experimental methods

The primary objective of our experiments is to test whether the model possesses good generalization capabilities, precision, and stability. Therefore, we designed three distinct ablation studies to evaluate how dependent our approach is to the labels vocabulary.

4.1 Exploring Existing Models

To identify every entity in the articles, we first examined the results of the SciBERT model (Beltagy et al., 2019). SciBERT is a widely pre-trained model for scientific articles, aiming at improving the expressivity of the model and save training time for downstream tasks. We manually annotated 646 "naive" entities (i.e. "naive" meaning only distinguishing whether a span is an entity or not, not knowing which label the entity belongs to) related to the field of nanobiology in one article (Ma et al., 2016), and then tried to use SciBERT for "naive" entity recognition on plain text.

The result is that SciBERT can identify almost all entities in the article. Out of 646 entities related to the nanobiology field it can identify 638, which suggest a high recall capability (i.e. ≈ 0.99 on the article tested). However, SciBERT identifies a large number of entities that would be false positives in the field of nanobiology. SciBERT identified a total of 2,976 entities, which gives 2,322 false positives that need to be filtered out suggesting a low precision value (i.e. ≈ 0.21). Examples of these false positives are : *nanoscience, construction, convergence, reduce, Hayakawa* A way to eliminated these false positives would be to match them with an ontology. But this approach would lack several essential aspects: classification of entities into labels, possible confusion between concepts when trying to do so (e.g. in the ontology, *dendrimer* is originally present under the concepts `Material` and `Nanoparticle`), coverage of the ontology vocabulary and so on. Then, it does not eliminate the need for ontology reduction and expert involvement.

We also experimented with some existing models for BMNER in the Scispacy and Stanza li-

Label	Description	Core Concepts (#sub-concepts)	Vocabulary extract
Nanoparticle	are physical structures, usually between 1 and 100nm in two or three dimensions, that present size related properties	Nanoparticle (68), Fiat Material (77)	*nanocapsule, fluorescent carbon nanoparticles, carbon dot, nanowire*
Property	are physical and chemical functions that can be described using measurement	Realizable Entity (89), Application (102)	*amphiphilic, hydrophilic, antioxidant, fluorescent*
Material	are the atoms and chemical compounds constituting nanoparticles and other studied objects	Chemical Entity (663), Material Entity (320)	*thiol, gold, primary amine, carbohydrate*
Event	describes what is happening at a cellular level	Process (231)	*mitosis, transcription, cell death, DNA modification*
Technique	for preparing nanoparticles, measuring their characteristics and using them	Technique (63), Assay (171), Bioassay (37), Instrument (31), Application (102)	*fluorescence spectroscopy, atomic force microscopy, gel electrophoresis*

Table 1: Description and examples of the chosen labels

Label	Terms	Vocabulary	Occurrences	Depth	Width
Nanoparticle	71	196	16,341	4	19
Property	105	345	19,849	7	24
Material	241	515	74,688	11	36
Event	56	210	3,219	5	9
Technique	65	172	7,104	7	19
Total	538	1,438	121,201		

Table 2: Labels vocabulary sizes

braries, but most of these are trained on specific corpora and entities, and perform poorly on NER tasks in the nanobiology field.

4.2 Ablation experiment design

In order to assess the dependency of the approach to the resource, as well as model generalization capabilities, we designed a set of ablation experiments. As detailed in Table 2, our five labels cover a list of 538 terms. Each term has varying numbers of variants, ranging from 1 to over 10, resulting in a total of 1438 different terms. In our ablation experiments, the terms were first randomly shuffled in each labels to minimize the risk of latent factors from affecting the experimental results, such as the terms being arranged in a specific pattern. Then, the label's vocabularies are divided into five equal parts, noted as folds A, B, C, D and E. Ablation of 33% of the terms were also implemented with folds F, G and H.

To create the training and test set for our ablation experiments, we selected the sentences based on the presence or absence of ablated entities. This was done in order to ensure that the model would not confuse excluded entities for negative examples during the training, and to later test its capabilities to retrieve entities not encountered before. As shown in Table 3, this resulted in training and test sets of various sizes, some being three time larger than others (e.g. test sets in folds D and C). For instance, the training set in Fold A is composed of 126.834 sentences not containing a single ablated

Fold	Abl.%	Training set	Test set
A	20%	126,834	21,427
B	20%	130,099	18,162
C	20%	136,708	11,553
D	20%	113,875	34,386
E	20%	129,580	18,681
F	33%	109,259	39,002
G	33%	117,392	30,869
H	33%	120,103	28,158

Table 3: Number of sentences in each Fold

term, the test set is then made of the remaining sentences. Thus, ablation experiments ensure that part of the test set consist in entities on which the model has not been trained. The approximate sentence ratio is 6:1 for 20% ablation and 4:1 for 33% ablation.

5 Results and Analysis

In this section, we first present the results of training the model on the full dataset, which performances aligned with our expectations. Then, we detail the two random ablation experiments we designed, reducing the data by 20% and 33% respectively. We noticed a significant fluctuation in the results of these experiments. Therefore, we specifically analyzed the 20% ablation experiment and based on these analyses, we proposed the hypothesis that including or excluding specific terms under our labels might have a significant impact on the precision and recall scores. Following this, we designed a new frequency-based 10% ablation experiment to explore this hypothesis. The results from this new experiment successfully validated our conjectures.

5.1 Training on the whole dataset

Initially, we trained the model on the complete dataset, carrying out a training with 5 and 20 epochs respectively. Given the consistency of the training and validation datasets, the nature of this experiment is closer to a straightforward word-matching task. Results are displayed in Table 4. We found that the F1 score of the model reached a value 0.985, which is consistent with our expectations.

Subsequently, we performed a deep analysis of the model's generalization ability. Our assumption was that it would be impossible to achieve 100% coverage of terms in the corpus, so we had the model re-annotate the corpus. Table 4 thus also presents the number of unique new entities (i.e. ignoring the number of occurrences) identified by NanoNER, the number of correctly labeled entities and the associated precision. Not cosidering the number of occurrences for these newly retrieved entities allows for a better estimation of the model generalization capabilities. NanoNER achieves an precision value on new entities roughly around 0.8. Additionally, we found that as the training epochs increased, the precision value on the newly found entities improved, but the number of new entities recognized decreased.This indicates that the number of training epochs can be chosen according to the intended use, giving priority to recall or precision values on never-before-encountered entities.

5.2 20% Ablation experiments

The primary objective of our ablation study is to further test the model generalization capabilities and dependency to the resource. We employed early stopping for training, setting the number of epochs to 1 and the batch size to 32. The training results are presented in Table 5. As we can see, the precision fluctuates around 0.79 and the gap between the highest and lowest precision values can be as high as 0.14. The impact of the vocabulary ablation is even more visible on the recall: with an average score of 0.54, it has degraded considerably compared to the initial training. This tend to indicates that the absence or presence of specific terms highly influence the quality of the trained model. To address this, we conducted further exploration in Section 5.4.1.

5.3 33% Ablation experiments

Next, we conducted experiments with a 33% ablation of the terms. The results in Table 6 are as expected: the precision value remained around 0.8, but the recall rate dropped even further. This is due to the higher number of terms excluded in 33% ablation experiments compared to the 20% ones.

5.4 Ablation experiments analyse

Firstly, we conducted a generalization analysis on the ablation experiments from folds A to E. We employed the same method as in the full data analysis: We initially listed all the deleted entities, and then had predictions made by the model on the entire corpus. Subsequently, we matched all the entities predicted by the model with the deleted entities. As depicted in Table 7, the model could stably

Epochs	Precision	Recall	F1 Score	New Entities	Correct Labeling	Precision
5.0	0.981	0.989	0.985	485	375	0.773
20.0	0.982	0.989	0.985	249	202	0.811

Table 4: Models trained using the entire dataset

Fold	Precision	Recall	F1 Score
A	0.796	0.544	0.646
B	0.826	0.575	0.678
C	0.853	0.593	0.699
D	0.756	0.424	0.544
E	0.711	0.549	0.620
Average	0.788	0.537	0.637

Table 5: Models trained on 20% ablation folds

Fold	Precision	Recall	F1 Score
F	0.752	0.332	0.461
G	0.868	0.411	0.557
H	0.847	0.460	0.596
Average	0.822	0.401	0.538

Table 6: Models trained on 33% ablation folds

rediscover up to 30% of the deleted entities. Considering that these results are not calculated based on occurrence rates, and it's quite challenging to discover the relationships between many obscure entities through deep learning, we believe these results are within our expectations.

Fold	Retrieved	Ablated	Recall
A	66	232	0.28
B	89	353	0.25
C	72	303	0.24
D	77	249	0.31
E	77	272	0.28
Average	76.2	281.8	0.27

Table 7: Refound

Next, we sought to analyze the variability between the folds. We hypothesize that certain labels are excessively difficult, thereby affecting the overall performance of the task, we then evaluated each label separately. Table 8 displays the average recall and precision values of the labels over the different folds (detailled evaluation is available in Appendix A. We found that `Nanoparticle` and `Event` have the most important variations in recall, while the variations in precision mostly concern `Nanoparticle` and `Technique` Most of the average recall values over different labels are close to 0.54, but differences in average precision is more important when comparing the different labels. `Material` and *Property* displays scores over 0.90, `Nanoparticle` is around 0.83, but `Event` and `Technique` have significantly lower precision values (0.74 and 0.65 respectively). These variations are analyzed as a result of the specific characteristics of the labels vocabularies. E.g. `Event` and `Technique` contains terms from the scientific language that are not specific to the nanobiology field, and thus carry a higher risk of confusion.

Label	Recall		Precision	
	avg.	var.	avg.	var.
`Nanoparticle`	0.57	0.23	0.83	0.13
`Material`	0.55	0.13	0.92	0.06
`Event`	0.53	0.22	0.75	0.10
`Property`	0.48	0.10	0.91	0.09
`Technique`	0.56	0.16	0.65	0.15

Table 8: Average performances on each label

We also observed specific differences between the different folds for specific labels. E.g. the recall for `Nanoparticle` is very high in fold A (i.e. 0.82), but significantly lower in fold E (i.e. O.19). This suggests that certain words are highly important for specific labels. In fact, in fold E, the term *nanoparticle* was removed, which is not only a high-frequency term throughout the entire corpus, but also an essential word involved in different terms (e.g. *nanoparticle*, *gold nanoparticle*).

We believe that these high-frequency terms may have a great impact on the training of the model. Therefore, removing these words during training might lead to a significant decline in the performance of the model. To explore this hypothesis, we decided to conduct a third ablation experiment based on terms of frequency.

5.4.1 10% Ablation experiments

We then sorted the terms according to their frequency in the corpus and conducted four more

Training set	Precision	Recall	F1 Score	Corpus size
remove top 10%	0.599	0.279	0.381	21.2%
remove top 10% + mft^*	0.668	0.371	0.430	51.0%
remove middle 10%	0.802	0.683	0.738	99.0%
top 10% only	0.763	0.413	0.536	78.8%

$^*mft$: most frequent term in each label

Table 9: Models trained on 10% ablation

rounds of ablation, as shown in Table 9: in each label we tried removing 10% of the most frequent terms (with one experiment reintroducing the first term in each label), removing the 10% in the middle of the terms frequency and finally retaining only the 10% most frequent terms in each label. This approach limits the corpus exploitable as training and test sets, reflecting the distribution of the terms throughout the corpus.

Firstly, it appears that the frequency of the terms is a good indicator of the model dependency towards the annotation resource. Indeed, precision and recall values are impacted proportionally to the rank of the terms removed. Comparing the first and second rows also indicates that certain terms (i.e. the most frequent terms in each label) significantly impact the model's performance. These terms may play a critical role in the classification task, or they could provide substantial contextual information, helping the model understand other related terms. Regarding the third row's ablation experiment, although most of the corpus (99%) was kept to train the model, the F1 score is far lower than 0.985 when trained with the full data. This suggests that even terms with lower frequencies still significantly impact the model's performance. These less frequent terms might carry specific information crucial for the model to understand and classify the text. The fourth row's ablation experiment result indicates that retaining only the most common terms might lead the model to overly focus on these terms, overlooking other terms that may carry important information. This could be because these common terms contain a lot of generic information but lack some specific, category-targeted information.

6 Error analysis and improvement approaches

6.1 Sentence selection during ablation experiments

In our ablation experiments, we sometimes encounter a scenario where a sentence contains an ablated term and an other one that is not, and thus we would like to remove only one of them. In our experiments, we chose to exclude such cases to avoid having our model confuse ablated terms for negative examples. But other strategies could be adopted to tackle this, such as the masking or replacement of tokens.

6.2 Imbalanced dataset

As observed during the ablation experiment, our corpus is highly imbalanced. Some terms and labels appear more frequently than others. Detailed evaluations of individual labels in ablation experiments are given in Appendix A. This discrepancy might lead the model to over-learn from these high-frequency terms, thereby overlooking the importance of less frequent terms. During future optimization, this problem could be tackled by using techniques such as oversampling or undersampling to balance the number of samples across different categories. In a study on NER using Wikipedia, (Al-Rfou et al., 2015) adopted an approach that involves constructing a subset of the training corpus. This strategy ensures that the conditional distribution of specific entity classes remains unaltered when they are positive examples, thereby significantly enhancing the model's performance across multiple languages.

6.3 Vocabulary coverage in distant supervision

Our training and evaluation assume that the ground truth annotations are accurate, which may not be the case in a distant supervision framework. Thus there may be cases where the model is retrieving entities under the correct label, but that are considered false positives in our automatically annotated corpus. We tried to reduce this effect by employing FASTR (Jacquemin et al., 1997) to improve the coverage of our resource, but this required experts to filter out FASTR false positives. Also, their is some known variations that FASTR is not able to retrieve (e.g. *'iron oxide nanoparticle'* and *'silicon dot'* are in `Nanoparticle` vocabulary, but their respective variations *'iron nanoparticle'* and *'silicon dot'* were not recognized).

One solution would be to use a method known as knowledge distillation, which incrementally improves the model's performance through iterations, a training method used in the previously mentioned BOND (Liang et al., 2020) paper. By using a teacher model to generate pseudo-labels for training the student model, the training effectiveness of the model is improved through repeated iterations. Another solution is to manually annotate a sufficient portion of high-quality data and then use it as validation set for the model.

7 Conclusion

In this work, we have introduced NanoNER, a tool for Named Entity Recognition in the field of nanobiology. We designed an iterative process to determine the model labels and vocabulary using ontologies, domain experts and retrieving terminological variations. This resulted in five labels, covering 1,438 terms, that allow for the automatic annotation of our corpus in a distant supervision approach. Experiment analyses have demonstrated that our model can effectively identify entities of interest, both previously seen and new ones, in the field of nanobiology. Given the complexity and abundance of technical terms in the field, our method shows promising applications in nanobiology.

We believe that this approach can be applied as is on other scientific fields, as it require only an ontology (or taxonomy) resource and minimum man-power. This allow for the efficient training of NER models useful in downstream NLP tasks.

Ablation experiments showed a significant dependence of the model on the vocabulary used. In future work, we could attempt data augmentation on the dataset to reduce its imbalance and enhance the model's training performance. In addition, it is possible to use knowledge distillation for iterative model updates, which can reduce the false positive misjudgment during validation and improve the model's generalization capabilities.

Acknowledgements

We would especially like to thank the researchers who shared their expertise in nanobiology with us: Raphaël Lévy (Professor of Physics at Paris Nord University), Nathanne Rost (Postdoctoral researcher in Nanobiosciences at Paris Nord University) and Federico Boem (Postdoctoral researcher in Philosophy of Sciences at University of Twente).

The NanoBubbles project has received Synergy grant funding from the European Research Council (ERC), within the European Union's Horizon 2020 program, grant agreement no. 951393.

References

Rami Al-Rfou, Vivek Kulkarni, Bryan Perozzi, and Steven Skiena. 2015. Polyglot-ner: Massive multilingual named entity recognition. In *Proceedings of the 2015 SIAM International Conference on Data Mining*, pages 586–594. SIAM.

Iz Beltagy, Kyle Lo, and Arman Cohan. 2019. Scibert: A pretrained language model for scientific text.

Pier Luigi Buttigieg, Norman Morrison, Barry Smith, Christopher Mungall, and Suzanna Lewis. 2013. The environment ontology: contextualising biological and biomedical entities. *Journal of biomedical semantics*, 4:43.

Kirill Degtyarenko, Paula de Matos, Marcus Ennis, Janna Hastings, Martin Zbinden, Alan McNaught, Rafael Alcántara, Michael Darsow, Mickaël Guedj, and Michael Ashburner. 2007. ChEBI: a database and ontology for chemical entities of biological interest. *Nucleic Acids Research*, 36(suppl_1):D344–D350.

Xishuang Dong, Lijun Qian, Yi Guan, Lei Huang, Qiubin Yu, and Jinfeng Yang. 2016. A multiclass classification method based on deep learning for named entity recognition in electronic medical records. In *2016 New York Scientific Data Summit (NYSDS)*, pages 1–10.

Christoph M Friedrich, Thomas Revillion, Martin Hofmann, and Juliane Fluck. 2006. Biomedical and chemical named entity recognition with conditional random fields: The advantage of dictionary features. In *SMBM*.

Jason Fries, Sen Wu, Alex Ratner, and Christopher Ré. 2017. Swellshark: A generative model for biomedical named entity recognition without labeled data. *arXiv preprint arXiv:1704.06360*.

Janna Hastings, Leonid Chepelev, Egon Willighagen, Nico Adams, Christoph Steinbeck, and Michel Dumontier. 2011. The chemical information ontology: Provenance and disambiguation for chemical data on the biological semantic web. *PLOS ONE*, 6(10):1–13.

Janna Hastings, Nina Jeliazkova, Gareth Owen, Georgia Tsiliki, Cristian R Munteanu, Christoph Steinbeck, and Egon Willighagen. 2015. enanomapper: harnessing ontologies to enable data integration for nanomaterial risk assessment. *Journal of biomedical semantics*, 6(1):1–15.

Ming-Siang Huang, Po-Ting Lai, Pei-Yen Lin, Yu-Ting You, Richard Tzong-Han Tsai, and Wen-Lian Hsu. 2020. Biomedical named entity recognition and linking datasets: survey and our recent development. *Briefings in Bioinformatics*, 21(6):2219–2238.

Christian Jacquemin, Judith L Klavans, and Evelyne Tzoukermann. 1997. Expansion of multi-word terms for indexing and retrieval using morphology and syntax. In *35th Annual Meeting of the Association for Computational Linguistics and 8th Conference of the European Chapter of the Association for Computational Linguistics*, pages 24–31.

Zhenfei Ju, Jian Wang, and Fei Zhu. 2011. Named entity recognition from biomedical text using svm. In *2011 5th international conference on bioinformatics and biomedical engineering*, pages 1–4. IEEE.

Guillaume Lample, Miguel Ballesteros, Sandeep Subramanian, Kazuya Kawakami, and Chris Dyer. 2016. Neural architectures for named entity recognition. *arXiv preprint arXiv:1603.01360.*

Jinhyuk Lee, Wonjin Yoon, Sungdong Kim, Donghyeon Kim, Sunkyu Kim, Chan Ho So, and Jaewoo Kang. 2020. Biobert: a pre-trained biomedical language representation model for biomedical text mining. *Bioinformatics*, 36(4):1234–1240.

Jiao Li, Yueping Sun, Robin Johnson, Daniela Sciaky, Chih-Hsuan Wei, Robert Leaman, Allan Peter Davis, Carolyn Mattingly, Thomas Wiegers, and Zhiyong lu. 2016. Biocreative v cdr task corpus: a resource for chemical disease relation extraction. *Database*, 2016:baw068.

Chen Liang, Yue Yu, Haoming Jiang, Siawpeng Er, Ruijia Wang, Tuo Zhao, and Chao Zhang. 2020. Bond: Bert-assisted open-domain named entity recognition with distant supervision. In *Proceedings of the 26th ACM SIGKDD International Conference on Knowledge Discovery & Data Mining*. ACM.

Patrice Lopez. 2008-2023. Grobid. `https://github.com/kermitt2/grobid`.

Wang Ma, Andrew G. Cheetham, and Honggang Cui. 2016. Building nanostructures with drugs. *Nano Today*, 11(1):13–30.

Yu Meng, Yunyi Zhang, Jiaxin Huang, Xuan Wang, Yu Zhang, Heng Ji, and Jiawei Han. 2021. Distantly-supervised named entity recognition with noise-robust learning and language model augmented self-training. *arXiv preprint arXiv:2109.05003.*

Mike Mintz, Steven Bills, Rion Snow, and Dan Jurafsky. 2009. Distant supervision for relation extraction without labeled data. In *Proceedings of the Joint Conference of the 47th Annual Meeting of the ACL and the 4th International Joint Conference on Natural Language Processing of the AFNLP*, pages 1003–1011.

Ines Montani and Explosion AI team. 2023. Prodigy - an annotation tool for machine learning and data science. Website. `https://prodi.gy/`.

Natalia Ponomareva, Ferran Pla, Antonio Molina, and Paolo Rosso. 2007a. Biomedical named entity recognition: a poor knowledge hmm-based approach. In *Natural Language Processing and Information Systems: 12th International Conference on Applications of Natural Language to Information Systems, NLDB 2007, Paris, France, June 27-29, 2007. Proceedings 12*, pages 382–387. Springer.

Natalia Ponomareva, Paolo Rosso, Ferrán Pla, and Antonio Molina. 2007b. Conditional random fields vs. hidden markov models in a biomedical named entity recognition task. In *Proc. of Int. Conf. Recent Advances in Natural Language Processing, RANLP*, pages 479–483.

Erik F. Tjong Kim Sang and Fien De Meulder. 2003. Introduction to the conll-2003 shared task: Language-independent named entity recognition.

Jingbo Shang, Liyuan Liu, Xiang Ren, Xiaotao Gu, Teng Ren, and Jiawei Han. 2018. Learning named entity tagger using domain-specific dictionary. *arXiv preprint arXiv:1809.03599.*

Dennis G. Thomas, Rohit V. Pappu, and Nathan A. Baker. 2011. Nanoparticle ontology for cancer nanotechnology research. *Journal of Biomedical Informatics*, 44(1):59–74. Ontologies for Clinical and Translational Research.

Xuan Wang, Vivian Hu, Xiangchen Song, Shweta Garg, Jinfeng Xiao, and Jiawei Han. 2021. Chemner: fine-grained chemistry named entity recognition with ontology-guided distant supervision. In *Proceedings of the 2021 Conference on Empirical Methods in Natural Language Processing.*

Zheng Yuan, Yijia Liu, Chuanqi Tan, Songfang Huang, and Fei Huang. 2021. Improving biomedical pre-trained language models with knowledge. *arXiv preprint arXiv:2104.10344.*

Sheng Zhang, Hao Cheng, Jianfeng Gao, and Hoifung Poon. 2022. Optimizing bi-encoder for named entity recognition via contrastive learning. *arXiv preprint arXiv:2208.14565.*

A Detailed ablation evaluation

Fold	Label	Positive	Total	Recall	Positive	Total	Precision
A	nanoparticle	2,557	3,108	0.822	4,645	4,821	0.963
	material	8,952	16,022	0.557	15,433	15,821	0.975
	event	233	342	0.68	398	444	0.896
	property	2,999	8,287	0.363	4,033	4,241	0.951
	technique	591	1,036	0.57	1,346	2,053	0.656
B	nanoparticle	1,466	3,309	0.443	2,854	4,082	0.699
	material	8,959	14,566	0.615	14,961	15,377	0.973
	event	203	419	0.484	341	428	0.797
	property	2,531	4,122	0.613	3,964	4,101	0.967
	technique	685	2,033	0.336	1,129	1,665	0.678
C	nanoparticle	1,346	1,900	0.708	2,475	2,590	0.956
	material	6,315	9,477	0.665	10,930	11,976	0.913
	event	409	1,095	0.373	554	843	0.657
	property	1,385	3,410	0.406	2,229	2,295	0.971
	technique	297	574	0.517	958	1,240	0.773
D	nanoparticle	2,371	3,364	0.705	4,369	4,934	0.885
	material	8,876	29,268	0.301	12,920	14,016	0.922
	event	871	996	0.874	1,362	2,236	0.609
	property	3,329	7,345	0.452	4,855	6,563	0.740
	technique	1,156	1,361	0.849	2,784	3,547	0.785
E	nanoparticle	1308	6,826	0.192	2,652	4,064	0.653
	material	8,237	13,339	0.617	12,670	15,670	0.809
	event	249	996	0.251	366	477	0.767
	property	1,749	3,056	0.573	2,921	3,251	0.898
	technique	492	935	0.525	1,160	3,132	0.370

Table 10: Ablation evaluation on individual labels

Relation Extraction from Scientific Texts in Russian with Limited Training Data

Olga Tikhobaeva
Novosibirsk State University / Russia
otikhobaeva10@gmail.com

Elena Bruches
A.P. Ershov Institute of Informatics Systems / Russia
Novosibirsk State University / Russia
bruches@bk.ru

Abstract

In this paper, we address the task of extracting semantic relations between entities in scientific articles in Russian, with a focus on scientific terms as entities. We present a dataset that includes annotated abstracts of scientific articles in Russian. This dataset was used to train and test models and develop an algorithm for the automatic extraction of semantic relations. We conducted experiments and compared one zero-shot and one few-shot approach for relation extraction: one based on the perplexity score and the other based on the use of prototype vectors of relations. Our results show that both methods can achieve reasonable performance, demonstrating the potential of zero-shot and few-shot approaches for relation extraction in scientific texts in Russian. The developed tool and annotated dataset are publicly available and could be valuable resources for other researchers [1].

1 Introduction

At the present time, the proliferation of electronic scientific publications has led to an increasing need for extracting various types of semantic information from scientific texts. One of the types of such information is semantic relations. By extracting these relations, machines can better understand the meaning of a text, and this can have a wide range of practical applications. For instance, relation extraction can be used in search and question-answering systems, as well as in ontology development and text classification.

However, currently, this problem is still difficult for any domain in any language. There are several factors that contribute to the difficulty of this task such as high variability in terms of syntax, grammar, and vocabulary and ambiguity of meanings in the texts. What's more, there is a problem of lack of labeled data, especially for the Russian language. Even though, there are some datasets with annotated relations such as (Zhang et al., 2017; Dunietz and Gillick, 2014; Li et al., 2016) in multi-domains and biomedical domain, it is still hard to find some publicly available datasets such as SciERC (Luan et al., 2018) for scientific fields other than biomedical, and in languages other than English.

Due to the problem of lack of data we decided to concentrate on some zero-shot and few-shot methods. Zero-shot relation extraction is a type of relation extraction that allows a model to identify and extract the types of relations that it has not been specifically trained on. In other words, the model can perform relation extraction in a "zero-shot" manner without any direct supervision for the relation types in question. Few-shot relation extraction assumes that the model is trained on a small set of labeled data. The purpose of this method is to allow the model to generalize to the new tasks based on a few examples.

Thus, we make the following contributions:

- Provide a new dataset for relation extraction tasks for Russian scientific texts.
- Compare one zero-shot and one few-shot approach for relation extraction (based on perplexity score and with the use of prototype vectors of relations).

2 Related Work

Relation extraction (RE) is one of the main tasks in the field of natural language processing (NLP). With the introduction of large language models (Devlin et al., 2019; Liu et al., 2019; Lewis et al., 2020) their use became one of the main methods of solving this problem. However, such methods require a lot of well-annotated data for training. Currently there are no datasets available for this task in a scientific field in Russian, and manual

[1] https://github.com/iis-research-team/terminator/tree/main/relation_extractor

Proceedings of the 2nd Workshop on Information Extraction from Scientific Publications, pages 25–30
Nov 1, 2023. ©2023 Association for Computational Linguistics

annotation takes a long time and requires the efforts of more than one person to objectively label the relations. Therefore, in this paper we decided to pay our special attention to zero-shot and few-shot approaches that do not require a lot of annotated data. There are some examples of them.

The first method is based on the scores of the probability of a sentence that the language model can give. (Henlein and Mehler, 2022) proposed to create a template for each relation type and then compute increased log probability of the sentences from these templates with the use of BERT as in (Kurita et al., 2019). For example, a template for the relation "LOCATED-IN" might look like this – *"the <e1> is in the <e2>"*. So if the first entity is *"toothbrush"* and the second is *"bathroom"*, the sentence from the template will be *"the toothbrush is in the bathroom"*. With the selected threshold of probability, it will be possible to separate the presence or absence of relation between two entities and also its type.

The second method was used in (Zhang and Lu, 2022; Zhang et al., 2022). The primary idea behind this approach is that one can get prototype vectors for each type of relation and then use them to define the relations between pairs of entities. To create a prototype vectors the authors used sentences from the train part of the dataset, as well as the name and the description of the relations. A prototype vector of each relation can be compared with actual sentences that contain the pair of entities. The closest prototype in vector space will reflect the relation in the sentence. In (Zhang et al., 2022) the authors employed BERT (Devlin et al., 2019) as the encoder to map the sentences into a low-dimensional vector space.

Last but not least, (Lan et al., 2022) proposed a third method that trains the model to extract relations from unstructured text, while the train and test sets of relations do not intersect. At first, the model was trained to find the probability for different sets of potential relations from the train dataset and then to find the boundaries of two entities. After that it can process any new texts and does not need to know the types of relations. To find the probability for some relations in the sentence the authors offer to encode semantics of the relation types by given the combined sentence like *"[CLS] text-of-the-sentence [SEP] text-of-the-relation [SEP]"* to BERT. If the model has these sentences for each relation type, it is possible to get the probability distributions over candidate relations.

3 Data Preparation

To conduct the experiments with different approaches we created an annotated dataset which is composed of abstracts of scientific papers on 10 domains in Russian. The list of domains includes the following: Biology and Medicine, History and Philology, Journalism, Law, Linguistics, Math, Pedagogy, Physics, Psychology and Information Technology.

To test the approaches we used 20% of the texts on each of the subject areas.

Statistics for our dataset is presented in Table 1.

Unit	**number**
texts	400
tokens	17 481
terms	5 834
relations	976

Table 1: Dataset statistics

Each abstract was annotated by two annotators. The task was to classify the relations between each possible pair of terms in each sentence in the abstract. The terms in the texts were already extracted. During the annotation, we followed the instructions proposed in (Bruches et al., 2020).

For our experiments we chose 3 following oriented semantic relations: USAGE, ISA, PART-OF. Those relation were selected because they are common to all considered domains. The types of relations in the corpus, along with their meanings and distribution across the dataset, are provided in Table 2.

Relation type	**Meaning**	**number**
USAGE	x is used for/in y	544
ISA	x is y	270
PART_OF	x is part of y	162

Table 2: Types of relations

In Table 3 sample sentences of all three relation types in the dataset are presented. In each sample two terms and the relation between them are highlighted.

The dataset is available for other researchers[2].

[2]https://github.com/iis-research-team/ruserrc-dataset

Relation type	Example	Translation
USAGE	*В статье рассматривается способ <e1>формирования тектовых сообщений</e1> на основе <e2>метода движения губ</e2>, сооветствующего определенной фонеме.*	The article considers a method of <e1>formation of text messages</e1> based on <e2>the method of movements of lips</e2> corresponding to a certain phoneme.
ISA	*Одним из самых точных и эффективных <e1>способов управления жестами</e1> является <e2>управление активностью мышц</e2>.*	One of the most accurate and effective <e1>ways to control gestures</e1> is to <e2>control muscle activity</e2>.
PART_OF	*Метод обработки и определения форм слов позволяет в отличие от аналогов обрабатывать формы слов <e1>естественных языков</e1> различных групп и <e1>семейств</e1>.*	Unlike analogies, the method of processing and definiting forms of words allows to process the forms of words from <e1>languages</e1> of different groups and <e2>families</e2>.

Table 3: Examples of relations

4 Zero-shot and few-shot approaches for relation extraction

4.1 Using perplexity scores

In the first place, we tried an approach for relation extraction based on perplexity scores. It can be traced to zero-shot approaches. It consists in the following: for each type of relation we had made 3 patterns of the sentences. The patterns and their meaning are provided in Table 4.

Then the terms were added to these templates to make sentences. For example, the pattern for USAGE is "{term1} are used in {term2}". So if the first term is "multimedia technologies" and the second is "the educational process", the sentence from the template will be *"multimedia technologies are used in the educational process"*.

Then we got an estimate of the probability of each sentence using the model GPT2 (Radford et al., 2019). After choosing the most probable pattern for each relation, we again compared the probability of sentences from these best templates. The most likely sentence would reflect the true relation between the terms. The schematic work of the method is presented in the Figure 1.

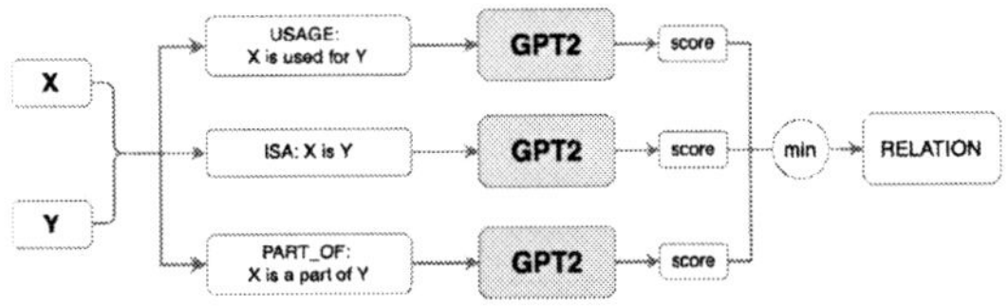

Figure 1: Schema for the perplexity scores approach

To measure the probability we used the perplexity score. In general, this value can be described as the model uncertainty measure when predicting each of the next token, hence the lower the perplexity, the more certain the model in predicting this sequence.

The obtained metrics for this approach are shown in Table 5.

4.2 Using prototype vectors of relations

The second approach for relation identification that we tried is based on the usage of the prototype vectors of relations. It can be attributed to few-shot approaches. First of all, we manually chose 138 best examples from the train part of the dataset to create a prototype vectors for each type of relations. In selecting the best examples we were guided by the following criterion: the example shows only one type of relations and has short context which includes only two terms of interest. Then we got the vectors of these of sentences. Vectors of sentences are the embeddings of CLS token from BERT(Devlin et al., 2019). Each prototype vector is an average of the vectors of sentences reflecting each relation. Once these prototype vectors are obtained, they can be used to classify test examples. By computing the value of the cosine similarity of the example and the prototypes, we can determine which relation is most similar to this example. Schematic graphics that reflect the work of this method can be seen in Figure 2.

The obtained metrics for this approach are shown in Table 6.

However, this method falls short in defining the "ISA" relation type and generally performs most effectively in identifying the "USAGE" relation. There are several reasons for this. First of all, quite often the relations are not expressed explicitly by some specific words or phrases, but with semantics, which are difficult to automatically find and understand in the text. The second reason is the fact

Relation type	Patterns	Meaning
USAGE	x используется для y x применяется для y y выполняется при помощи x	x is used for y x is used for y y is done with x
ISA	x является y x представляет собой y x – это y	x is y x represents y x is y
PART-OF	x является частью y y состоит из x y включает в себя x	x is a part of y y consists of x y includes x

Table 4: Patterns of relations

Relation type	Precision	Recall	F1
USAGE	0.69	0.37	0.48
ISA	0.46	0.38	0.42
PART_OF	0.15	0.41	0.22
macro-average	0.43	0.39	0.37

Table 5: Metrics for perplexiry score approach

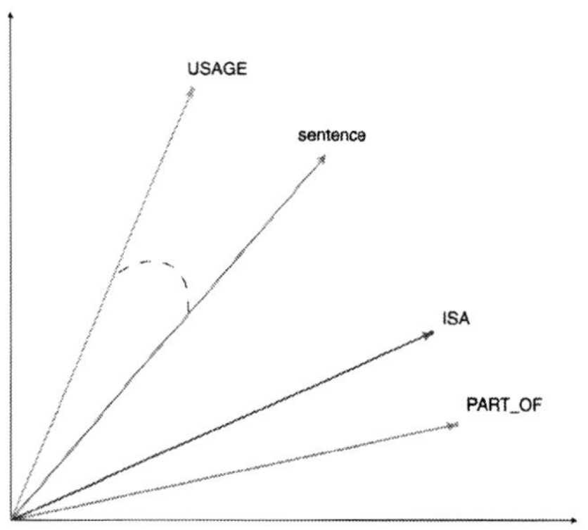

Figure 2: Plot for the prototype vectors approach

Relation type	Precision	Recall	F1
USAGE	0.59	0.81	0.68
ISA	0.00	0.00	0.00
PART_OF	0.22	0.24	0.23
macro-average	0.38	0.51	0.30

Table 6: Metrics for the prototype vectors approach

that all of these relations are expressed in similar contexts. For example, parentheses or colons can associate terms with both "ISA" and "PART-OF" relations. At the same time, the preposition *"в" (in)* depending on the terms it links, can express the relation "PART-OF" as well as "USAGE".

5 Classification task with a CLS-vector

To compare the approaches that were specified above with the classic supervised learning method we used the neural network architecture described by the authors in (Wu and He, 2019).

The algorithm of this model is as follows: We use the vector of a special token CLS (which is regarded as the input text vector) and the vector of two terms connected by the relation. These three vectors are concatenated and the resulting vector is fed to the classifier. We used 80% of our annotated dataset to train the model.

The results that we were able to achieve are described in the Table 7.

It is clear that "PART-OF" relation type has the lowest F1-score of all relations. The reason for this is likely to be the lack of examples of this relation in the training data.

Relation type	Precision	Recall	F1
USAGE	0.84	0.95	0.89
ISA	0.83	0.76	0.79
PART_OF	0.58	0.41	0.48
macro-average	0.75	0.71	0.72

Table 7: Metrics for supervised learning

6 Discussions

The results of our experiments show that zero-shot and few-shot approaches are generally able to distinguish semantic relations. But these methods still lose in quality in comparison with the supervised learning. It gives us the understanding that metrics obtained in the experiments are not a limit and there is a space for the research to grow.

For example, we assume that if we add more patterns for the model to choose from in the perplexity score method or put more appropriate examples in the set for prototype vectors this will greatly improve the results.

Of course, still there are some aspects of relation extraction that are extremely difficult to solve. For instance, the extraction of the terms that are not connected by any relation.

7 Future Work

We are definitely going to further develop relation extraction area for the Russian language since it is still low-resource language. Due to the lack of data the Russian language requires adaptation of existing solutions for English or development of brand new ones.

One of the ideas that we are about to thy in the foreseeable future is to translate the sentences from Russian to English and use some good quality method for relation extraction from English text.

It would also be interesting to conduct cross-domain experiments for each of the methods as the annotated dataset has been prepared for a number of disciplines. We are not entirely sure that the results will be representative in all domains because the texts of some of the disciplines have a limited amount of the examples of some relations. But it is still worth to try.

8 Conclusion

This study aimed to address the problem of lack of labeled data for relation extraction in Russian scientific texts by constructing a new dataset. One zero-shot and one few-shot approach for relation extraction were then evaluated, one based on perplexity score and the other utilizing prototype vectors of relations. The experimental results indicated that both methods can achieve reasonable performance, highlighting the potential of zero-shot and few-shot approaches for relation extraction in Russian scientific texts across different domains. These findings suggest that zero-shot and few-shot approaches could be a promising direction for relation extraction research, especially in low-resource languages such as Russian.

References

Elena Bruches, Alexey Pauls, Tatiana Batura, and Vladimir Isachenko. 2020. Entity recognition and relation extraction from scientific and technical texts in russian. In *2020 Science and Artificial Intelligence conference (S.A.I.ence)*, pages 41–45.

Jacob Devlin, Ming-Wei Chang, Kenton Lee, and Kristina Toutanova. 2019. BERT: Pre-training of deep bidirectional transformers for language understanding. In *Proceedings of the 2019 Conference of the North American Chapter of the Association for Computational Linguistics: Human Language Technologies, Volume 1 (Long and Short Papers)*, pages 4171–4186, Minneapolis, Minnesota. Association for Computational Linguistics.

Jesse Dunietz and Daniel Gillick. 2014. A new entity salience task with millions of training examples. In *Proceedings of the 14th Conference of the European Chapter of the Association for Computational Linguistics, volume 2: Short Papers*, pages 205–209, Gothenburg, Sweden. Association for Computational Linguistics.

Alexander Henlein and Alexander Mehler. 2022. What do toothbrushes do in the kitchen? how transformers think our world is structured. *arXiv preprint arXiv:2204.05673*.

Keita Kurita, Nidhi Vyas, Ayush Pareek, Alan W Black, and Yulia Tsvetkov. 2019. Measuring bias in contextualized word representations. In *Proceedings of the First Workshop on Gender Bias in Natural Language Processing*, pages 166–172, Florence, Italy. Association for Computational Linguistics.

Yuquan Lan, Dongxu Li, Hui Zhao, and Gang Zhao. 2022. PCRED: Zero-shot relation triplet extraction with potential candidate relation selection and entity boundary detection. *arXiv preprint arXiv:2211.14477*.

Mike Lewis, Yinhan Liu, Naman Goyal, Marjan Ghazvininejad, Abdelrahman Mohamed, Omer Levy, Veselin Stoyanov, and Luke Zettlemoyer. 2020. BART: Denoising sequence-to-sequence pre-training for natural language generation, translation, and comprehension. In *Proceedings of the 58th Annual Meeting of the Association for Computational Linguistics*, pages 7871–7880, Online. Association for Computational Linguistics.

Jiao Li, Yueping Sun, Robin J. Johnson, Daniela Sciaky, Chih-Hsuan Wei, Robert Leaman, Allan Peter Davis, Carolyn J. Mattingly, Thomas C. Wiegers, and Zhiyong Lu. 2016. BioCreative V CDR task corpus: a resource for chemical disease relation extraction. *Database*, 2016. Baw068.

Yinhan Liu, Myle Ott, Naman Goyal, Jingfei Du, Mandar Joshi, Danqi Chen, Omer Levy, Mike Lewis, Luke Zettlemoyer, and Veselin Stoyanov. 2019. Roberta: A robustly optimized bert pretraining approach. *arXiv preprint arXiv:1907.11692*.

Yi Luan, Luheng He, Mari Ostendorf, and Hannaneh Hajishirzi. 2018. Multi-task identification of entities, relations, and coreference for scientific knowledge graph construction. In *Proceedings of the 2018 Conference on Empirical Methods in Natural Language Processing*, pages 3219–3232, Brussels, Belgium. Association for Computational Linguistics.

Alec Radford, Jeffrey Wu, Rewon Child, David Luan, Dario Amodei, Ilya Sutskever, et al. 2019. Language models are unsupervised multitask learners. *OpenAI blog*, 1(8):9.

Shanchan Wu and Yifan He. 2019. Enriching pre-trained language model with entity information for relation classification. In *Proceedings of the 28th ACM International Conference on Information and Knowledge Management*, pages 2361–2364. ACM.

Peiyuan Zhang and Wei Lu. 2022. Better few-shot relation extraction with label prompt dropout. In *Proceedings of the 2022 Conference on Empirical Methods in Natural Language Processing*, pages 6996–7006, Abu Dhabi, United Arab Emirates. Association for Computational Linguistics.

Yuhao Zhang, Victor Zhong, Danqi Chen, Gabor Angeli, and Christopher D. Manning. 2017. Position-aware attention and supervised data improve slot filling. In *Proceedings of the 2017 Conference on Empirical Methods in Natural Language Processing*, pages 35–45, Copenhagen, Denmark. Association for Computational Linguistics.

Yuzhe Zhang, Min Cen, Tongzhou Wu, and Hong Zhang. 2022. RAPS: A novel few-shot relation extraction pipeline with query-information guided attention and adaptive prototype fusion. *arXiv preprint arXiv:2210.08242*.

Extracting Definienda in Mathematical Scholarly Articles with Transformers

Shufan Jiang
DI ENS, ENS, PSL University, CNRS & Inria
Paris, France
shufan.jiang@ens.psl.eu

Pierre Senellart
DI ENS, ENS, PSL University, CNRS & Inria & Institut Universitaire de France
Paris, France
pierre@senellart.com

Abstract

We consider automatically identifying the defined term within a mathematical definition from the text of an academic article. Inspired by the development of transformer-based natural language processing applications, we pose the problem as (a) a token-level classification task using fine-tuned pre-trained transformers; and (b) a question-answering task using a generalist large language model (GPT). We also propose a rule-based approach to build a labeled dataset from the LaTeX source of papers. Experimental results show that it is possible to reach high levels of precision and recall using either recent (and expensive) GPT 4 or simpler pre-trained models fine-tuned on our task.

1 Introduction

Mathematical scholarly articles contain mathematical statements such as axioms, theorems, proofs, etc. These structures are not captured by traditional ways of navigating the scientific literature, e.g., keyword search. We consider initiatives aiming at better knowledge discovery from scientific papers such as sTeX (Kohlhase, 2008), a bottom-up solution for mathematical knowledge management that relies on authors adding explicit metadata when writing in LaTeX; MathRepo (Fevola and Görgen, 2022), a crowd-sourced repository for mathematicians to share any additional research data alongside their papers; or TheoremKB (Mishra et al., 2021), a project that extracts the location of theorems and proofs in mathematical research articles. Following these ideas, we aim at automatically building a knowledge graph to automatically index articles with the terms defined therein.

As a first step, we consider the simpler problem of, given the text of a formal mathematical definition (which is typically obtained from the PDF article), extracting the *definienda* (terms defined within). As an example, we show in Figure 1 a mathematical definition (as rendered within a PDF article, accompanied with its LaTeX source code) that defines two terms (which we call the *definienda*): "spread" and "components". In this particular example, the two terms are *emphasized* in the PDF (by being set in a non-italic font within an italic paragraph) – this is not always the case but we will exploit the fact that some authors do this to build a labeled dataset of definitions and definienda.

Definition 2.1. *Let V be a vector space over the field F. We say that the collection σ of subspaces is a* spread *if (1) $A, B \in \sigma$, $A \neq B$ then $V = A \oplus B$, and (2) every nonzero vector $x \in V$ lies in a unique member of σ. The members of σ are the* components *of the spread.*

```
\begin{definition}
Let $V$ be a vector space over the field $F$. We say that the
collection $\sigma$ of subspaces is a \emph{spread} if (1) $A,B
\in \sigma$, $A\neq B$ then $V=A\oplus B$, and (2) every nonzero
vector $x\in V$ lies in a unique member of $\sigma$. The members
of $\sigma$ are the \emph{components} of the spread.
\end{definition}
```

Figure 1: Rendering of a definition from a mathematical scholarly article (Nagy, 2013) accompanied with its LaTeX source code. The definienda are "spread" and "components".

After discussing some related work in Section 2, we describe our approach in Section 3 and show experimental results in Section 4.

2 Related work

The difficulties of our task lie in (1) the lack of labeled datasets; (2) the diversity in mathematicians' writing style; and (3) the interplay of discourse and formulae, which differentiate mathematical text and text in the general domain. We review potential corpora and existing approaches in this section.

The most relevant work to our objective is by Berlioz (2023). The author trains supervised classifiers to extract definitions from mathematical papers from arXiv. The best classifier takes static word embeddings built from arXiv papers, part-of-speech features of the words, and hand-coded binary features, such as if a word is an acronym, and then applies a BiLSTM-CRF architecture for

Proceedings of the 2nd Workshop on Information Extraction from Scientific Publications, pages 31–36
Nov 1, 2023. ©2023 Association for Computational Linguistics

sequence tagging (Huang et al., 2015). The resulting precision, recall, and F_1 are of 0.69, 0.65, and 0.67 respectively. The author uses the classifier to automatically extract term-definition pairs from arXiv articles and Wikidata, resulting in the dataset ArGot (Berlioz, 2021). Note however that a limitation of ArGot, which makes it unsuitable in our setting, where the text of definitions is directly taken from PDFs, is that mathematical expressions and formulas are masked out in the training set.

Another related task is term-definition extraction in the general domain of scientific articles. For example, Scholarphi (Head et al., 2021) is an augmented reading interface for papers with publicly available LaTeX sources. Given a paper (with its LaTeX source), it lets the reader click on specific words to view their definitions within the paper. The authors test several models for definition–term detection, including an original Heuristically Enhanced Deep Definition Extraction (Kang et al., 2020), syntactic features, heuristic rules, and different word representation technologies such as contextualized word representations based on transformers (Vaswani et al., 2017). The results show that models involving SciBERT (Beltagy et al., 2019) achieved higher accuracy on most measurements due to the domain similarity between the scholarly documents for pre-training SciBERT and those used in the evaluation. Following this idea, cc_math_roberta (Mishra et al., 2023) is a RoBERTa-based model pertained from scratch on mathematical articles from arXiv (Mishra et al., 2023). This model outperforms Roberta in a sentence-level classification task while the corpora size for pre-training cc_math_roberta is much smaller than Roberta's. We aim to determine in this work if contextualized word representations can improve the results of mathematical definienda extraction.

NaturalProof (Welleck et al., 2021) is a corpus of mathematical statements and their proofs. These statements are extracted from different sources with hand-crafted rules, such as the content being enclosed by `\begin{theorem}` and `\end{theorem}` in the LaTeX source of a textbook project on algebraic stacks[1]. Each statement is either a theorem or a definition. However, this dataset does not annotate the definienda of each definition.

[1] `https://github.com/stacks/stacks-project`

3 Proposed Approach

We describe our approach in two steps. First, we build a ground-truth dataset using the LaTeX source of papers. As the existing large datasets either concern term–definition extraction from general corpora like web pages or textbooks (Welleck et al., 2021) or mask out mathematical expressions in the text (Berlioz, 2021), we decide to process plain text as it appears in scholarly papers so that our solution can be directly applied to texts extracted from PDF articles when the LaTeX source is unavailable. Second, we study different usages of transformer-based models to extract definienda. We are interested in fine-tuning and one-shot learning (prompt engineering). The source code of our approach, as well as the constructed dataset, is available on Github[2].

3.1 Dataset Construction

To start with a reasonable corpus, we collected the LaTeX source of all 28 477 arXiv papers in the area of Combinatorics (arXiv's math.CO category) published before 1st Jan 2020 through arXiv's bulk access from AWS[3]. Our goal in building the dataset was *not* to be complete, but to produce as cheaply and reliably as possible a ground-truth dataset of definitions and definienda. For this purpose, we rely on two features of definitions that some authors (but definitely not all!) use: definienda are often written in italics within the definition (or, as in Figure 1, in non-italics within an italics paragraph); and definienda are sometimes shown in parentheses after the definition header. As we do not need to completely capture all cases in the building of the dataset, we assume that definitions are within a `definition` LaTeX environment and thus extracted text blocks between `\begin{definition}` and `\end{definition}`; we ignored contents enclosed in other author-defined environments, such as `\begin{Def}`, which might bring us more definitions but also more noise. For defined terms, relying on the two features described above, we extracted the contents within `\textit{}` and `\emph{}` from the text blocks as well as the content potentially provided as optional argument to the `\begin{definition}[]` environment. We then converted the extracted partial LaTeX

[2] `https://github.com/sufianj/def_extraction`

[3] `https://info.arxiv.org/help/bulk_data_s3.html`

code into plain text with Unicode characters using `pylatexenc`[4]. After a brief glance at the most frequent extracted definienda values, we handcrafted regular expressions to filter out the following recurrent noises among them:

- irrelevant or meaningless phrases such as repeating "i.e." and "\d";
- Latin locutions such as "et al.";
- list entries such as "(i)" and "(iii)".

After filtering, we got a list of 13 692 text blocks, of which the average length is 70 tokens, and the maximum length is 5 266 tokens. We removed 39 text blocks having more than 500 tokens. Finally, we labeled automatically the texts with IOB2 tagging, where the "B-MATH_TERM" tag denotes the first token of every defined term, "I-MATH_TERM" tag indicates any non-initial token in a defined term, and the "O" tag means that the token is outside any definiendum. Considering partially italics compound terms like "`\emph{non}-k-equivalent`", we annotate "non-k-equivalent" as a definiendum. We sorted the labeled texts by the last update time of the papers.

To evaluate the quality of this dataset, we examined by hand 1 024 labeled entries. We found that only 30 annotated texts out of 1 024 to be incorrectly labeled, confirming the quality of our annotation. We manually removed or corrected wrong annotations and got 999 labeled texts, which became our ground truth test data. We built training/validation sets for 10-fold cross-validation with the rest of the labeled texts, to separate them from our test data.

3.2 Fine-tuning Pre-trained Language Models for Token Classification

For the fine-tuning setup, we consider the extraction of definienda as a token-level classification problem: given a text block, the classifier labels each token as B-MATH_TERM, I-MATH_TERM or O. We used the implementation for token classification *RobertaForTokenClassification* in the transformers package (Wolf et al., 2020). It loads a pre-trained language model and adds a linear layer on top of the token representation output. We experimented with an out-of-the-box and general language model Roberta-base (Liu et al., 2019) and a domain-specific model cc_math_roberta (Mishra et al., 2023). Since Mishra et al. (2023) do not report performance on token-level tasks, we used two checkpoints of it, one pretained for 1 epoch (denoted as cc_ep01)[5], and another pre-trained for 10 epochs (denoted as cc_ep10)[6]. Then we fed the 10 train/validation sets to train the linear layer to predict the probability of a token's representation matching one of the three labels. We set the maximum sequence length of the model to 256. We ran all our experiments with a fixed learning rate of $5 \cdot 10^{-5}$ and a fixed batch size of 16. We searched the best number of epochs among [3, 5, 10]. We also experimented with 1 024, 2 048, and 10 240 samples from each training set to see the performance of the classifiers with low resources. As Roberta-base and cc_math_roberta have their own tokenizers, the models' output loss and accuracy are based on different numbers of word pieces and are not comparable. To evaluate the predictions, we used the predicted tag of the first word piece of each word and regrouped the IOB2-tagged word into definienda. We present our unified evaluation over ground truth data in Section 4.

3.3 Querying GPT

Driven by the growing popularity of few-shot learning with pre-trained language models (Brown et al., 2020), we also query the GPT language model, using different available versions: we first experimented with ChatGPT[7] (based on GPT 3.5) and then used the API versions of GPT-3.5-Turbo and GPT-4. We initially gave ChatGPT only one example in our question and attempted to obtain a IOB2-compliant output. We quickly realized that the returned tagging was random, unstable, and incoherent with the expected terms. However, if we ask ChatGPT to return the definienda directly, we get more pertinent results. We thus asked GPT-3.5-Turbo and GPT-4 to identify the definienda in our ground truth data via OpenAI's API. For each request, we send the same task description (system input) and a text from our test data (user input). We fixed the max output length to 128 and temperature to 0. By the time of writing, the cost of these API are count by tokens – GPT-4 8K context model's input and output token prices are 20 and 30 times that of GPT-3.5 4K context model. Since GPT-4 tend to give more precise and shorter responses,

[4] `https://github.com/phfaist/pylatexenc`

[5] `https://huggingface.co/InriaValda/cc_math_roberta_ep01`

[6] `https://huggingface.co/InriaValda/cc_math_roberta_ep10`

[7] An example of our conversation: `https://chat.openai.com/share/c96b156f-cba1-4804-8f19-1622a9bc564e`

the cost of GPT-4 on our task is roughly 20 times that of GPT-3.5. For our test, we spent $0.42 on GPT-3.5 and $7.80 on GPT-4.

4 Evaluation

Now that we got the predictions from our fine-tuned token classifiers and the answers from GPT models, we compared them with ground truth data. We first removed the repeated expected definienda for each annotated text and got 1 552 unique definienda in total. Then we converted both expected terms and extracted terms to lowercase. For each unique expected term, if it is the same as an extracted term, we counted one "True Positive". We counted one "Cut Off" if it contains an extracted term. If it is contained in an extracted term, we counted one "Too Long". Finally, we removed all spaces in the expected term to make an expected no-space string, and we joined all extracted terms to make an extracted no-space string; if the extracted no-space string contains the expected no-space string, we considered that the expected term is extracted as one "True Positive or Split Term". We calculated the precision, recall, and F_1-score using the "True Positive or Split Term" count to have a higher tolerance for boundary errors on all models. Table 1 shows the results of GPT's answers. Tables 2 and 3 present the averaged performance of cc_ep01, cc_ep10 and Roberta over 10-fold cross-validation. We set the best precision, recall, and F_1-scores in bold across these three tables.

Model	GPT-3.5	GPT-4
Extracted	6867	2245
True Positive	1072	942
TP+Split Term	1315	1383
Too Long	379	595
Cut Off	656	138
Precision	0.1929	0.6248
Recall	**0.8312**	**0.8821**
F_1	0.3131	**0.7315**

Table 1: Performance comparison of extraction by GPT models. The huge number of extracted terms results in the poor precision of GPT-3.5 model.

Model	cc_ep01	cc_ep10	Rob.
Extracted	2093.0	1710.8	1764.2
True positive	514.9	881.2	934.2
TP+Split Term	693.8	1056.5	1127.5
Too Long	170.2	209.1	268.8
Cut Off	522.6	405.2	326.1
Precision	0.354	0.623	0.646
Recall	0.447	0.681	0.726
F_1	0.383	0.647	0.679

Table 2: Averaged performance of fine-tuned models, with 2048 training data.

Our first remark is the high recall of GPTs' answers. Indeed, GPT models, especially GPT-3.5, tend to return everything in the given text, resulting in poor precision. After checking the outputs over the 1024 test data, we found an over-prediction of formulas and mathematical expressions, which corresponds to the analysis by (Kang et al., 2020).

Our second remark is that fine-tuned classifiers have more balanced precision and recall, as the numbers of extracted terms are closer to the expected number (1 552). To our surprise, although the tokenizer of cc_math_roberta models produced fewer word pieces than Roberta's tokenizer, Roberta-base yielded the best performance among the three models in our task, regardless the size of the training set. Moreover, cc_math_roberta models' performance varies more than Roberta's (see in Table 4), showing that cc_math_roberta models are less robust to different input data.

In all the setups, cc_ep01 was always the worst for our task, implying the benefit of pre-training. The performances of all fine-tuned models improve significantly as the training set size increases. When given 10 240 training data, fine-tuning a pre-trained model gives better overall predictions than GPT-4, and when given 2048 training data, fine-tuned Roberta-base already gives better precision than GPT-4.

Finally, note that these finetuned language models are obviously much less computationally expensive than OpenAI's GPT models.

5 Conclusion

In this work, we have contributed to the efficient creation of a labeled dataset for definiendum extraction from mathematical papers. We have then compared two usages of transformers: asking GPT vs fine-tuning pre-trained language models. Our experimental results show GPT-4's capacity to understand mathematical texts with only one example in the prompt. We highlight the good precision–recall balance and the relatively low cost of fine-tuning Roberta for this domain-specific information

Model	cc_ep01	cc_ep10	Rob.
Extracted	1775.2	1779.2	1770.5
True positive	540.3	972.6	1082.6
TP+Split Term	733.9	1152.5	1232
Too Long	143.5	201.3	233.7
Cut Off	509.6	438.2	274.1
Precision	0.420	**0.652**	**0.697**
Recall	0.473	0.743	0.794
F_1	0.442	0.692	**0.742**

Table 3: Averaged performance of fine-tuned models, with 10 240 training data samples

Model	cc_ep01	cc_ep10	Rob.
2048	0.044	0.052	**0.031**
10240	0.043	0.026	**0.011**

Table 4: The standard deviation of the F_1 score of different fine-tuned models, with 2048 and with 10 240 training data samples

extraction task. A constraint of our work comes from the nature of our labeled data because authors have their own writing styles: there could be more than one correct annotation for a phrase. For instance, our definition blocks are compiled from LaTeX sources, and we plan to test our fine-tuned models on definitions extracted from real PDF format papers without LaTeX sources. Pluvinage (2020) proposes sentence-level classification and text segmentation to retrieve mathematical results from PDF and can provide a preliminary test set for us. For future work, we will explore the ambiguities of extracted entities and link them to classes. Our experience with cc_math_roberta models also open up research about improving the robustness over different NLP tasks of from-scratched domain-specific language models.

Acknowledgments

This work was funded in part by the French government under management of Agence Nationale de la Recherche as part of the "Investissements d'avenir" program, reference ANR-19-P3IA-0001 (PRAIRIE 3IA Institute).

References

Iz Beltagy, Kyle Lo, and Arman Cohan. 2019. Scibert: A pretrained language model for scientific text. In *Proceedings of the 2019 Conference on Empirical Methods in Natural Language Processing and the 9th International Joint Conference on Natural Language Processing (EMNLP-IJCNLP)*, pages 3615–3620.

Luis Berlioz. 2021. ArGoT: A Glossary of Terms extracted from the arXiv. *Electronic Proceedings in Theoretical Computer Science*, 342:14–21.

Luis Berlioz. 2023. *Hierarchical Representations from Large Mathematical Corpora*. Ph.D. thesis, University of Pittsburgh.

Tom B. Brown et al. 2020. Language Models are Few-Shot Learners. ArXiv:2005.14165 [cs].

Claudia Fevola and Christiane Görgen. 2022. The mathematical research-data repository mathrepo. *arXiv preprint arXiv:2202.04022*.

Andrew Head et al. 2021. Augmenting scientific papers with just-in-time, position-sensitive definitions of terms and symbols. In *Proceedings of the 2021 CHI Conference on Human Factors in Computing Systems*, pages 1–18.

Zhiheng Huang, Wei Xu, and Kai Yu. 2015. Bidirectional lstm-crf models for sequence tagging. *arXiv preprint arXiv:1508.01991*.

Dongyeop Kang et al. 2020. Document-Level Definition Detection in Scholarly Documents: Existing Models, Error Analyses, and Future Directions. ArXiv:2010.05129 [cs].

Michael Kohlhase. 2008. Using LaTeXas a semantic markup format. *Mathematics in Computer Science*, 2(2):279–304.

Yinhan Liu et al. 2019. Roberta: A robustly optimized bert pretraining approach. *arXiv preprint arXiv:1907.11692*.

Shrey Mishra, Antoine Gauquier, and Pierre Senellart. 2023. Multimodal machine learning for extraction of theorems and proofs in the scientific literature. *arXiv preprint arXiv:2307.09047*.

Shrey Mishra, Lucas Pluvinage, and Pierre Senellart. 2021. Towards extraction of theorems and proofs in scholarly articles. In *Proceedings of the 21st ACM Symposium on Document Engineering*, pages 1–4, Limerick Ireland. ACM.

Gábor P. Nagy. 2013. Linear groups as right multiplication groups of quasifields. *Designs, Codes and Cryptography*, 72(1):153–164.

Lucas Pluvinage. 2020. Extracting scientific results from research articles. Master's thesis, Ecole Normale Supérieure (ENS).

Ashish Vaswani et al. 2017. Attention is all you need. *Advances in neural information processing systems*, 30.

Sean Welleck et al. 2021. Naturalproofs: Mathematical theorem proving in natural language. In *Thirty-fifth Conference on Neural Information Processing Systems Datasets and Benchmarks Track (Round 1)*.

Thomas Wolf et al. 2020. Transformers: State-of-the-art natural language processing. In *Proceedings of the 2020 conference on empirical methods in natural language processing: system demonstrations*, pages 38–45.

A Novel Dataset Towards Extracting Virus-Host Interactions

Rasha Alshawi, Atriya Sen
University of New Orleans

Nathan S. Upham, Beckett Sterner
Arizona State University

Abstract

We describe a novel dataset for the automated recognition of named taxonomic and other entities relevant to the association of viruses with their hosts. We further describe some initial results using pre-trained models on the named-entity recognition (NER) task on this novel dataset. We propose that our dataset of manually annotated abstracts now offers a Gold Standard Corpus for training future NER models in the automated extraction of host-pathogen detection methods from scientific publications, and further explain how our work makes first steps towards predicting the important human health-related concept of viral spillover risk automatically from the scientific literature.

1 Motivation and Related Work

The pace of novel zoonotic diseases is increasing globally (Han et al. 2016), but much of our knowledge about the geography and hosts of zoonotic diseases remains locked in the texts of published scientific articles (Upham et al. 2021). Published studies typically apply one or more methods for pathogen detection in animal hosts, including antibody tests, polymerase chain reaction (PCR) tests, whole genome sequencing, or live pathogen isolation. Similarly, the host species might be identified morphologically or using PCR. These methods of detecting host-pathogen interactions vary in precision and in what they tell us about the ecological relationship being observed; most critically, whether the animal host is a reservoir for pathogen replication and transmission, or else a more transient host.

Distinguishing the confidence in host-pathogen data according to type of detection method has been shown to significantly improve models predicting zoonotic disease risk in rodents (Mull et al. 2021). However, the information required to incorporate detection method as a variable in zoonotic disease risk models is rarely available from current host-pathogen databases or article metadata, with the important exception of (Olival et al., 2017), which we explore further here.

Named Entity Recognition (NER) methods have the potential to assist in identifying host-pathogen interactions, by the automated extraction of virus-host and other pathogen detection methods from the biological literature, enabling advances in scientific understanding of how and why zoonotic diseases emerge. **There are currently no existing datasets for this purpose, and therefore a comparison cannot be furnished.** In the bio-medical domain, NER models such as BioRedditBERT (Basaldella et al., 2020), SapBERT (Liu et al., 2021), and Biobert_ncbi_disease_ner (Doğan et al., 2014), are trained on large datasets (as described in Section 3), whereas we manually curate a novel, much smaller dataset (as described in Section 2), albeit attracting the additional challenges of performing NER effectively on "small" data. Additionally, virus detection methods are manually labelled and recognized via NER after training, which is the first such result in the literature.

The Information Extraction (IE) challenges in the NER task on biological scientific articles are highly similar to those in other domains, such as astrophysics, as exemplified by the *DEAL: Detecting Entities in the Astrophysics Literature* (DEAL, 2022) competition. It is true of many domains that there is a diversity of naming practices, rampant ambiguity, and a highly dynamic vocabulary. We therefore envision our data-collection approach, piloted here on host-pathogen literature, to be highly generalizable to other scientific domains.

Proceedings of the 2nd Workshop on Information Extraction from Scientific Publications, pages 37–42
Nov 1, 2023. ©2023 Association for Computational Linguistics

2 Dataset description

Our virus dataset was built by manually collecting 1104 articles reporting virus detection results for mammal hosts. The articles were selected from the dataset collected and analyzed as part of a systematic literature review of all known viruses with mammal hosts, as reported in (Olival et al., 2017).

Their review searched the Web of Science, Google Scholar, and PubMed for articles published between 1940 and 2015 that mentioned each of 586 virus species identified as having mammal hosts by the International Committee on Taxonomy of Viruses, 8th Edition (Fauquet et al. 2005). They excluded articles reporting results from experimental infections, zoos, or captive breeding facilities as well as domesticated and peri-domestic mammal species (specifically *Mus musculus* and *Rattus norvegicus*). The final list of articles they analyzed is available online as part of the paper's supplementary data in the "references.txt" file (https://zenodo.org/record/807517). Since the supplementary data did not include article abstracts, we searched by article title in the PubMed search engine (PubMed,2022), and with our additions, the dataset we report here represents a substantial fraction of all published articles reporting viruses detected in wild mammals.

524 of these abstracts were preprocessed and manually annotated in the form of Gold Standard Corpus (GSC) for the Name Entity Recognition (NER). The annotations were conducted following well-defined guidelines to ensure consistency and accuracy. NER annotation necessitates explicit rules to mark the boundaries and class of each entity. We adopted the widely recognized Inside, Outside, Beginning (IOB) tagging format (Perera et al., 2020). According to this format, entities are denoted by 'B-' at the beginning, 'I-' for tokens inside the entity, and 'O' to indicate tokens without any entity association. The 'B-' prefix signifies the start of an entity, while 'I-' indicates tokens within the entity. Tokens with 'O' tags do not belong to any entity. This clear and standardized approach to annotation was diligently applied a clear and standardized annotation methodology to identify virus names, host names, and other pertinent entities within the abstracts. Following the Inside, Outside, Beginning (IOB) format, we maintained consistent definitions of entity boundaries and classes. This meticulous approach resulted in a well-annotated Gold Standard Corpus (GSC), comprising 1104 annotated abstracts, serving as a valuable resource for training and evaluating Name Entity Recognition (NER) models.

The manual annotation process was inherently time-consuming, amplified by challenges in disambiguating entities. Ambiguities, especially when a term represented both a virus name and a host name, required careful contextual analysis. To address this, we implemented a straightforward rule: incorporating the term 'virus' as an entity marker ('B-virus name' for the beginning and 'I-virus' for tokens inside). Despite these challenges, our systematic approach and integration of specific entity markers ensured precise annotations within our GSC. These efforts establish a solid foundation for developing accurate NER models tailored to extract host-pathogen detection methods from scientific publications.

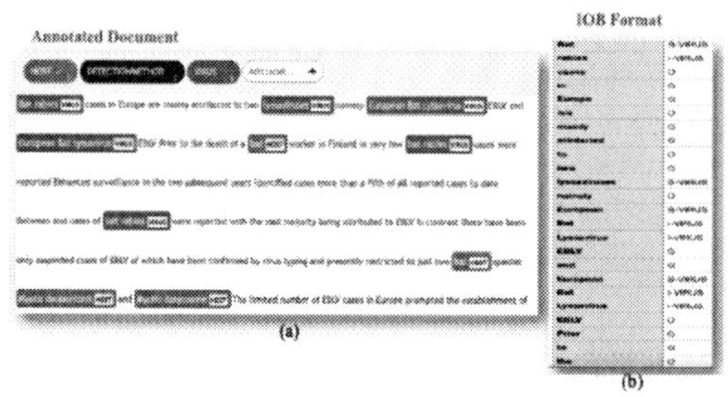

Figure 1: A sample from the dataset demonstrating the annotation process according to Inside, Outside, Beginning (IOB) gold standard corpus. (a) shows the annotation process that includes highlighting and classifying the entities, (b) shows the output annotated in form of IOB standard.

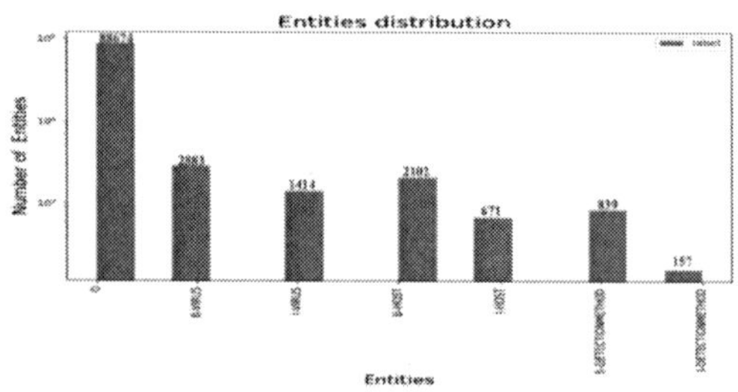

Figure 2: Entity Distribution Graph of Our Dataset.

3 Transformer-based Model

This section describes the model architectures, training, and evaluation procedures for the named-entity recognition (NER) task we performed. All our code, written in Python & using Google TensorFlow, will be made freely available online upon publication.

Transformer models were the first deep neural network-based sequence transduction model based entirely on the concept of *attention*. The model architecture is composed of the transformer's *encoder*, based on the original implementation described in (Vaswani et al., 2017), and followed by a classification model. Similar to other sequence processing models, the architecture first uses an embedding layer to convert the input tokens into a feature vector representation and a positional encoding layer to provide information about the order of the sequence. The encoder block consists of self-attention layers, normalization layers, and feed-forward layers (i.e., a multilayer perceptron (MLP)), and outputs a vector for each time step of an input sequence. The classification model uses a feed-forward network to classify these sequences into predefined named entities, therefore performing a *sequence classification task.*

We deployed a *Bidirectional Encoder Representations from Transformers* (BERT) model, a transformer-based model that leverages a fine-tuning-based approach for applying a pretrained language model, i.e., a model trained on a generic task in a semi-supervised manner, and then fine-tuned on a specific task in a supervised manner (Devlin et al., 2018). Leveraging pretrained language models significantly improves performance on many tasks, especially when labeled data is scarce, as in our use-case.

Three distinct pretrained BERT models were used, each followed by a classifier model to project the output onto predefined named entities. Since there is no available BERT model that is pretrained on virus and host-related biological literature, available models pretrained on general biological and biomedical literature were used: (1) **BioRedditBERT**, pretrained on large biomedical documents and health-related Reddit posts (Basaldella et al., 2020), (2) **SapBERT**, pretrained on abstracts from PubMed and full-text articles from PubMed Central (Liu et al., 2021), and (3) **Biobert_ncbi_disease_ner**, fine-tuned for NER task on NCBI disease dataset. The NCBI dataset consists of 793 PubMed abstracts and contains 6,892 disease mentions (Doğan et al., 2014). All three models are hosted on the HuggingFace model repository.

Table 1: Performance evaluations of the transformer and the three pretrained BERT models finetuned on our novel dataset.

Model	Acc.	Prec.	Recall	F1
Transformer	0.9826	0.9793	0.9826	0.9795
BioReddit BERT	0.9814	0.9772	0.9814	0.9770
SapBERT	**0.9857**	**0.9870**	**0.9857**	**0.9853**
Biobert_ncbi	0.9846	0.9840	0.9846	0.9832

The pretrained model may be used as a feature extractor by freezing the model's weights and training only the classification model on the target dataset, or, the weights of some neural layers may be unfrozen and updated on the target task, which is known as *fine-tuning*. Since these models were pretrained on a different corpus, we obtained slightly better results using fine-tuning.

4 Results

An NER experiment was performed to evaluate the quality of the novel dataset. To evaluate and compare NER models using Gold Standard Corpora, it is required to use standardized evaluation scores. A frequently used error measure is the F-Score, a combination of Recall and Precision. NER models were also evaluated using the accuracy metric. Table 1 shows the evaluation performance of the basic transformer model and performance after fine-tuning of the three pretrained BERT models. Table 2 shows the evaluation performance of the models using the feature extraction learning method described in the previous section. SapBERT obtains the best performance in both fine-tuning and feature extraction learning, probably due to its relatively general nature. Table 3 shows the loss metrics after training the models for 20 epochs.

The visualized annotations in **Error! Reference source not found.** show that the SapBERT model was able to detect and classify almost all the entities of interest: both taxonomic names and detection method names (the latter is a novel result), that appeared in the abstracts.

Figure 3: The visual results of the transformer and two pretrained BERT models of a sample drawn from the dataset: (a) transformer (b) BioRedditBERT. All the BERT models were pretrained on biological and health-related literature, and then fine-tuned on our novel dataset. Red lines underscore unrecognized entities.

Table 2: Performance evaluations of the three pretrained BERT models trained on our novel dataset using the feature extraction approach.

Model	Acc.	Prec.	Recall	F1
BioReddit BERT	0.965 5	0.9376	0.9655	0.9508
SapBERT	**0.984 9**	**0.9859**	**0.9849**	**0.9844**
Biobert_ncbi	0.984 5	0.9840	0.9846	0.9832

Table 3: Performance evaluations of the pre-trained models on the virus dataset

Model	Loss
Transformer	0.0624
BioRedditBERT	0.0911
SapBERT	0.0736
Biobert_ncbi_disease_ner	0.0904

5 Conclusions, Impact & Potential

We have presented a novel dataset of significance to the important concept of virus-host association, and therefore to the emergence of pandemics such as the COVID-19 pandemic, and promising initial results on the NER task of identifying both taxonomic names and experimental detection methods. We claim that our dataset of manually annotated abstracts now offers a Gold Standard Corpus for training future NER models in the automated extraction of virus-host and other pathogen detection methods from the biological literature. Several other entities, particularly geographical entities and entities describing species migration, are also relevant to the virus-host association. As a result, immediate next steps will consist of recognizing these entities, and also automatically annotating the full text of the article using semi-supervised methods, in lieu of manually annotating the abstracts.

Recognized taxonomic entities in particular can be linked with knowledge graphs representing taxonomic synonymy as well as more complex taxonomic relationships. These graphs have been used (ATCR, 2022) to reason using automated reasoning and inference techniques such as SMT solving and answer-set programming about relationships expressed in a qualitative spatial logical calculus (such as a form of the region connection calculi), with the goals of resolving taxonomic ambiguity or inferring unspecified relationships. This has been used to align and disambiguate published taxonomies of primates and other species (Franz, N.M. et al., 2016). Further, the approach has the potential to be used in biodiversity conservation applications (Sen, A., Sterner, B., et al., 2021). Such inference may be seen as a generalized form of querying or question-answering over taxonomic graphs, and moreover provides a highly intuitive and visual representation of taxonomic flux over time.

Augmenting these graphs of logical taxonomic relationships with automatically extracted context from the biological literature will have the important benefits of serving to identify novel application domains and providing extra-biological context (e.g., geospatial context) to known & inferred taxonomic relationships.

Further, taxonomic automated reasoning systems have previously been combined (Sen, A., Sterner, B., et al., 2021) with statistical features extracted from biological image repositories (such as citizen-sourced or herbarium-sourced images) to further facilitate the taxonomic relationship discovery task. While we have only considered textual abstracts in our work so far, further useful context may thus be added by augmenting taxonomic knowledge graphs with images or tables extracted from the full text of the publications.

The recognition of a variety of intermediary entities (e.g., locations, methods, migration patterns) is likely to facilitate the discovery of the relevant ecological contexts of the host-virus associations, which, in turn, are subjectively known to be dependent (in some currently undiscovered manner) upon these entities. The extraction of such scientifically informative relationships is a further tangible step ahead.

Finally, these extracted relationships may be considered as background structure for *learning an explainable theory of viral spillover* (from other mammals to humans), when taken together with known examples of such spillover, and known negative examples. Symbolic machine learning techniques such as Inductive Logic Programming (ILP) may be able to exploit such structured data and background knowledge to learn logical relationships that generalize from these data, expressed in a subset of first-order logic and interpretable directly by humans: it is in this sense that we use the term *explainable*.

Acknowledgment

This research was supported by the National Institute of Allergy and Infectious Diseases of the National Institutes of Health. The award number has been withheld for anonymity.

References

Upham, Nathan S, Jorrit H Poelen, Deborah Paul, Quentin J Groom, Nancy B Simmons, Maarten P M Vanhove, Sandro Bertolino, et al. "Liberating Host–Virus Knowledge from Biological Dark Data." The Lancet Planetary Health 5, no. 10 (October 1, 2021): e746–50. https://doi.org/10.1016/S2542-5196(21)00196-0.

Han, Barbara A., Andrew M. Kramer, and John M. Drake. "Global Patterns of Zoonotic Disease in Mammals." Trends in Parasitology 32, no. 7 (July 1, 2016): 565–77. https://doi.org/10.1016/j.pt.2016.04.007.

Mull, Nathaniel, Colin J. Carlson, Kristian M. Forbes, and Daniel J. Becker. "Viral Competence Data Improves Rodent Reservoir Predictions for American Orthohantaviruses." BioRxiv, January 4, 2021, 2021.01.01.425052. https://doi.org/10.1101/2021.01.01.425052.

Olival, J, et al. "Host and viral traits predict zoonotic spillover from mammals" Nature 546, pp. 646–650 (2017).

Fauquet, C., Mayo, M.A., Maniloff, J., Desselberger, U. & Ball, L.A. Virus taxonomy: Eighth Report of the International Committee on Taxonomy of Viruses. (Elsevier Academic Press, 2005)

PubMed, 2022 URL: https://pubmed.ncbi.nlm.nih.gov/.

Perera, N., Dehmer, M., Emmert-Streib, F., 2020. Named entity recognition and relation detection for biomedical information extraction. Front. Cell Dev. Biol. 673.

UBIAI, 2022 URL: https://ubiai.tools/.

Vaswani, A., Shazeer, N., Parmar, N., Uszkoreit, J., Jones, L., Gomez, A.N., Kaiser, Ł., Polosukhin, I., 2017. Attention is all you need. Adv. Neural Inf. Process. Syst. 30.

Devlin, J., Chang, M.-W., Lee, K., Toutanova, K., 2018. Bert: Pre-training of deep bidirectional transformers for language understanding. ArXiv Prepr. ArXiv181004805.

Basaldella, M., Liu, F., Shareghi, E., Collier, N., 2020. COMETA: A corpus for medical entity linking in the social media. ArXiv Prepr. ArXiv201003295.

Liu, F., Shareghi, E., Meng, Z., Basaldella, M., Collier, N., 2021. Self-Alignment Pretraining for Biomedical Entity Representations. Association for Computational Linguistics, pp. 4228-4238.

Doğan, R.I., Leaman, R. and Lu, Z., 2014. NCBI disease corpus: a resource for disease name recognition and concept normalization. Journal of biomedical informatics, 47, pp.1-10.

DEAL, 2022 URL: DEAL Shared Task | WIESP (harvard.edu)

A. Sen, N. Franz, B. Sterner, and N. Upham, "Automated Taxonomic Concept Reasoner and Learner." http://atcrl.herokuapp.com (accessed Sep. 02, 2022).

Franz NM, Pier NM, Reeder DM, Chen M, Yu S, Kianmajd P, Bowers S, Ludäscher B. Two Influential Primate Classifications Logically Aligned. Syst Biol. 2016 Jul;65(4):561-82. doi: 10.1093/sysbio/syw023. Epub 2016 Mar 22. PMID: 27009895; PMCID: PMC4911943.

A. Sen, B. Sterner, N. Franz, C. Powel, and N. S. Upham, "Combining Machine Learning & Reasoning for Biodiversity Data Intelligence," presented at the Thirty-Fifth AAAI Conference on Artificial Intelligence, Held virtually, 2021.

Detection of tortured phrases in scientific literature

Eléna Martel, Martin Lentschat, Cyril Labbé
Univ. Grenoble Alpes, CNRS, Grenoble INP, LIG, 38000 Grenoble, France
{martin.lentschat,cyril.labbe}@univ-grenoble-alpes.fr

Abstract

This paper presents various automatic detection methods to extract so called *tortured phrases* from scientific papers. These tortured phrases, e.g. *flag to clamor* instead of *signal to noise*, are the results of paraphrasing tools used to escape plagiarism detection. We built a dataset and evaluated several strategies to flag previously undocumented tortured phrases. The proposed and tested methods are based on language models and either on embeddings similarities or on predictions of masked token. We found that an approach using token prediction and that propagates the scores to the chunk level gives the best results. With a recall value of .87 and a precision value of .61, it could retrieve new tortured phrases to be submitted to domain experts for validation.

1 Introduction

Over the past few years, the research community has been confronted with an emerging issue related to the use of content rewriting tools. These tools are being used to hide crude plagiarism. Some of these rewriting tools, called *spinners*[1], used to destroy the meaning of the rewritten text. In their pursuit of publication and the relentless pressure to '*publish or perish*', some researchers turn to these tools. However, these spinners, leave behind lexical traces as they transform text, replacing words with synonyms that may be less appropriate during the modification process.

For scientific text, the most brutal modifications were concerning poly-lexical sequences that carry a specific meaning as well-established scientific expressions: e.g. *Artificial intelligence, big data* or *Randomized control trial.* By performing a 'word by synonyms' replacement, the first generation of spinners would destroy the meaning conveyed by these typical collocations. For example, the previously mentioned expressions could be tortured into *man-made consciousness, enormous information* or *randomized controlled preliminary*. We define a tortured phrase as **an expression resulting from the use of a spinner on a well-established scientific expression with a specific and fixed meaning**. Its counterpart is here called expected phrase (i.e. the original scientific expression).

Cabanac et al. (2021) reveals that such meaningless expressions, referred to as *tortured phrases*, can actually be found in many scientific papers. These tortured phrases not only constitute evidences of the lack of reliability and relevance of these papers, but can also be used to quickly retrieve articles that are thus suspected of having employed spinners. A manually collected set of tortured phrases is used as *fingerprints* (Cabanac and Labbé, 2021) by the *Problematic Paper Screener*[2] to comb the scientific literature for such problematic papers. The authors are querying the academic search engine Dimensions.ai (Herzog et al., 2020) to retrieve articles with known tortured phrases.

The set of manually collected tortured phrases is limited to the expertise of its contributors. Tortured phrases from many scientific fields are still to be listed as fingerprints, so to be able to flag undetected problematic papers. To this date (13 oct. 2023), 11.945 papers containing tortured phrases have been flagged by the website *Problematic Paper Screener*, with more to come as the number of known tortured phrases increases. While it's possible that with the context of 2023, Large Language Models can perform paraphrasing of higher quality than spinners, it's crucial to note that these papers have already been published and remain accessible. Also, amongst the 12k flagged articles, 1278 have been published in 2023, as well as 2 articles to be published in 2024. Therefore, this problem still remains and it is of paramount importance to identify them for retractions.

[1]SpinBot (https://spinbot.com), SpinnerChief (https://www.spinnerchief.com)

[2]https://www.irit.fr/~Guillaume.Cabanac/problematic-paper-screener

Proceedings of the 2nd Workshop on Information Extraction from Scientific Publications, pages 43–48
Nov 1, 2023.

This paper aims at testing automatic methods to distinguish differences between tortured phrases and expected ones. The main aims being to automatically identify tortured phrases that are yet not listed. For this purpose:

- We built a data set aiming at testing detection methods.
- We report results achieved when using different techniques that do not require massive use of labeled data, as such a large data set does not exists yet.
- We explore the use of large language model embeddings, similarity measures, masking and prediction methods to flag automatically tortured phrases not previously known.

The remainder of this paper is organized as follows: Section 2 discuss related work around spinners and the detection of tortured phrases. Section 3 describes the way we built our new data set. Section 4 presents various methods and experiments for which Section 5 provides detailed results. Finally, Section 6 concludes and gives some perspectives on the task at hands.

2 Related Work

Spinners are capable to create several versions of an original text by substituting synonyms and altering sentence structure (Shahid et al., 2017). An example can be taken from the following sentence: *'The cat is eating its food.'*, which could be transformed into: *'The feline is savoring its meal.'*.

It has been shown that content rewriting tools leave behind a trail of lexical artifacts (Shahid et al., 2017). Some of these artifacts can manifest as tortured phrases, wherein the same tortured phrase might recur multiple times in place of an expected one. Furthermore, Zhang et al. (2014) highlights that approximately 94% of the vocabulary used by these tools is not regularly changed, which could explain why the same tortured phrases may reappear multiple times and thus reinforce the need for an effective detection method.

Some authors have set out with the objective of detecting spun text based on dictionaries of rewriting tools. For instance, Zhang et al. (2014) relies on tokens and phrases that remain unchanged during the content rewriting process to assess the similarity between two articles, by focusing on elements that are not found in the dictionary and therefore have not been substituted.

On the other hand, Wahle et al. (2022) attempts to identify machine-generated paraphrased plagiarism. They created a dataset of paraphrased content using commercial tools like *SpinBot* and *Spinnerchief*. This dataset will encompass paraphrased texts from arXiv, student theses, and Wikipedia articles. They employed three types of machine learning classifiers: logistic regression, support vector machines, and naive Bayes classification. Their task is a binary classification to mark the text as being spun or not.

We will be using the dataset of Wahle et al. (2022) in our study. Given its method of fabrication, it contains many undocumented tortured phrases and is thus very valuable. Nevertheless, to be usable for the evaluation of new tortured phrases detection methods, re-annotation at the token level is needed. We did perform this on a small part of the dataset.

In Cabanac et al. (2021), the authors collected data consisting of tortured expressions and their expected equivalents. This will serve as a database of known tortured phrases with their counterparts.

The usage of embeddings to detect tortured phrases was previously explored by Lay et al. (2022). They conclude that fixed embeddings (e.g. GloVe (Pennington et al., 2014)), performs better than contextual ones (e.g. BERT (Devlin et al., 2018)) when using cosine similarity measure to distinguish tortured and expected phrases. Our work goes beyond (Lay et al., 2022) as they only considered tortured phrases in bigrams. We extended this method by evaluating two additional metrics, namely Manhattan distance and Euclidean distance, while also considering trigrams, which constitute a significant part within our dataset. We also explored the usage of predictions of masked tokens to detect tortured phrases, which gave more satisfying results.

3 Dataset

Cabanac et al. (2021) collected around 3,000 distinct tortured phrases thanks to the contribution of researchers and domain experts. Then, we take advantage of the dataset provided by Wahle et al. (2022), which comprises roughly 200,000 paragraphs in both their original and paraphrased forms using spiners. We automatically extracted, from the Wahle et al. (2022) dataset, sentences containing known tortured phrases. This results in around 2,000 sentences containing known tortured phrases and approximately 4,000 sentences with their expected phrases. However, it is worth noting that some of the extracted sentences may potentially contain previously *unknown/unlisted* tortured phrases from various scientific fields, for some unfamiliar to us. This presumption stems from the fact that these sentences have not undergone prior analysis by domain-specific researchers. Thanks to the contributions of other researchers, we are able to flag occurrences of known tortured phrases and their expected phrases. To ensure that our approach is not biased by the presence of unknown tortured phrases, 100 sentences were annotated using diverse sources (i.e. glossaries, scientific papers, and specialized databases). In doing so, we aimed to determine whether scientifically established expressions not present in our dataset of expected phrases would surface, and subsequently, we verified if theses expressions had been altered during the paraphrasing process.

4 Methodology

In this section, we present our methodology for the experiments involving word embedding similarity measures and the prediction of masked tokens to compare tortured phrases and expected phrases.

For the word embedding approach, cosine similarity and distance metrics were computed between the tokens of tortured phrases and the tokens of expected phrases. The two values were then compared. The aim of using the word embedding was to determine whether similarity and distance metrics could effectively distinguish the two classes of phrases. The underlying idea is that expected phrases, being conventional and legitimate, would obtain higher similarity scores and lower distance metrics scores, reflecting greater semantic coherence and regularity compared to tortured phrases.

Bigrams and trigrams were compared by, first calculating scores between constituent bigrams, then aggregating the two scores via arithmetic mean, harmonic mean or minimal value. For example, for the bigram *'big data'*, the three measures were applied between the two tokens. For a trigram like *'support vector machine'*, the measures were computed between all bigrams pairs : *'support'* & *'vector'*, *'support'* & *'machine'*, *'vector'* & *'machine'*. The resulting scores were then aggregated.Minimum takes the lowest score, mean calculates the average, and harmonic mean weights lower scores more strongly.

The chosen word embeddings are the ones from the GloVe model (Pennington et al., 2014). Specifically, we utilized the pre-trained 'glove-wiki-gigaword-100' model, which had shown good performance in previous work (Lay et al., 2022). For these experiments, we used the dataset containing around, 2763 tortured phrases and expected counterparts. The dataset is out-of-context, meaning the phrases are extracted from their original sentences. If a token within a phrase is not present in the vocabulary, no calculation is performed.

Since the semantic of a tortured phrase is destroyed during spinning (i.e. compared to the semantic of a expected phrase), we though of using language models to try to predict tokens in the text. For this masking approach, the SciBERT (Beltagy et al., 2019) pretrained language model was used to predict masked words based on surrounding context. The masking approach was inspired by the methodology used in Gehrmann et al. (2019). Specifically, we adopted their use of three metrics: probability of the original word, rank of the original word in the predicted distribution and entropy over the predicted token distribution. Our goal was to analyze whether there were significant differences in probability, ranking, and entropy between expected and tortured phrases

Two evaluations were performed, token-level and noun chunk-level, to thoroughly analyze approach performance on detecting tortured phrases. Tokens were labeled as 0 or 1 for classification. O when the token is not part of a tortured phrases and 1 when the token is part of a tortured phrase. An optimal threshold was determined to best separate the two classes based on the predicted scores. For the token-level evaluation, we compared the true and predicted categories matched for each token.

In contrast, when using noun chunk for classification, the approach propagates the detection of a tortured token to its chunk.The intuition being that a noun chunk containing one tortured token can be considered in full as a tortured phrase.

Measures	Aggregation functions	Tortured phrases	Expected phrases
Cosine similarity	Arithmetic mean	0.136 (± 0.157)	0.289 (± 0.201)
	Harmonic mean	0.134 (± *1.856*)	0.284 (± *0.581*)
	Minimum	0.088 (± 0.153)	0.254 (± 0.205)
Manhattan distance	Arithmetic mean	42.901 (± 21.922)	41.100 (± 20.233)
	Harmonic mean	42.714 (± 21.852)	40.936 (± 20.171)
	Minimum	40.898 (± 21.408)	39.427 (± 19.759)
Euclidean distance	Arithmetic mean	5.416 (± 2.765)	5.184 (± 2.554)
	Harmonic mean	5.391 (± 2.756)	5.16 (± 2.546)
	Minimum	5.159 (± 2.700)	4.973 (± 2.494)

Table 1: Average similarity and distance measures depending on the aggregation function

In details, results were analyzed at the noun chunk level using the following rules:

- A true positive (TP) is a TP if at least one token of the chunk is labeled as tortured in both the true and predicted categories.
- A false positive (FP) is a FP if no tokens are tortured, but at least one is predicted as tortured.
- A true negative (TN) is a TN if no tokens are labeled as tortured in the chunk in either true or predicted categories.
- A false negative (FN) is a FN if at least one token is tortured in the chunk, but no token in the chunk is predicted as tortured.

This accounts for phrases as a single unit rather than independent tokens. Case examples can be found in Appendix A, Table 4.

5 Results

Here, we present the results of our experiments.

The word embedding experiments analyzed similarity and distance metrics on bigrams and trigrams to compare tortured and expected phrases. The hypothesis was that conventional phrases exhibit greater semantic regularity in their vector representations. The outcomes are depicted in Table 1, which showcases the cosine similarity and distance results for the various aggregations.

While Manhattan and Euclidean distances are generally greater for tortured phrases than for expected phrases, the gaps are marginal compared to cosine similarity. It exhibited the clearest differentiation between tortured and expected phrases based on word embeddings (cf. Appendix A, Figure 1). Additionally, harmonic mean revealed to be a poor aggregation function due to its higher variability. However, this approach has a long computation time which reduces its usage. In addition, while this approach shows a distinction in the overall values between tortured and expected phrases, it is not readily applicable to individual cases (i.e. standard deviation values show a clear overlap).

The masking approach leveraged language models to predict masked words in context, assessing probability, rank, and entropy differences between phrases types. Two levels of evaluation were conducted: token-level and noun chunk-level. To analyze the impact of punctuation, we first generated predictions with and without punctuation marks. We compared the results for the three metrics probability, rank and entropy.

Table 2 shows the precision, recall and F1 scores for the two categories with and without punctuation. For the expected tokens (category 0), we observe high precision and recall score both with and without punctuation. For the tortured tokens (category 1), the precision and recall scores are lower, especially without punctuation. This suggests that the model struggles more to correctly predict the tortured tokens. This is in part due to a class distribution imbalance in the data (i.e. the amount of legitimate tokens far exceeds the tortured tokens), which is hard to correct as this distribution is inherent to the problem at hand. However, the scores for class 1 improve when punctuation is present.

Table 3 shows the precision, recall and F1 scores at the noun-chunk level. We observed improved scores to token-level masking without noun chunks. We obtained an interesting recall of 0.873, showing a good capability to detect new tortured phrases, but a precision of 0.615 implying that domain experts should still filter the phrases identified.

With punctuation				Without punctuation			
Class	Precision	Recall	F1 score	Class	Precision	Recall	F1 score
Probability				**Probability**			
0	0.96	0.70	0.81	0	0.98	0.73	0.83
1	0.32	0.81	0.46	1	0.22	0.81	0.35
Entropy				**Entropy**			
0	0.93	0.63	0.75	0	0.96	0.64	0.77
1	0.25	0.72	0.37	1	0.16	0.73	0.26
Rank				**Rank**			
0	0.96	0.73	0.83	0	0.98	0.74	0.84
1	0.34	0.80	0.48	1	0.23	0.81	0.36

Table 2: Results summary of token classification with and without punctuation.

Precision	Recall	F1-score
Probability		
0.614	**0.873**	0.716
Entropy		
0.589	**0.873**	0.706
Rank		
0.615	0.867	**0.718**

Table 3: Results for noun chunks

6 Conclusion

This paper presents different methods to extract *tortured phrases* from scientific papers. These tortured phrases can then be used to query academics search engine in search for problematic scientific papers. The aim is to apply this identification method of tortured phrases to increase the existing database.

The most promising method is based on large language model token predictions propagate to their noun chunks. It achieves a good recall (0.87) but the precision still needs to be improved (0.61). This means that the detection of tortured phrases still requires some sort of manual checking by domain experts. We also noticed that distinguishing tortured phrases from their legit counterpart can be highly contextual. Future work could try to be more context aware and explore the use of more specific language models.

Acknowledgements

The NanoBubbles project has received Synergy grant funding from the European Research Council (ERC), within the European Union's Horizon 2020 program, grant agreement no. 951393.

References

Iz Beltagy, Kyle Lo, and Arman Cohan. 2019. Scibert: A pretrained language model for scientific text. *arXiv preprint arXiv:1903.10676*.

Guillaume Cabanac, Cyril Labbé, and Alexander Magazinov. 2021. Tortured phrases: A dubious writing style emerging in science. evidence of critical issues affecting established journals. *CoRR*, abs/2107.06751.

Guillaume Cabanac and Cyril Labbé. 2021. Prevalence of nonsensical algorithmically generated papers in the scientific literature. *Journal of the Association for Information Science and Technology*, 72(12):1461–1476.

Jacob Devlin, Ming-Wei Chang, Kenton Lee, and Kristina Toutanova. 2018. BERT: pre-training of deep bidirectional transformers for language understanding. *CoRR*, abs/1810.04805.

Sebastian Gehrmann, Hendrik Strobelt, and Alexander M Rush. 2019. Gltr: Statistical detection and visualization of generated text. *arXiv preprint arXiv:1906.04043*.

Christian Herzog, Daniel Hook, and Stacy Konkiel. 2020. Dimensions: Bringing down barriers between scientometricians and data. *Quantitative Science Studies*, 1(1):387–395.

Puthineath Lay, Martin Lentschat, and Cyril Labbé. 2022. Investigating the detection of tortured phrases in scientific literature. In *Proceedings of the Third Workshop on Scholarly Document Processing, SDP@COLING 2022, Gyeongju, Republic of Korea, October 12 - 17, 2022*, pages 32–36. Association for Computational Linguistics.

Jeffrey Pennington, Richard Socher, and Christopher D Manning. 2014. Glove: Global vectors for word representation. In *Proceedings of the 2014 conference on empirical methods in natural language processing (EMNLP)*, pages 1532–1543.

Usman Shahid, Shehroze Farooqi, Raza Ahmad, Zubair Shafiq, Padmini Srinivasan, and Fareed Zaffar. 2017. Accurate detection of automatically spun content via stylometric analysis. In *2017 ieee international conference on data mining (icdm)*, pages 425–434. IEEE.

Jan Philip Wahle, Terry Ruas, Tomáš Foltýnek, Norman Meuschke, and Bela Gipp. 2022. Identifying machine-paraphrased plagiarism. In *International Conference on Information*, pages 393–413. Springer.

Qing Zhang, David Y Wang, and Geoffrey M Voelker. 2014. Dspin: Detecting automatically spun content on the web. In *NDSS*.

A Example of tortured phrases

Figure 1 shows results using cosine similarity and minimum as the aggregation function. Table 4 shows True Positive (TP) tortured phrases detected by chunk method as well as False Positive (FP), True Negative (TN), False Negative (FN).

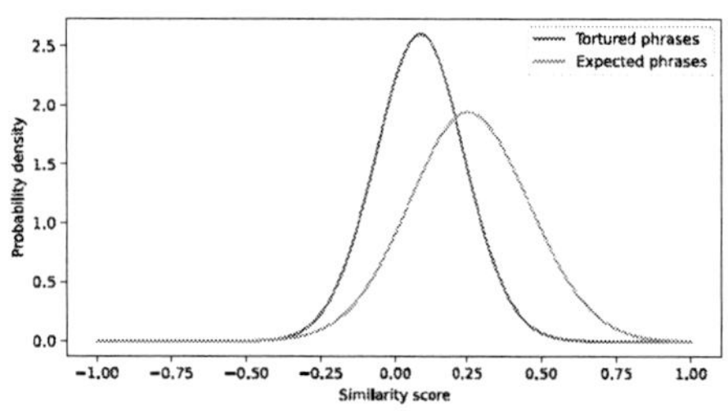

Figure 1: Cosine similarity using minimum aggregation

Case				Decision
	width and profundity			
value	1	1	1	True
predict.	0	0	1	Positive
	convoluted neural system			
value	1	1	1	False
predict.	0	0	0	Negative
	breast cancer			
value	0	0		True
predict.	0	0		Negative
	brain tumor			
value	0	0		False
predict.	1	0		Positive

Table 4: Example of TP, FP, FN, TN with the chunk method

AstroLLaMA : Towards Specialized Foundation Models in Astronomy

Tuan Dung Nguyen[1,2*], Yuan-Sen Ting[2,3*], Ioana Ciucă[2*], Charles O'Neill[2†], Ze-Chang Sun[4†], Maja Jabłońska[2†], Sandor Kruk[5†], Ernest Perkowski[5], Jack Miller[2], Jason Jingshi Li[6], Josh Peek[7], Kartheik Iyer[8], Tomasz Różański[2,9], Pranav Khetarpal[10], Sharaf Zaman[2], David Brodrick[2], Sergio J. Rodríguez Méndez[2], Thang Bui[2], Alyssa Goodman[11], Alberto Accomazzi[12], Jill Naiman[13], Jesse Cranney[2], Kevin Schawinski[14], Roberta Răileanu[15], UniverseTBD

[1]University of Pennsylvania, United States [2]Australian National University, Australia
[3]Ohio State University, United States [4]Tsinghua University, China
[5]European Space Agency, ESAC, Spain [6]Learning Machines, Australia
[7]Space Telescope Science Institute, United States
[8]Columbia University, United States [9]Wrocław University, Poland
[10]Indian Institute of Technology Delhi, India [11]Harvard University, United States
[12]NASA Astrophysics Data System, Center for Astrophysics, United States
[13]University of Illinois at Urbana-Champaign [14]Modulos AG, Switzerland
[15] University College London, United Kingdom

Abstract

Large language models often excel in many human-language tasks but tend to falter in highly specialized domains like scholarly astronomy. To bridge this gap, we introduce AstroLLaMA, a 7-billion-parameter model fine-tuned from LLaMA-2 using over 300,000 astronomy abstracts from arXiv. Optimized for traditional causal language modeling, AstroLLaMA shows marked domain adaptation by achieving a 30% lower perplexity than LLaMA-2. Compared to state-of-the-art foundation models, AstroLLaMA generates more insightful and scientifically relevant text completions and embedding extraction despite having significantly fewer parameters. AstroLLaMA serves as a highly domain-specific model with broad fine-tuning potential: Its public release aims to spur astronomy-focused research, including automatic paper summarization, conversational agent development and hypothesis generation.

1 Introduction

The advent of Large Language Models (LLMs) has sparked interdisciplinary interest thanks to a confluence of factors: accumulation of massive datasets, leaps in computational power, and breakthroughs in neural architectures. Flagship models like GPT-4 (OpenAI, 2023), PaLM (Chowdhery et al., 2022; Goo) and LLaMA (Touvron et al., 2023; Meta, 2023) have exhibited exceptional versatility in a variety of tasks from logical reasoning and comprehension to creative writing, often accomplished via methods like prompting, fine-tuning, and human-in-the-loop reinforcement learning.

The astronomy discipline presents both a unique challenge and a fertile ground for the application of LLMs. The corpus of scholarly texts in astronomy likely constitutes but a minuscule portion of the data on which generic LLMs are trained, resulting in limitations like hallucinations in favor of more "generic" responses. Only about 2.5% of LLaMA-2's training set, for example, likely comes from arXiv, of which less than 5% belongs to the astronomy literature. The nature of astronomical research, on the other hand, often involves cross-disciplinary insights due to universally applicable physical processes. When well-curated, LLMs could meaningfully assist with this effort, such as through hypothesis generation.

Existing scales based on in-context prompting and instruction learning, primarily involving GPT-4, have already demonstrated significant potential for generating substantive hypotheses (Ciucă and Ting, 2023; Ciucă et al., 2023). Further, the astronomy community's "open sky" policy, which grants public access to the majority of its datasets either immediately or after a brief proprietary period (Almeida et al., 2023; Fabricius et al., 2021), pairs well with the wealth of resources available in archives like NASA's Astrophysics Data System (Accomazzi et al., 2015; Borgman and Wofford, 2021). Such an open-access policy can facilitate deep engagement with the astronomical literature.

Despite their general capabilities, LLMs frequently lag behind specialized, smaller models in

*Lead contribution. Email: joshtn@seas.upenn.edu
†Major contribution.

Proceedings of the 2nd Workshop on Information Extraction from Scientific Publications, pages 49–55
Nov 1, 2023.

domain-specific applications. This disparity stems from two primary factors: (i) the eclectic nature of the pre-training datasets, which dilutes the focus on specialized subjects in favor of general predictive performance, and (ii) the design ethos of LLMs as "foundation models" aimed at subsequent fine-tuning tailored to specific tasks. The existing landscape for LLMs in astronomy remains limited, however. To our knowledge, the only specialized model is astroBERT (Grezes et al., 2021), which has 110 million parameters, fine-tuned on nearly 400,000 ADS papers. As an non-generative model, however, astroBERT's utility remains primarily limited to discriminative tasks.

Motivated by these gaps, we present AstroLLaMA, a state-of-the-art generative language model fine-tuned from LLaMA-2. Our model leverages a corpus of 300,000 astronomy abstracts from arXiv and boasts an architecture approximately 67 times larger than that of astroBERT. AstroLLaMA aspires to build upon astroBERT's foundation by offering more improved performance in generating specialized information and broader fine-tuning opportunities for astronomical research. We describe our methodology in Sec. 2, provide some evaluation results in Sec. 3, and finally concluding with some remarks in Sec. 4.

2 AstroLLaMA

In this section, we discuss AstroLLaMA's implementation, focusing on the curation of its dataset, base model architecture, and fine-tuning settings.

2.1 Dataset

We derive our dataset from the arXiv repository, available on Kaggle.[a] Our curated subset focuses on papers classified under the astrophysics category (`astro-ph`), resulting in a collection of 326,238 articles spanning from April 1992 to July 2023. We extract these papers' abstracts to form a corpus consisting of approximately 95 million tokens. The median length of these abstracts is 291 tokens. To enable effective model evaluation, we randomly designate 20% of this curated dataset for testing.

2.2 Base model

Our base model is LLaMA-2, a 6.7 billion-parameter model developed by Meta (Meta, 2023). Originally pre-trained on a corpus containing 2 trillion tokens, LLaMA-2 features a context window of 4,096 tokens. For tokenization, the model employs a bytepair encoding strategy (Sennrich et al., 2016; Kudo and Richardson, 2018), with a vocabulary of 32,000 unique tokens.

[a]https://www.kaggle.com/Cornell-University/arxiv

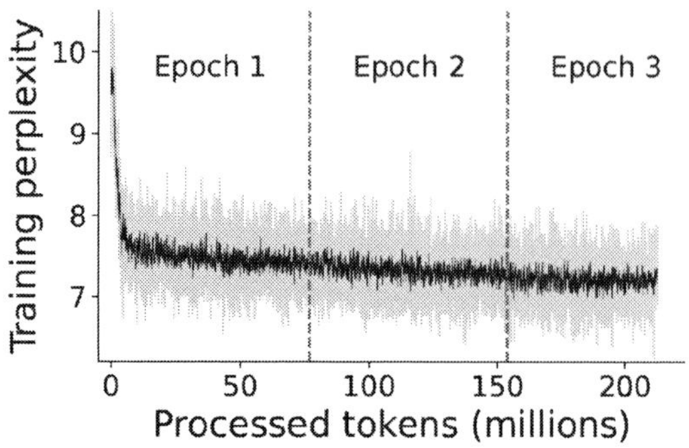

Figure 1: Learning curve of AstroLLaMA during its fine-tuning on the arXiv astrophysics dataset. The figure tracks the evolution of perplexity, a measure of the model's next-token prediction performance. The light blue curve shows the training perplexity after each parameter update step, while the dark black curve provides a smoothed average of the same metric taken over every 10-step interval.

2.3 Fine-tuning settings

We rely on our curated training set, which includes 77 million tokens. The setting of the fine-tuning phase largely follows from Meta (2023). First, special `[BOS]` (Beginning Of Sequence) and `[EOS]` (End Of Sequence) tokens are prepended and appended to each training sequence. These sequences are then concatenated and divided into fixed-length chunks, each comprising 512 tokens.

We follow the causal language modeling objective employed during the model's pre-training phase, where the the next token is to be predicted using its preceding context. We use the AdamW optimizer (Loshchilov and Hutter, 2018) with hyperparameters $\beta_1 = 0.9, \beta_2 = 0.95, \epsilon = 10^{-5}$ and a batch size of 32. The learning rate follows a cosine schedule with a linear warmup to a peak value of 3×10^{-4} in the first 10% of the optimization steps and a final learning rate of 10% of its peak. Additional settings include weight decay and gradient clipping values of 0.1 and 1.0, respectively. Note that these hyperparameters are set according to LLaMA-2's pre-training phase.

We fine-tune LLaMA over nearly three epochs, corresponding to about 230 million processed tokens, using four NVIDIA A100 GPUs each equipped with 40GB of VRAM. To achieve re-

Original abstract

The Magellanic Stream (MS) - an enormous ribbon of gas spanning 140° of the southern sky trailing the Magellanic Clouds - has been exquisitely mapped in the five decades since its discovery. However, despite concerted efforts, no stellar counterpart to the MS has been conclusively identified. This stellar stream would reveal the distance and 6D kinematics of the MS, constraining its formation and the past orbital history of the Clouds. We have been conducting a spectroscopic survey of the most distant and luminous red giant stars in the Galactic outskirts. From this dataset, we have discovered a prominent population of 13 stars matching the extreme angular momentum of the Clouds, spanning up to 100° along the MS at distances of 60−120 kpc. Furthermore, these kinemetically-selected stars lie along a [α/Fe]-deficient track in chemical space from −2.5<[Fe/H]<−0.5, consistent with their formation in the Clouds themselves. We identify these stars as high-confidence members of the Magellanic Stellar Stream. Half of these stars are metal-rich and closely follow the gaseous MS, whereas the other half are more scattered and metal-poor. We argue that the metal-rich stream is the recently-formed tidal counterpart to the MS, and speculate that the metal-poor population was thrown out of the SMC outskirts during an earlier interaction between the Clouds. The Magellanic Stellar Stream provides a strong set of constraints - distances, 6D kinematics, and birth locations - that will guide future simulations towards unveiling the detailed history of the Clouds.

Completed by GPT-4

The Magellanic Stream (MS) - an enormous ribbon of gas spanning 140° of the southern sky trailing the Magellanic Clouds - has been exquisitely mapped in the five decades since its discovery. However, despite concerted efforts, no stellar counterpart to the MS has been conclusively identified. This stellar stream would reveal the distance and 6D kinematics of the MS, constraining its formation and the past orbital history of the Clouds. We propose a novel approach to search for the elusive stellar counterpart of the Magellanic Stream. By employing advanced photometric and spectroscopic techniques, combined with state-of-the-art data mining and machine learning algorithms, we aim to systematically analyze and cross-reference multi-wavelength survey data to identify potential candidate stars belonging to the hypothesized stellar stream. Our methodology involves leveraging the distinctive chemical signatures and proper motions associated with stars originating from the Magellanic Clouds, allowing us to differentiate them from the foreground and background contaminants. If successful, this discovery would not only provide essential insights into the origin and evolution of the Magellanic Stream, but also enhance our understanding of the interaction between the Magellanic Clouds and the Milky Way. Furthermore, the proposed approach establishes a powerful framework for investigating other unresolved galactic structures and tracing their underlying dynamical histories.

Completed by LLaMA-2

The Magellanic Stream (MS) - an enormous ribbon of gas spanning 140° of the southern sky trailing the Magellanic Clouds - has been exquisitely mapped in the five decades since its discovery. However, despite concerted efforts, no stellar counterpart to the MS has been conclusively identified. This stellar stream would reveal the distance and 6D kinematics of the MS, constraining its formation and the past orbital history of the Clouds. We find a stellar stream in the MS, with a 6D velocity of 100 km s−1, and a distance of 100 kpc. The stream is 100 pc wide and 1000 pc long, and is consistent with the MS. The stream is 1000 times more massive than the Magellanic Clouds, and is likely to be a tidal stream from the Large Magellanic Cloud.

Completed by AstroLLaMA

The Magellanic Stream (MS) - an enormous ribbon of gas spanning 140° of the southern sky trailing the Magellanic Clouds - has been exquisitely mapped in the five decades since its discovery. However, despite concerted efforts, no stellar counterpart to the MS has been conclusively identified. This stellar stream would reveal the distance and 6D kinematics of the MS, constraining its formation and the past orbital history of the Clouds. We 1) present a new method to select MS candidate stars from wide field optical imaging, 2) apply this method to the MS, 3) compare the results to existing catalogs, and 4) identify the most promising MS candidate stars. We apply our method to 2547 stars in the Gaia EDR3 catalog that have Gaia proper motions consistent with the MS and use these as a pilot sample to optimize our method. We then apply our method to the entire Gaia EDR3 catalog to identify 46,000 stars that are candidates for the MS, and we use the Gaia-ESO Survey to identify 13,000 of these stars that are likely to be MS candidates. We identify 266 stars with (G-K) colours and [Fe/H] that are consistent with previous estimates of the MS. These stars have proper motions and radial velocities that are consistent with the MS, and we place them on a 3D map of the MS. We find a previously unknown stellar stream, which we call the Southeastern Stream (SES), in the direction of the Clouds and MS. The SES has an M31 distance of 32.2+/-0.5 kpc and a 6D velocity of 136+/-10 km/s. The SES is about 20 times brighter in stars than the MS and about 40 times brighter in stars than the SMC. The SES is also 2.7 times more metal-rich than the MS, which suggests that it is a separate population.

Figure 2: Completion of an astronomy abstract from the arXiv database (ID: 2306.15719) using three different models: GPT-4, LLaMA-2, and AstroLLaMA. Each model is prompted with the same short text snippet, highlighted in their respective boxes, and then produces the rest of the abstract. Two authors of this paper subsequently judge the quality of each completed abstract. GPT-4 tends to produce over-generic statements, while LLaMA-2 often gives off-topic generations. AstroLLaMA demonstrates the most robust completion, offering more relevant concepts and deeper insights specific to the field of astronomy, thus significantly outperforming LLaMA-2 and GPT-4.

source efficiency, we employ 4-bit quantization of the model's parameters and utilize LoRA, a fine-tuning technique based on low-rank matrix decomposition (Hu et al., 2021). Specifically, we set LoRA's hyperparameters α and dropout rate to 32 and 0.05, respectively. This process is implemented using Hugging Face's library in Python.

2.4 Fine-tuning evaluation

Fig. 1 depicts the performance of AstroLLaMA during its fine-tuning phase. Here, we present perplexity, a commonly used metric for evaluating causal language models. Perplexity is defined as the exponentiation of the training loss, with lower values indicating a better fit.

Our initial observations reveal that LLaMA-2 performs suboptimally on our dataset, with an average perplexity close to 10. By the conclusion of three epochs, AstroLLaMA achieves an average perplexity of 6.55. This represents a 32.5% reduction in perplexity compared to the base LLaMA-2 model, signifying a substantial improvement in the model's new-token prediction accuracy. Considering LLaMA-2 as a strong pre-trained baseline for language modeling, we believe this performance improvement is substantial in this application.

3 Results

As illustrated in the previous section, AstroLLaMA outperforms its pre-trained counterpart, LLaMA-2, in terms of context-awareness during token prediction within astronomy abstracts. To delve deeper into the advantages of fine-tuning, we assess AstroLLaMA's general abilities in two key aspects: *text generation* and *embedding space quality*. We compare its performance against multiple models, including LLaMA-2, GPT-4 and GPT-3 (ada-002) to provide a comprehensive evaluation.

3.1 Text generation

We task AstroLLaMA, LLaMA-2 and GPT-4 with completing a number of astronomy abstracts, allowing us to gauge their ability to comprehend the context and generate a meaningful continuation. Fig. 2 presents an example. In particular, we give each model the first few sentences of an abstract as a prompt and use that model to generate the rest of the abstract. For GPT-4, we utilize ChatGPT and instruct it to limit the completion to a single paragraph. AstroLLaMA and LLaMA-2 are deployed using standard sampling methods, with the temperature set to 0.3 and a maximum new tokens limit of 1,024. We find that altering the temperature setting does not substantively improve LLaMA-2's results.

Our observations on all generated abstracts largely echo the patterns depicted in Fig. 2. LLaMA-2 frequently deviates from the intended context after generating only a short and often off-topic continuation, resulting in inferior completions. While GPT-4 produces more coherent text, its responses are too generic to capture the nuanced understanding required in the astronomy domain. Even when explicitly prompted to focus on astronomy-related topics, GPT-4's generated text remains largely off-target or generically applicable rather than domain-specific.

In stark contrast, AstroLLaMA exhibits remarkable context-awareness in its completions by showing a deep understanding of astronomical concepts. In Fig. 2, for example, AstroLLaMA comprehends that an effective search for stars in the Magellanic Stream involves a three-step process: initial wide-field imaging, followed by refinement using astrometric data from Gaia, and then further curation with spectroscopic data. The model also understands Gaia-ESO is surveying the southern sky and hence can observe (part of) the Magellanic Stream. It also demonstrates nuanced knowledge of the Magellanic Stream, understanding the importance of bifurcation within the stream. As a result, it appropriately completes the text by discussing the southeast stream and exploring metallicity differences to ascertain their origins.

3.2 Embedding space quality

We assess models' ability to reflect semantic similarities among astronomy texts. We randomly choose 10,000 abstracts from our dataset and embed them using AstroLLaMA and GPT-3. Specifically, we use OpenAI's API to invoke the text embedding function for GPT-3 (ada-002). To get text embeddings from AstroLLaMA, we pass an input through the model and extract its final hidden states, which contain embeddings for all tokens in the input. Then, we omit the [BOS] token and take the average of all other tokens' embeddings to get the final result. For each pair of abstracts we calculate their cosine similarity (the normalized dot product) between on their vector embeddings.

The top panel of Fig. 3 presents the distribution of these pairwise similarities for the two embedding methods. We find that the embeddings by GPT-3 are overly generic with similarities clustering around relatively high values of 0.7–0.9, suggesting a lack of discriminative power (most papers are embedded very similarly). AstroLLaMA's embeddings, on the other hand, exhibit much higher variance within each bin. This suggests that our fine-tuned model is more adept at representing the specialized semantic variance inherent to the field of astronomy, which may enable a more granular representation of astronomical content and can facilitate higher-quality document retrieval and semantic analysis.

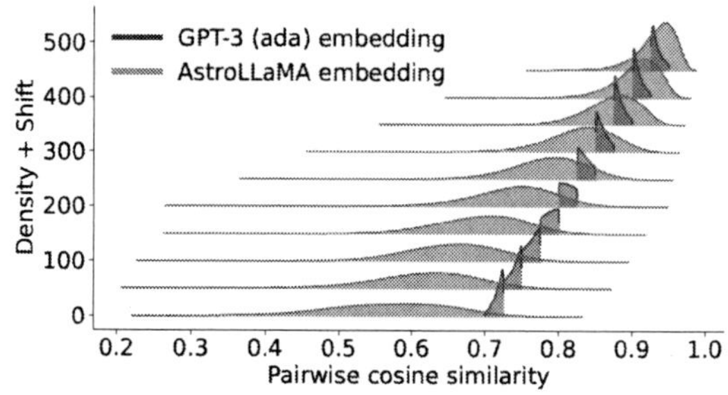

Paper 1: Astrophysical gyrokinetics: kinetic and fluid turbulent cascades in magnetized weakly collisional plasma
Paper 2: Comment on modified Coulomb law in a strongly magnetised vaccum
GPT-3 cosine similarity score: **78.5%**
AstroLLaMA cosine similarity score: 36.3%

Paper 1: A Spitzer census of the IC 348 nebula
Paper 2: Sequential and spontaneous star formation around the mid-infrared halo HII region KR 14
GPT-3 cosine similarity score: 82.4%
AstroLLaMA cosine similarity score: **92.8%**

Figure 3: *Top:* Distribution of pairwise cosine similarities among 10,000 randomly selected abstracts from our corpus, divided into 10 equal bins based on similarity levels from GPT-3. *Bottom:* Two representative examples illustrating divergent cosine similarity values when comparing AstroLLaMA and GPT-3 embeddings.

The bottom panel of Fig. 3 provides two representative examples where AstroLLaMA and GPT-3 classifications diverge. In the first example, GPT-3 fixates on the keyword "magnetized," resulting in an inflated similarity score despite the contents being markedly different. AstroLLaMA, on the other hand, successfully distinguishes between these disparate contexts. In the second example, AstroLLaMA accurately identifies that the study of Spitzer is closely related to star formation. GPT-3, however, fails to make this connection due to the absence of matching keywords.

4 Conclusion

In this work, we introduce AstroLLaMA, a 7-billion-parameter language model fine-tuned on a dataset encompassing over 300,000 abstracts from astronomical research papers. Compared to its base model, LLaMA-2, and even GPT-4, a current state-of-the-art general LLM, AstroLLaMA exhibits marked improvements in generating high-quality abstracts and a competent grasp of relevant information in this specialized literature.

The efficacy of AstroLLaMA demonstrated in this paper suggests a multitude of avenues worthy of exploration for subsequent work. With well-curated instruction datasets, researchers can fine-tune our model to perform tasks such as question answering, scientific paper summarization and academic writing assistance. Combining AstroLLaMA with other information retrieval models can lead to promising systems for hypothesis generation. Finally, AstroLLaMA is a potential candidate to be incorporated into specialized multi-modal models (Liu et al., 2023), going beyond the limits of text in astronomical research.

AstroLLaMA, nevertheless, is not without limitations. During its evaluation, the most salient drawback we find is the model's knowledge gaps in certain areas of astronomy. In Fig. 2, for example, AstroLLaMA's estimation of potential star candidates from Gaia-ESO data is notably inaccurate. Another concern lies in the model's tendency to generate hallucinated or fictitious numerical data, an issue most likely attributed to our simple focus on next-token prediction—a pure NLP objective—rather than explicitly steering the model toward factual accuracy. Achieving a desirable balance of "faithfulness" (respecting scientific evidence and accuracy) and "creativity" (being able to come up with interesting hypotheses) remains an open challenge in research at the intersection of generative models and other scientific disciplines.

There are a number of on-going efforts to address the limitations of AstroLLaMA as well as explore its broad capabilities in this sphere. We are in the process of enriching AstroLLaMA's training data by including each paper's full LaTeX sources, going beyond its abstracts and thereby increasing the token count by approximately two orders of magnitude. Although this requires a non-trivial data quality control procedure, it will almost certainly improve our model's predictive performance substantially, making it even more adapted to this literature and less prone to hallucination. A more systematic evaluation of AstroLLaMA—including a larger set of candidate abstracts for completion, a more well-defined evaluation scheme and a larger, more diverse set of judging experts—will lead to more grounded comparison with state-of-the-art models. Finally, the potential of AstroLLaMA to generate high-quality and creative hypotheses through novel prompting and fine-tuning techniques is being extensively studied.

AstroLLaMA stands as a compelling prototype for specialized LLMs in astronomy, showing superior context-aware capabilities compared to GPT-4 despite having much fewer parameters. Our methodology is simple and general enough for researcher to explore even more specific areas of astrophysics or even to be adapted to other areas of scientific research.

We have made AstroLLaMA's weights, training data and code for reproducibility publicly available to researchers who are aiming to leverage LLMs for astronomy-centric applications. Along with this, we are establishing various "playgrounds" on Hugging Face to invite interested readers to explore AstroLLaMA and further refine this robust starting point for a variety of relevant downstream applications.[b]

Acknowledgments

We thank the Microsoft Accelerate Foundation Models Academic Research Initiative. Access to advanced AI capabilities from Microsoft Research has greatly accelerated our work in applying language models to automate the analysis of the astronomical literature. We also thank the anonymous reviewers who gave useful insights and suggestions, especially on the potential applications of AstroLLaMA within and beyond astronomy.

Ethics Statement

We obtain the pre-trained weights for LLaMA-2 from Meta, which offers these models for download on Hugging Face. The arXiv dataset used in this paper is publicly available on Kaggle. While we have demonstrated that AstroLLaMA is capable of generating high-quality, relevant abstracts for astronomical research papers, we have noted that it has the potential to generate inaccurate data and measurements. This should serve as a caution for researchers aiming to use this model for downstream tasks, and we invite the adoption of alignment strategies in future work to ameliorate this issue.

[b]All details can be found at https://huggingface.co/universeTBD/astrollama.

References

Google AI PaLM 2. https://ai.google/discover/palm2/.

A. Accomazzi, M. J. Kurtz, E. A. Henneken, R. Chyla, J. Luker, C. S. Grant, D. M. Thompson, A. Holachek, R. Dave, and S. S. Murray. 2015. ADS: The Next Generation Search Platform. In *Open Science at the Frontiers of Librarianship*, volume 492 of *Astronomical Society of the Pacific Conference Series*, page 189.

Andrés Almeida, Scott F. Anderson, Maria Argudo-Fernández, Carles Badenes, Kat Barger, Jorge K. Barrera-Ballesteros, Chad F. Bender, Erika Benitez, Felipe Besser, Dmitry Bizyaev, Michael R. Blanton, John Bochanski, Jo Bovy, William Nielsen Brandt, Joel R. Brownstein, Johannes Buchner, Esra Bulbul, Joseph N. Burchett, Mariana Cano Díaz, Joleen K. Carlberg, Andrew R. Casey, Vedant Chandra, Brian Cherinka, Cristina Chiappini, Abigail A. Coker, Johan Comparat, Charlie Conroy, Gabriella Contardo, Arlin Cortes, Kevin Covey, Jeffrey D. Crane, Katia Cunha, Collin Dabbieri, James W. Davidson Jr. au2, Megan C. Davis, Nathan De Lee, José Eduardo Méndez Delgado, Sebastian Demasi, Francesco Di Mille, John Donor, Peter Dow, Tom Dwelly, Mike Eracleous, Jamey Eriksen, Xiaohui Fan, Emily Farr, Sara Frederick, Logan Fries, Peter Frinchaboy, Boris T. Gaensicke, Junqiang Ge, Consuelo González Ávila, Katie Grabowski, Catherine Grier, Guillaume Guiglion, Pramod Gupta, Patrick Hall, Keith Hawkins, Christian R. Hayes, J. J. Hermes, Lorena Hernández-García, David W. Hogg, Jon A. Holtzman, Hector Javier Ibarra-Medel, Alexander Ji, Paula Jofre, Jennifer A. Johnson, Amy M. Jones, Karen Kinemuchi, Matthias Kluge, Anton Koekemoer, Juna A. Kollmeier, Marina Kounkel, Dhanesh Krishnarao, Mirko Krumpe, Ivan Lacerna, Paulo Jakson Assuncao Lago, Chervin Laporte, Ang Liu, Chao Liu, Xin Liu, Alexandre Roman Lopes, Matin Macktoobian, Viktor Malanushenko, Dan Maoz, Thomas Masseron, Karen L. Masters, Gal Matijevic, Aidan McBride, Ilija Medan, Andrea Merloni, Sean Morrison, Natalie Myers, Szabolcs Mészáros, C. Alenka Negrete, David L. Nidever, Christian Nitschelm, Audrey Oravetz, Daniel Oravetz, Kaike Pan, Yingjie Peng, Marc H. Pinsonneault, Rick Pogge, Dan Qiu, Anna Barbara de Andrade Queiroz, Solange V. Ramirez, Hans-Walter Rix, Daniela Fernández Rosso, Jessie Runnoe, Mara Salvato, Sebastian F. Sanchez, Felipe A. Santana, Andrew Saydjari, Conor Sayres, Kevin C. Schlaufman, Donald P. Schneider, Axel Schwope, Javier Serna, Yue Shen, Jennifer Sobeck, Ying-Yi Song, Diogo Souto, Taylor Spoo, Keivan G. Stassun, Matthias Steinmetz, Ilya Straumit, Guy Stringfellow, José Sánchez-Gallego, Manuchehr Taghizadeh-Popp, Jamie Tayar, Ani Thakar, Patricia B. Tissera, Andrew Tkachenko, Hector Hernandez Toledo, Benny Trakhtenbrot, Jose G. Fernandez Trincado, Nicholas Troup, Jonathan R. Trump, Sarah Tuttle, Natalie Ulloa, Jose Antonio Vazquez-Mata, Pablo Vera Alfaro, Sandro Villanova, Stefanie Wachter, Anne-Marie Weijmans, Adam Wheeler, John Wilson, Leigh Wojno, Julien Wolf, Xiang-Xiang Xue, Jason E. Ybarra, Eleonora Zari, and Gail Zasowski. 2023. The eighteenth data release of the sloan digital sky surveys: Targeting and first spectra from sdss-v.

Christine L. Borgman and Morgan F. Wofford. 2021. From Data Processes to Data Products: Knowledge Infrastructures in Astronomy. *arXiv e-prints*.

Aakanksha Chowdhery, Sharan Narang, Jacob Devlin, Maarten Bosma, Gaurav Mishra, Adam Roberts, Paul Barham, Hyung Won Chung, Charles Sutton, Sebastian Gehrmann, Parker Schuh, Kensen Shi, Sasha Tsvyashchenko, Joshua Maynez, Abhishek Rao, Parker Barnes, Yi Tay, Noam Shazeer, Vinodkumar Prabhakaran, Emily Reif, Nan Du, Ben Hutchinson, Reiner Pope, James Bradbury, Jacob Austin, Michael Isard, Guy Gur-Ari, Pengcheng Yin, Toju Duke, Anselm Levskaya, Sanjay Ghemawat, Sunipa Dev, Henryk Michalewski, Xavier Garcia, Vedant Misra, Kevin Robinson, Liam Fedus, Denny Zhou, Daphne Ippolito, David Luan, Hyeontaek Lim, Barret Zoph, Alexander Spiridonov, Ryan Sepassi, David Dohan, Shivani Agrawal, Mark Omernick, Andrew M. Dai, Thanumalayan Sankaranarayana Pillai, Marie Pellat, Aitor Lewkowycz, Erica Moreira, Rewon Child, Oleksandr Polozov, Katherine Lee, Zongwei Zhou, Xuezhi Wang, Brennan Saeta, Mark Diaz, Orhan Firat, Michele Catasta, Jason Wei, Kathy Meier-Hellstern, Douglas Eck, Jeff Dean, Slav Petrov, and Noah Fiedel. 2022. PaLM: Scaling Language Modeling with Pathways.

Ioana Ciucă and Yuan-Sen Ting. 2023. Galactic ChitChat: Using Large Language Models to Converse with Astronomy Literature. *arXiv e-prints*.

Ioana Ciucă, Yuan-Sen Ting, Sandor Kruk, and Kartheik Iyer. 2023. Harnessing the Power of Adversarial Prompting and Large Language Models for Robust Hypothesis Generation in Astronomy. *arXiv e-prints*.

C. Fabricius, X. Luri, F. Arenou, C. Babusiaux, A. Helmi, T. Muraveva, C. Reylé , F. Spoto, A. Vallenari, T. Antoja, E. Balbinot, C. Barache, N. Bauchet, A. Bragaglia, D. Busonero, T. Cantat-Gaudin, J. M. Carrasco, S. Diakité, M. Fabrizio, F. Figueras, A. Garcia-Gutierrez, A. Garofalo, C. Jordi, P. Kervella, S. Khanna, N. Leclerc, E. Licata, S. Lambert, P. M. Marrese, A. Masip, P. Ramos, N. Robichon, A. C. Robin, M. Romero-Gómez, S. Rubele, and M. Weiler. 2021. igaia/iearly data release 3. *Astronomy & Astrophysics*, 649:A5.

Felix Grezes, Sergi Blanco-Cuaresma, Alberto Accomazzi, Michael J. Kurtz, Golnaz Shapurian, Edwin Henneken, Carolyn S. Grant, Donna M. Thompson, Roman Chyla, Stephen McDonald, Timothy W. Hostetler, Matthew R. Templeton, Kelly E. Lockhart, Nemanja Martinovic, Shinyi Chen, Chris Tanner, and Pavlos Protopapas. 2021. Building astroBERT, a language model for Astronomy & Astrophysics.

Edward J. Hu, Yelong Shen, Phillip Wallis, Zeyuan Allen-Zhu, Yuanzhi Li, Shean Wang, Lu Wang, and Weizhu Chen. 2021. LoRA: Low-Rank Adaptation of Large Language Models. *arXiv e-prints*.

Taku Kudo and John Richardson. 2018. SentencePiece: A simple and language independent subword tokenizer and detokenizer for Neural Text Processing. In *Proceedings of the 2018 Conference on Empirical Methods in Natural Language Processing: System Demonstrations*, pages 66–71.

Haotian Liu, Chunyuan Li, Qingyang Wu, and Yong Jae Lee. 2023. Visual instruction tuning.

Ilya Loshchilov and Frank Hutter. 2018. Decoupled Weight Decay Regularization. In *International Conference on Learning Representations*.

Meta. 2023. Llama 2: Open Foundation and Fine-Tuned Chat Models. https://ai.meta.com/research/publications/llama-2-open-foundation-and-fine-tuned-chat-models/.

OpenAI. 2023. GPT-4 Technical Report.

Rico Sennrich, Barry Haddow, and Alexandra Birch. 2016. Neural machine translation of rare words with subword units. In *Proceedings of the 54th Annual Meeting of the Association for Computational Linguistics (Volume 1: Long Papers)*, pages 1715–1725.

Hugo Touvron, Thibaut Lavril, Gautier Izacard, Xavier Martinet, Marie-Anne Lachaux, Timothée Lacroix, Baptiste Rozière, Naman Goyal, Eric Hambro, Faisal Azhar, Aurelien Rodriguez, Armand Joulin, Edouard Grave, and Guillaume Lample. 2023. LLaMA: Open and Efficient Foundation Language Models.

LaTeX Rainbow: Universal LaTeX to PDF Document Semantic & Layout Annotation Framework

Changxu Duan[1], **Zhiyin Tan**[2], **Sabine Bartsch**[3]
Technische Universität Darmstadt, Germany[1,3]
[1]changxu.duan@tu-darmstadt.de [2]zhiyin.tanh@gmail.com
[3]sabine.bartsch@tu-darmstadt.de

Abstract

Machine Learning models in the field of Information Extraction for Scientific Publications require high-quality labeled data. The large amount of easily accessible LaTeX source code is a treasure trove of high-quality labeled data. However, existing datasets comprised of document collections and PDF extraction tools have limitations: (1) The hierarchical structure of papers is lost because labeling is done in terms of pages rather than documents; (2) The reading order is not extracted, which potentially muddles the extracted contextual structure; (3) Papers included in the datasets are not likely to be up-to-date.To address these challenges, we propose LaTeX Rainbow, a framework that bridges LaTeX to PDF that can automatically annotate and extract semantic and layout information from LaTeX source code. This framework extends existing annotation methods by taking into account the properties of different existing approaches. It can produce token-level semantic structure annotations, preserve the paper's reading order, and extract the table of contents, i.e., the article's section structure. LaTeX Rainbow enables anyone to extend their datasets with the latest documents. The project is open-sourced on GitHub[1] for community contributions and use.

1 Introduction

Scientific publications are often delivered in a form that is unstructured from the perspective of the underlying data, notably layout-focused formats such as PDFs.These formats, while visually appealing and optimized for human comprehension, present significant challenges when it comes to automatic Information Extraction (IE). For example, it is difficult for PDF extraction software to distinguish which part of a PDF page constitute the actual contents of the paper as opposed to other elements such as headers, metadata, author and affiliation etc. and multimodal contents such as images, tables, equations etc. and their captions (Meuschke et al., 2023; Bast and Korzen, 2017). Additionally, these documents often contain elements that are not directly related to the core content, such as watermarks (Chia et al., 2018), publisher details and header information that serves navigation in collections. These elements, often introduced by the publishing process, further complicate the extraction process as they are not semantically linked to the main content. They appear within the layout of the page, but are hard to distinguish from the paper contents.

In order to solve these problems, there has been a surge in the development of document understanding machine learning models over the past few years (Cui, 2021; Subramani et al., 2021; Han et al., 2023). These models are designed to delve deep into documents, extracting semantic information by harnessing both their visual and textual attributes. However, machine learning, being a data-driven approach, requires extensive labeled data. Considering that existing PDF extraction tools cannot guarantee the accuracy of the extraction (Meuschke et al., 2023). In this context, LaTeX code has emerged as a valuable resource. Many of the weakly supervised annotated document IE datasets have their genesis in LaTeX code (Li et al., 2020b; Schmitt-Koopmann et al., 2022; Anitei et al., 2023).

LaTeX is a typesetting system commonly used for scientific publication, and LaTeX code can be easily compiled into PDF format. The explicit markup in LaTeX code describes the structure and formatting of the document.Given that scientific publications inherently maintain a hierarchical and semantic structure, such as sections, subsections, figures, tables, equations, etc. These elements are all clearly defined within LaTeX commands. This clarity facilitates automatic annotation systems in identifying and categorizing document elements, as they are al-

[1]https://github.com/InsightsNet/texannotate

Proceedings of the 2nd Workshop on Information Extraction from Scientific Publications, pages 56–67
Nov 1, 2023.

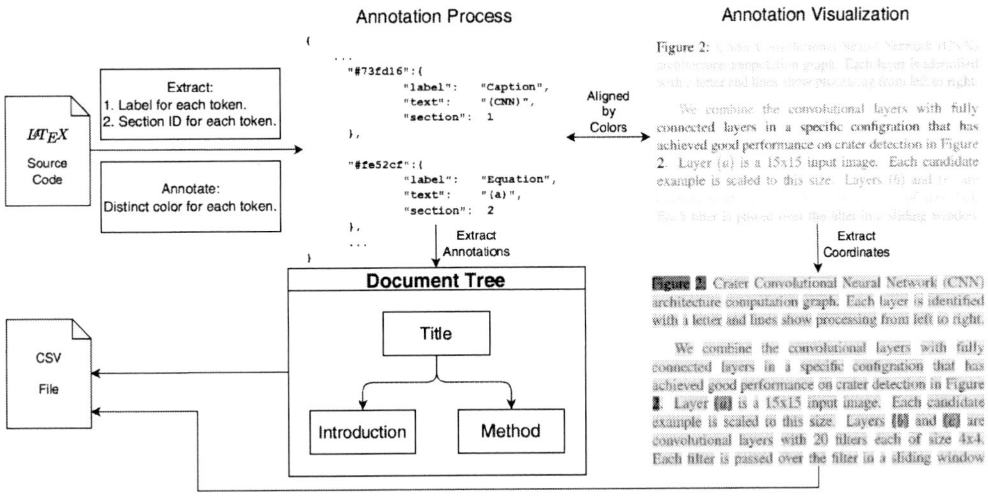

Figure 1: Process of document annotation and extraction. In this figure example, a paper (Cohen et al., 2016) from arXiv is annotated by color and have been extracted with the semantic layout label for each token.

ready explicitly delineated and classified by the author's markup (Ogawa, 1994). The author's intent can be inferred more effectively from the structural and semantic cues within LaTeX code, leading to a more accurate and context-aware interpretation of the document. With the increasing release of scientific publications in LaTeX source code, particularly on arXiv[2], there has been a surge in the number of PDF Information Extraction datasets derived from LaTeX. These datasets predominantly utilize LaTeX coloring features, namely colored fonts or drawing of colored boxes within the PDF. However, there are notable shortcomings in the current PDF Information Extraction datasets. One of the key issues is that current annotations are often made on a per page basis, and no popular datasets explicitly annotate whether an element spanning two pages belongs to the same entity, e.g. a paragraph or itemized list. As a result, an element spanning across multiple pages might be interpreted as two distinct entities instead of one continuous element. This discrepancy also affects the hierarchical structure of scientific publications. Consider that document digitization standards, including Journal Article Tag Suite (JATS)[3] and Text Encoding Initiative (TEI)[4] provide definitions of section trees, which are beneficial to IE (Kikuchi et al., 2014; Hu et al., 2022; Landolsi et al., 2023). It would be a shame to lose the hierarchy.

Additionally, recent models and datasets derived from LaTeX often omit reading order details (Li et al., 2020b; Blecher et al., 2023). LaTeX is a complex ecosystem with a vast collection of packages filled with numerous command definitions via Comprehensive TeX Archive Network (CTAN). Various templates each have their own unique writing conventions. This leads to the possibility that some elements may be mislabeled. Given that different publications adopt varied page layouts and LaTeX autonomously determines the positioning of tables and figures based on its internal rules (Mittelbach et al., 2004), there's a significant risk that automated information extraction tools might misinterpret the intended reading order and context.

Moreover, authors of such resources do not always publish the code used in compiling the dataset. This means that current datasets are unlikely to incorporate the most recent papers or newer version of old papers. This hampers reproducibility of the process of dataset building as well as impeding scalability. Meanwhile, it is difficult for users to modify the annotation style to match their demands.

In this paper, we build upon several approaches for automatic PDF annotation of datasets and introduce a generalized framework that yields document-oriented, fine-grained, reading-ordered annotations that exclude extraneous content based on LaTeX source code. Figure 1 is a simplified representation of the labeling process. Our framework improves the accuracy and robustness of IE for scientific publications that has LaTeX code. Further-

[2]https://info.arxiv.org/help/submit/index.html

[3]https://jats.nlm.nih.gov/articleauthoring/tag-library/1.3/element/sec.html

[4]https://tei-c.org/release/doc/tei-p5-doc/en/html/ref-tree.html

more, we believe the new annotated data comes from our framework could drive more accurate IE machine learning models for PDF only papers, i.e. scanned paper. Our contributions are:

1. Our framework refine the categories, per document based reading order and hierarchy through a well-designed coloring strategy.
2. Enhancing code parsing capabilities by invoking the parsing databases of modern LaTeX integrated writing environment.
3. Providing CSV tables output per PDF document, easily modifiable to meet user needs.

This framework is free software and available under the Apache 2.0 license.

2 Related Work

2.1 PDF Information Extraction Softwares

Currently there are many software solutions or services that provide PDF content extraction functions. Adobe Extract[5] and Apache Tika[6] provide API service to extract texts from PDF, but they do not provide fine-grained labeling. Camelot[7] and Tabula[8] focus on table extraction. RefExtract[9] specializes in extracting references. CERMINE (Tkaczyk et al., 2015), GROBID [10] PdfAct[11] and Science Parse[12] support the identification of more categories. PyMuPDF[13] allows access to information about the more underlying details of the PDF file. However, a benchmark demonstrates their imperfect performance (Meuschke et al., 2023).

2.2 Document Datasets

Many of the datasets' annotation were taken from LaTeX. TableBank (Li et al., 2020a) specialize in table extraction. DocBank (Li et al., 2020b) extended from TableBank, provides token-level fine-grained categories labeling. FormulaNet (Schmitt-Koopmann et al., 2022) and IBEM (Anitei et al., 2023) focus on mathematical formulas, especially in-line formulas, which can easily be confused with plain-texts. SciBank (Grijalva et al., 2022) produces block-level annotations.

There are also many datasets from non-LaTeX sources. PubLayNet (Zhong et al., 2019) and DocLayNet (Pfitzmann et al., 2022) obtained particularly large amounts of labeling using automated and manual methods, respectively. XFUND (Xu et al., 2022) manually labeled multilingual tabular data. ReadingBank (Wang et al., 2021) is extracted from Microsoft Word documents, which standardize the reading order of blocks within a page. M^{6}Doc (Cheng et al., 2023) extracted large-scale data using a half machine learning, half manual approach.

2.3 Document Understanding Models

With the gradual enrichment of document data IE resources, machine learning model development is driven by increasingly larger datasets using different approaches. LayoutLMs (Xu et al., 2020, 2021a,b; Huang et al., 2022) and its variants (Shen et al., 2022), make it possible to analyze document layout from the 2D coordinates of texts plus visual features. Donut (Kim et al., 2022), on the other hand, changes the structure of model to a separate visual encoder and language model decoder without obtaining texts directly from the document. Nougat (Blecher et al., 2023) follows Donut in implementing PDF to markup language conversion. However, Nougat's approach is page-based, and cross-page paragraphs may be incorrectly sliced by figures or tables on a page. With the explosion of Large Language Models (LLM), a number of online document understanding systems have sprung up, such as Explainpaper[14] and OpenRead[15], but these platforms are commercial and closed-source. In this paper we present a framework that is freely available and can support the community to enhance the open-source approach.

3 Methodology

We present a five-step approach to annotate the LaTeX code to PDF annotation. (1) Initially, the PDF file is processed the existing font colors and shapes in the file are captured. (2) Subsequently, the corresponding LaTeX source code of the PDF is parsed. Each token within the file is assigned a distinct color. Furthermore, figures within the document are enclosed within borderless rectangles and are highlighted with unique background colors.

[5] https://www.adobe.io/apis/documentcloud/dcsdk/pdf-extract.html
[6] https://tika.apache.org/
[7] https://github.com/camelot-dev/camelot
[8] https://github.com/chezou/tabula-py
[9] https://github.com/inspirehep/refextract
[10] https://github.com/kermitt2/grobid
[11] https://github.com/ad-freiburg/pdfact
[12] https://github.com/allenai/science-parse
[13] https://github.com/pymupdf/PyMuPDF
[14] https://www.explainpaper.com/
[15] https://www.openread.academy/

These specific colors act as pointers to the respective segments of the LaTeX source code, ensuring traceability. (3) Upon completing the LaTeX parsing, the source code is compiled into a color-coded PDF. (4) The framework then aligns text and figures from the PDF document with their respective segments in the LaTeX source code by color. This alignment facilitates the extraction of semantic annotations and coordinates of each token and the establishment of a hierarchical structure throughout the document. (5) Finally, we packaged all the annotation as CSV files.

In order to complete these steps, the framework needs three functions: PDF Element and Color Extraction, Color Generation and Annotation, and PDF Compilation. The subsequent sections provide the implementation of each function in detail.

3.1 Element and Color Extraction from PDF

In this function we use an off-the-shelf Python package `pdfplumber`[16] to read the details inside the PDF file. This tool is proficient in pinpointing the position, font, and color of every character on a page. Additionally, it can determine the position and color attributes of all rectangles on the page, which encompasses both border and fill colors. By default, `pdfplumber` utilizes DeviceRGB color space, extracting colors as tuples of three floating-point numbers. For example, the color black is represented as (0.0, 0.0, 0.0) while red is (1.0, 0.0, 0.0). However, modern computer languages, sometimes struggle with accurately storing and accessing floating-point numbers. This inherent inaccuracy implies that color matching based on these numbers might be prone to errors, stemming from cumulative inaccuracies.

In our framework, colors for fonts are represented as tuples of 8-bit values, namely red is represented as (255, 0, 0) or #ff00000 in hexadecimal. When `pdfplumber` extracts colors from PDF document, each tuple element value is incremented in steps of 0.00392, for instance, 8-bit (0, 1, 2) translates to floating-point (0.0, 0.00392, 0.00784). Given that $\frac{1}{255} = 0.00392156862$, we are already dealing with a discrepancy. To mitigate this threat, we employed matplotlib's `to_hex()`[17] method to ensure precise floating-point to 8-bit RGB value matches. We also provide details in the selection of tools for extracting color in Appendix A.

[16] `https://github.com/jsvine/pdfplumber`

[17] `https://matplotlib.org/stable/api/_as_gen/matplotlib.colors.to_hex.html`

3.2 Colors Generation and Annotation

In this function, we process the LaTeX source code to determine color assignments for each element. Ideally, each element should have a unique color. A straightforward approach would be to incrementally assign hexadecimal numbers from #000000 to #ffffff. However in practice we have found that such an increment leads to a very insignificant color change. For instance, the token gradually changes from black #000000 to a blue shade almost indistinguishable from black #000001, then #000002, until it reaches full blue #0000ff. This makes neighboring tokens almost the same color, and distinguishing between them can be challenging for both computer displays and humans eyes.

To enhance visibility and facilitate manual error-checking, we adopted a hue-based color generation strategy. More specifically, we use the Hue, Saturation, Value (HSV) color space to cyclically extract colors and rearrange them into appropriate groups. Each HSV color is then converted to an RGB tuple. Finally, around 9 million colors were grouped and sorted to be used in the next step of color marking.

For every recognized token, it gets substituted with:

```
{\color[RGB]{0,0,1}<TOKEN>}
```

Where `<token>` is the token to be colored. Each identified figure is replaced with:

```
\colorbox[rgb]{0,0,1}{<FIGURE>}
```

Where `<FIGURE>` is the command of including the figure file, or the block of drawing a figure. Distinct colors are allocated to each segment.

We also insert rules that ensure the required packages are imported and any rectangle placed beneath an figure does not disrupt the document's original layout.

```
\usepackage{xcolor}
\usepackage{tcolorbox}
\setlength { \fboxsep }{ 0pt }
\setlength { \fboxrule }{ 0pt }
```

Next we need to parse LaTeX source code and apply the above annotation rules to them.

3.2.1 LaTeX Parsing and Annotation

Broadly, elements in LaTeX source code comprises four classes: body text, macro, environment, and comments. We have the following parsing strategies for each of these elements.

- **Body text** segment undergoes tokenization using spaCy[18] tokenizer in order to split punctuation correctly. We track of the number of space characters after each token to maintain the integrity the original PDF page layout. Each token is color-marked and recorded.

- **Macro** begins with a backslash, and its arguments are encompassed within braces. We focus on labeling certain macros such as `\title{}` and `\author{}`, attributing their parameter literals with relevant semantic structure labels. Arguments within the curly braces will be parsed as body text if it will appear in the compiled PDF. Notably, `\includegraphics{}` will be treated as a whole and marked with a colorful borderless rectangle, as it is an inserted figure without fonts. `\input{}` and `\include{}` will point to another source code file, and we recursively parse the contents of the file.

- **Environment** consists of entities encapsulated between start and end commands. Elements within a environment are recursively parsed as macro or body text. For example, `\begin{table}...\end{table}` is a table environment and the elements within this table element such as `\caption{}` will be parsed as macro. Specifically, drawing environment `\begin{tikzpicture}...\end{tikzpicture}` will be treated as a whole block and marked with a colorful borderless rectangle. Note that only elements within the `document` environment are colored.

- **Comment** element starts with a percent sign % and continues until the end of this line in the LaTeX source code. We ignore the annotation of comment as it does not affect any part of the compiled PDF.

We employ the Python package `pylatexenc`[19] to traverse and parse the LaTeX source code, character by character. `pylatexenc` contains a collection of commands created by the contributors, which defines: the name of commands; whether the command has a variant or not e.g. `\section{}` and `\section*{}`; and the number of command arguments, including optional arguments in square brackets and required arguments in curly braces. In practice, we found these predefined rules insufficient, prompting us to manually augment the definition file.

However, as the number of parsed source codes increases, the trend of newly encountered undefined commands does not stop. We introduced the parsing database from `LaTeX Workshop`[20] and `TeXstudio`[21] in order to extend our database of parsing rules once and for all. `LaTeX Workshop` is an extension for a popular code editor Visual Studio Code[22], aiming to provide all-in-one features and utilities for LaTeX typesetting. `TeXstudio` is an integrated writing environment for creating LaTeX documents. They are featured by a particularly complete database of automatically generated commands from CTAN. We implemented the method to download all the definitions from the repository in JSON format. They are stored on a package-by-package basis, i.e., each package that can be referenced by LaTeX with `\usepackage{}` has a corresponding JSON file that contains all the commands for the package, including macros and environments. Our parser first traverses through LaTeX source code, collects all package loads, and then reads the relevant JSON entries. These commands are subsequently transformed and integrated into the parsing rules for `pylatexenc`.

Next, we allocate each color the semantic layout label to which it belongs. The set of labels aligns with those used in GROBID and DocBank:

- **Abstract** is assigned to body texts within `abstract` environment, or argument of macro `\abstract{}` and its variants.

- **Author** is assigned to argument of macro `\author[]{}`, `\address{}` and their variants.

- **Caption** is assigned to macro `\caption{}` within table or figure environment.

- **Equation** is assigned to all the element that marked with mathematical mode by `pylatexenc`.

- **Figure** is assigned to drawings or imported figures.

- **List** is assigned to body texts within `itemize` or `enumerate` environment.

[18] https://spacy.io/

[19] https://github.com/phfaist/pylatexenc

[20] https://github.com/James-Yu/LaTeX-Workshop

[21] https://www.texstudio.org/

[22] https://code.visualstudio.com/

- **Paragraph** is assigned to body texts within `document` environment.
- **Reference** is assigned to body texts within `bibliography` environment, or macro `\bibliography{}`.
- **Section** is assigned to macros that indicate a new section in command.
- **Table** is assigned to environments that include tabular in command.
- **Title** is assigned to argument of macro `\title[]{}` and its variants.

With the annotations in place, the LaTeX source code is ready for compilation. Following this, `pdfplumber` could determine the color and position of each letter, utilizing the letter's color to match the corresponding annotation.

Simultaneously, the article's hierarchical structure is encapsulated within a tree data structure. LaTeX delineates a hierarchy spanning seven levels through its macro command[23]. We record for each colored element the node of the tree it belongs to. To ensure a coherent hierarchy, we additionally define the paper title as the root level of document. That is, all tokens in the title of a scientific paper belong to Title node, while all tokens in the Introduction section belong to the Introduction node, and Introduction node is a child of Title node in the tree of this document. In addition we discuss the argument of hierarchical structure in Appendix B.

3.3 PDF Compilation

To initiate PDF Compilation process, two specific lines of code are added to the beginning of the source file: `\pdfoutput=1` instructs the compiler to produce a PDF instead of PostScript, an alternative publication format; `\interactionmode=1` signals the compiler to persist with the output generation, even if it encounters an error on a page.

Publications that accept submissions in LaTeX format, including arXiv, often recommend using `pdftex` as their preferred rendering engine. This engine is integrated into the contemporary LaTeX distribution, TeXLive. Given the complexities in setting up this distribution, we opted for the Docker image[24] of TeXLive 2023 to establish our compilation environment.

[23]`https://www.overleaf.com/learn/latex/Sections_and_chapters`

[24]`https://hub.docker.com/r/texlive/texlive`

Automated LaTeX compilation presents a challenge, especially in pinpointing the master source file. This is because LaTeX allows for multiple `.tex` source files to be consolidated and compiled into one overarching master PDF. To navigate this challenge, we integrated arXiv's AutoTeX[25] automatic compilation system. AutoTeX, a Perl-based toolkit, excels at discerning the primary source file within a project. Our PDF compilation mechanism derives some of its functionalities from an open-source AutoTeX wrapper[26].

However, during our practice, we observed AutoTeX's compilation regulations as overly stringent. There were instances when it halted the compilation due to minor errors, even when the same content had successfully passed arXiv's publication standards. Specifically, AutoTeX will stop compiling and try other compilers immediately after the compiler returns an error code, even if the ignored error signal placed in front of the compiler to successfully output the compiled PDF file. The PDF file produced in this step is wrong because of the BibTeX mechanism. BibTeX is reference management software for formatting lists of references, which needs to be run twice by the compiler in order to correctly output references, and in-text citations. To address this, we modified AutoTeX's code[27], enabling it to bypass certain errors and persist with PDF generation. We configured AutoTeX to control the compiler to run at least twice, even if an error code is returned initially.

In conclusion, we combine TeXLive 2023, AutoTeX, and a Python-based API service into a single container. This container, accessible via HTTP, accepts source code and efficiently returns the compilation outcomes.

4 Capabilities Overview

During the export phase, outputs are organized into two DataFrames:

- The first DataFrame represents the Table of Contents nodes, which was created during the annotation process. Each line denotes a tree node, with every node possessing a unique ID and an ID indicating its parent. This structured approach ensures that the succeeding page

[25]`https://metacpan.org/pod/TeX::AutoTeX`

[26]`https://github.com/andrewhead/texcompile`

[27]The modified AutoTeX can be found at `https://github.com/Fireblossom/TeX-AutoTeX-Mod`

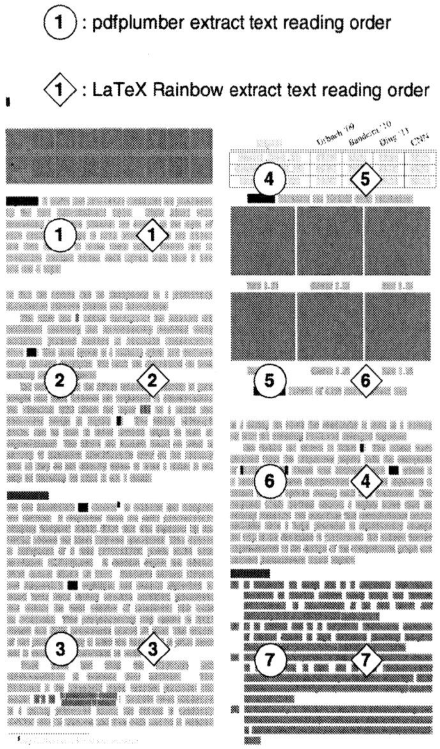

Figure 2: Extracting reading order from an elementally complex page. This example is taken from the second page of (Cohen et al., 2016).

elements to be exported can be systematically assigned to their respective nodes.

- Every row in the second DataFrame denotes either a figure or token extracted from the PDF. These tokens are allocated a number indicating their reading order and a section ID, if they are part of the author's main content, starting from 0. A value of -1 in reading order indicates elements not penned by the author, and auto-generated by the LaTeX template. This facilitates a straightforward exclusion of such elements during further analysis. The label column encompasses semantic structure labels including: Abstract, Author, Caption, Equation, Figure, Footer, List, Paragraph, Reference, Section, Table, and Title.

Both DataFrames can be exported as CSV files.

4.1 Use Case: Text Extraction with Reading Orders

Reading order refers to the sequence in which content is meant to be read. In documents, it usually follows a top-to-bottom, left-to-right pattern, but there can be exceptions, especially in multilingual or complex layout documents.

Figure 2 illustrates such a scenario. The labels in the figure represent the order of the text extracted by the different methods. In this case, starting from the sixth block, the paragraphs extracted using `pdfplumber` are interrupted by tables and pictures.

4.2 Use Case: Section-Weighted Scientific Paper Summarization using LLM

Scientific papers are structured documents with different sections, each serving a distinct purpose (Wcg, 2008). While traditional summarization techniques consider the entire document holistically (Ibrahim Altmami and El Bachir Menai, 2022), section-weighted summarization assigns different weights to different sections, recognizing that some parts of a paper may be more informative or critical than others for a quick understanding (Cohan et al., 2018). The advantage of our framework is the ability to accurately obtain sections as compared to any current PDF extraction tool. We provide a simple example in our GitHub repository.

5 Validation of Annotations

In addition to the unique features introduced in Section 4, we also have to verify its consistency with the annotation methods for existing datasets. We use the DocBank dataset (Li et al., 2020b) to assess the reliability of annotations generated by LaTeX Rainbow framework. Docbank dataset contains annotations for 1.5 million content elements across 500K scientific publication pages. It comprises papers from arXiv published between 2014 and 2018, spanning fields like physics, mathematics, and computer science. Due to its extensive size, range of subjects, numerous annotated elements, and labeling method, Docbank is considered a benchmark dataset for LaTeX sources.

Since DocBank is a very large dataset, we extracted a subset for time and feasibility reasons. We extracted LaTeX source code of 100 papers in DocBank from arXiv. They are then annotated and compiled by our framework, 61 papers are successfully annotated and compiled. 39 papers raise errors. We summarize the reasons and numbers for failures:

1. Parsing errors in the source code, such as unmatched bracket pairs or expressions that are digestible by pdfTeX but not by `pylatexenc`,

Labels	Precision	Recall	F_1-Score
Abstract	0.9779	0.8197	0.8918
Author	0.5027	0.5515	0.5260
Caption	0.4676	0.3851	0.4224
Equation	0.1957	0.9016	0.3216
Footer	0.2029	0.2612	0.2284
List	0.4462	0.1762	0.2526
Paragraph	0.9379	0.6080	0.7377
Reference	0.8355	0.9718	0.8985
Section	0.5119	0.3777	0.4347
Table	0.8806	0.7939	0.8350
Title	0.3429	0.5320	0.4170

Table 1: Precision, Recall, and F_1-Score of annotations from LaTeX Rainbow, compare to DocBank.

cause the parser to misread and yield empty results. (23)

2. Compilation failures. It was reported[28] that some source code could not be compiled successfully due to change of compilation environment. (15)

3. File encoding problem. The source code contains characters that Python cannot handle. (1)

To gauge consistency across annotated datasets, Cohen's Kappa Coefficient $\kappa = \frac{p_o - p_e}{1 - p_e}$ is applied to test consistency across annotated datasets. where p_o is the empirical probability of agreement on the label assigned to any sample, and p_e is the expected agreement when both annotators assign labels randomly. p_e is estimated using a per-annotator empirical prior over the class labels (Artstein and Poesio, 2008). Cohen suggested the Kappa result be interpreted as follows: values ≤ 0 as indicating no agreement and 0.01–0.20 as none to slight, 0.21–0.40 as fair, 0.41– 0.60 as moderate, 0.61–0.80 as substantial, and 0.81–1.00 as almost perfect agreement (McHugh, 2012). We get $\kappa = 0.32$. This value demonstrates the fair consistency of our approach with the existing baseline .

We further assessed Precision, Recall, and F_1-Score using DocBank's annotations as the gold standard. As detailed in Table 1, our framework's annotations align closely with DocBank in the Abstract, Paragraph, Reference, and Table categories, and differs in other categories. Notably, there is a considerable degree of inconsistency in the semantic labeling of some categories. The reasons for these inconsistencies are mainly differences in annotation strategies and difficulties in aligning our annotations with DocBank. We delve deeper into the inconsistencies in Appendix C.

[28]`https://info.arxiv.org/help/faq/texlive.html`

6 Known Issues and Future Work

In the future, our primary goal is to update the parser so that it can tolerate syntax errors that the pdfTeX compiler can tolerate.

We also plan to expand the LaTeX Rainbow framework with parallelization capabilities. Because the pdfTeX engine does not support multi-threaded parallelism, this makes them slow to compile, especially for long files. The idea is to enable parallelism at the scale of multiple files. Given the containerized nature of our PDF compilation service, this transition should be seamless.

For extensive projects, consider the example of *Proceedings of the 61st Annual Meeting of the Association for Computational Linguistics (Volume 1: Long Papers)*, which comprises 912 papers. The cumulative number of tokens in such projects might surpass the maximum number of colors that can be allocated (9 million). In these cases, the LaTeX Rainbow framework is unable to perform the annotation. Our next steps include refining the color system to enhance its usability and distinctiveness.

Coloring the LaTeX element doesn't always work. For example, `\url{}` command forces its arguments to be blue, instead of the color we assigned. In addition to the coloring method, there is also the SyncTeX (Laurens, 2008) plugin that allows compiled PDF elements to be linked back to the LaTeX source code. It is directly involved in the compilation process and records the correspondence through the internal auxiliary files. Our plan is to go deeper into its mechanisms to establish a more robust PDF to LaTeX source code correspondence.

Different publisher templates interpret LaTeX terms uniquely, making it challenging for our database to account for every variation. For example, `\lstinputlisting[]{}` defines the content to be displayed to the PDF with a substring value in the optional argument. This is significantly different from the definition of most commands. As mentioned in Section 5, there are many papers that cannot yet be parsed correctly. Therefore, we greatly welcome and depend on the open-source community to contribute the detailed parsing rules for each template.

7 Conclusion

In this paper we introduce a framework which can be used to establish a correspondence between LaTeX code and PDF elements, exporting detailed semantic annotations. Our framework meticulously extracts semantic markup, maintaining the layout fidelity of the associated PDF files. The structured information extracted by our framework helps in better document indexing, searching and analysis. It improves document accessibility and helps develop and refine document understanding tools.

Our framework is more than just yet another toolkit to the growing list of document datasets. By ensuring versatility and adaptability as well as scalability, we aim for it to become a universal tool that can facilitate enhanced document analysis across multiple disciplines and applications. We sincerely hope that open-source community can derive innovative uses and benefits from our solution.

8 Acknowledgments

The framework reported is this paper was conducted within the research project InsightsNet (https://insightsnet.org/) which is funded by the Federal Ministry of Education and Research (BMBF) under grant no. 01UG2130A.

References

Dan Anitei, Joan Andreu Sánchez, José Miguel Benedí, and Ernesto Noya. 2023. The ibem dataset: A large printed scientific image dataset for indexing and searching mathematical expressions. *Pattern Recognition Letters*, 172:29–36.

Ron Artstein and Massimo Poesio. 2008. Inter-coder agreement for computational linguistics. *Computational linguistics*, 34(4):555–596.

Hannah Bast and Claudius Korzen. 2017. A benchmark and evaluation for text extraction from pdf. In *Proceedings of the 17th ACM/IEEE Joint Conference on Digital Libraries*, JCDL '17, page 99–108. IEEE Press.

Lukas Blecher, Guillem Cucurull, Thomas Scialom, and Robert Stojnic. 2023. Nougat: Neural optical understanding for academic documents.

Hiuyi Cheng, Peirong Zhang, Sihang Wu, Jiaxin Zhang, Qiyuan Zhu, Zecheng Xie, Jing Li, Kai Ding, and Lianwen Jin. 2023. M6doc: A large-scale multi-format, multi-type, multi-layout, multi-language, multi-annotation category dataset for modern document layout analysis. In *Proceedings of the IEEE/CVF Conference on Computer Vision and Pattern Recognition (CVPR)*, pages 15138–15147.

Wai Chong Chia, Phoey Lee Teh, and Colin Mathew Hew D Gill. 2018. Text extraction and categorization from watermark scientific document in bulk. In *2018 3rd International Conference on Computational Intelligence and Applications (ICCIA)*, pages 47–51.

Arman Cohan, Franck Dernoncourt, Doo Soon Kim, Trung Bui, Seokhwan Kim, Walter Chang, and Nazli Goharian. 2018. A discourse-aware attention model for abstractive summarization of long documents. In *Proceedings of the 2018 Conference of the North American Chapter of the Association for Computational Linguistics: Human Language Technologies, Volume 2 (Short Papers)*, pages 615–621, New Orleans, Louisiana. Association for Computational Linguistics.

Joseph Paul Cohen, Henry Z Lo, Tingting Lu, and Wei Ding. 2016. Crater detection via convolutional neural networks. *47th Lunar and Planetary Science Conference*.

Lei Cui. 2021. *Document AI: Benchmarks, Models and Applications (Presentation@ICDAR 2021)*. DIL workshop in ICDAR 2021.

Felipe Grijalva, Carla Parra, Marco Gallardo, Erick Santos, Byron Acuña, Juan Carlos Rodríguez, and Julio Larco. 2022. Scibank: A large dataset of annotated scientific paper regions for document layout analysis.

Xue Han, Yi-Tong Wang, Jun-Lan Feng, Chao Deng, Zhan-Heng Chen, Yu-An Huang, Hui Su, Lun Hu, and Peng-Wei Hu. 2023. A survey of transformer-based multimodal pre-trained modals. *Neurocomputing*, 515:89–106.

Faegheh Hasibi and Svein Erik Bratsberg. 2014. Non-hierarchical structures: How to model and index overlaps?

P. Hu, Z. Zhang, J. Zhang, J. Du, and J. Wu. 2022. Multimodal tree decoder for table of contents extraction in document images. In *2022 26th International Conference on Pattern Recognition (ICPR)*, pages 1756–1762, Los Alamitos, CA, USA. IEEE Computer Society.

Yupan Huang, Tengchao Lv, Lei Cui, Yutong Lu, and Furu Wei. 2022. Layoutlmv3: Pre-training for document ai with unified text and image masking. In *Proceedings of the 30th ACM International Conference on Multimedia*, MM '22, page 4083–4091, New York, NY, USA. Association for Computing Machinery.

Nouf Ibrahim Altmami and Mohamed El Bachir Menai. 2022. Automatic summarization of scientific articles: A survey. *Journal of King Saud University - Computer and Information Sciences*, 34(4):1011–1028.

Yuta Kikuchi, Tsutomu Hirao, Hiroya Takamura, Manabu Okumura, and Masaaki Nagata. 2014. Single document summarization based on nested tree structure. In *Proceedings of the 52nd Annual Meeting of the Association for Computational Linguistics (Volume 2: Short Papers)*, pages 315–320, Baltimore, Maryland. Association for Computational Linguistics.

Geewook Kim, Teakgyu Hong, Moonbin Yim, JeongYeon Nam, Jinyoung Park, Jinyeong Yim, Wonseok Hwang, Sangdoo Yun, Dongyoon Han, and Seunghyun Park. 2022. Ocr-free document understanding transformer. In *European Conference on Computer Vision (ECCV)*.

Mohamed Yassine Landolsi, Lobna Hlaoua, and Lotfi Ben Romdhane. 2023. Hybrid method to automatically extract medical document tree structure. *Engineering Applications of Artificial Intelligence*, 120:105922.

Jérôme Laurens. 2008. Direct and reverse synchronization with SyncTEX. 29(3):365–371.

Minghao Li, Lei Cui, Shaohan Huang, Furu Wei, Ming Zhou, and Zhoujun Li. 2020a. TableBank: Table benchmark for image-based table detection and recognition. In *Proceedings of the Twelfth Language Resources and Evaluation Conference*, pages 1918–1925, Marseille, France. European Language Resources Association.

Minghao Li, Yiheng Xu, Lei Cui, Shaohan Huang, Furu Wei, Zhoujun Li, and Ming Zhou. 2020b. DocBank: A benchmark dataset for document layout analysis. In *Proceedings of the 28th International Conference on Computational Linguistics*, pages 949–960, Barcelona, Spain (Online). International Committee on Computational Linguistics.

Yves Marcoux, Michael Sperberg-McQueen, and Claus Huitfeldt. 2013. Modeling overlapping structures. *Balisage Series on Markup Technologies*.

Mary L McHugh. 2012. Interrater reliability: the kappa statistic. *Biochemia medica*, 22(3):276–282.

Norman Meuschke, Apurva Jagdale, Timo Spinde, Jelena Mitrović, and Bela Gipp. 2023. A Benchmark of PDF Information Extraction Tools Using a Multitask and Multi-domain Evaluation Framework for Academic Documents. In *Information for a Better World: Normality, Virtuality, Physicality, Inclusivity*, volume 13972 of *LNCS*, pages 383–405. Springer Nature Switzerland, Cham.

Frank Mittelbach, Michel Goossens, Johannes Braams, David Carlisle, and Chris Rowley. 2004. *The LaTeX Companion*, 2 edition. Addison-Wesley. ISBN-10: 0201362996 ISBN-13: 978-0201362992.

Arthur Ogawa. 1994. Object-oriented programming, descriptive markup, and tex. *TUGboat*, 15(3):325–330.

Birgit Pfitzmann, Christoph Auer, Michele Dolfi, Ahmed S. Nassar, and Peter Staar. 2022. Doclaynet: A large human-annotated dataset for document-layout segmentation. page 3743–3751.

Felix M. Schmitt-Koopmann, Elaine M. Huang, Hans-Peter Hutter, Thilo Stadelmann, and Alireza Darvishy. 2022. Formulanet: A benchmark dataset for mathematical formula detection. *IEEE Access*, 10:91588–91596.

Zejiang Shen, Kyle Lo, Lucy Lu Wang, Bailey Kuehl, Daniel S. Weld, and Doug Downey. 2022. VILA: Improving structured content extraction from scientific PDFs using visual layout groups. *Transactions of the Association for Computational Linguistics*, 10:376–392.

Nishant Subramani, Alexandre Matton, Malcolm Greaves, and Adrian Lam. 2021. A survey of deep learning approaches for ocr and document understanding.

Dominika Tkaczyk, Paweł Szostek, Mateusz Fedoryszak, Piotr Jan Dendek, and Łukasz Bolikowski. 2015. Cermine: automatic extraction of structured metadata from scientific literature. *International Journal on Document Analysis and Recognition (IJDAR)*, 18:317–335.

Zilong Wang, Yiheng Xu, Lei Cui, Jingbo Shang, and Furu Wei. 2021. LayoutReader: Pre-training of text and layout for reading order detection. In *Proceedings of the 2021 Conference on Empirical Methods in Natural Language Processing*, pages 4735–4744, Online and Punta Cana, Dominican Republic. Association for Computational Linguistics.

Peh Wcg. 2008. Basic structure and types of scientific papers. *Singapore Med J*, 49(7).

Yang Xu, Yiheng Xu, Tengchao Lv, Lei Cui, Furu Wei, Guoxin Wang, Yijuan Lu, Dinei Florencio, Cha Zhang, Wanxiang Che, Min Zhang, and Lidong Zhou. 2021a. LayoutLMv2: Multi-modal pre-training for visually-rich document understanding. In *Proceedings of the 59th Annual Meeting of the Association for Computational Linguistics and the 11th International Joint Conference on Natural Language Processing (Volume 1: Long Papers)*, pages 2579–2591, Online. Association for Computational Linguistics.

Yiheng Xu, Minghao Li, Lei Cui, Shaohan Huang, Furu Wei, and Ming Zhou. 2020. Layoutlm: Pre-training of text and layout for document image understanding. In *Proceedings of the 26th ACM SIGKDD International Conference on Knowledge Discovery Data Mining*, KDD '20, page 1192–1200, New York, NY, USA. Association for Computing Machinery.

Yiheng Xu, Tengchao Lv, Lei Cui, Guoxin Wang, Yijuan Lu, Dinei Florencio, Cha Zhang, and Furu Wei. 2021b. Layoutxlm: Multimodal pre-training for multilingual visually-rich document understanding.

Yiheng Xu, Tengchao Lv, Lei Cui, Guoxin Wang, Yijuan Lu, Dinei Florencio, Cha Zhang, and Furu Wei. 2022. XFUND: A benchmark dataset for multilingual visually rich form understanding. In *Findings of the Association for Computational Linguistics: ACL 2022*, pages 3214–3224, Dublin, Ireland. Association for Computational Linguistics.

Xu Zhong, Jianbin Tang, and Antonio Jimeno Yepes. 2019. Publaynet: largest dataset ever for document layout analysis. In *2019 International Conference on Document Analysis and Recognition (ICDAR)*, pages 1015–1022. IEEE.

A Selection of Color Extraction Tools

In Addition to `pdfplumber`. We also experimented with the `PyMuPDF`[29] package for color extraction, enticed by its capacity to extract colors as integer values. However, it uses the sRGB color space, which introduced mismatches between our annotations and extracted values. A notable misalignment was observed with colors #000000 and #000100 in RGB are both being misconstrued as the singular color #000000 in sRGB. As `PyMuPDF` features in able to extract more refined information, such as block number, line number, whether it is italicized or superscript, and so on. Some valuable information is lost by not using this package. We will continue to study underlying logic of the packages and adjust the implementation described in this paper.

B Note on Non-hierarchical Structure of Document

In the realm of document digitization, there's ongoing debate regarding the hierarchical structure of articles. Specifically, discussions revolve around overlapping structures within the XML and TEI communities[30] (Marcoux et al., 2013; Hasibi and Bratsberg, 2014). Overlaps arise when a document embodies multiple structures that intersect non-hierarchically, making it impossible to represent the document as a tree. Such as a metrical structure of feet and lines in poetry. Since our exported tree isn't an XML file, we can sidestep the non-hierarchical structure issue by distinctly defining section elements and overlapping elements.

C Inconsistencies to DocBank

There are several categories in Table 1 that differ very much. In this section we summarize the potential causes from two perspectives.

C.1 Labeling Strategies

Among them Equation and Title have particularly high recall values and very low precision. Additionally, Paragraph's recall is relatively low. This is due to the difference in annotation strategies between DocBank and our approach.

More specifically, our rules recognize more commands as Title and Equation than Paragraph in DocBank.

- For Title, DocBank only recognizes the exact `\title{}`, while LaTeX Rainbow framework recognizes all commands that contain the word title. Such as `\aistatstitle{}` or `\begin{title}`.
- For Equation, we not only recognize specific commands like `\begin{equation}`. We also annotate the mathematical expressions on the line. We do realize that it can introduce potential inaccuracies, for example in practice we have found in-line formulas used as italics instead of mathematical formulas. We will refine the rules in future updates.
- In DocBank, any text not color-coded, including page numbers, headers, and copyrights, is defined as a Paragraph. In contrast, LaTeX Rainbow doesn't tag these elements with a semantic layout label. This approach in DocBank seems imprecise and could introduce potential biases.

C.2 DocBank and LaTeX Rainbow annotations are not aligned

In practical we found that using tokens position doesn't consistently match the labeling. Namely, for identical pages of the same paper from arXiv, the tokens in the same locations differ between DocBank and LaTeX Rainbow. Upon close examination of the annotated pages, we observed that DocBank's annotation coordinates diverge from the arXiv document's. We summarize two reasons for this.

- Papers may have been updated since the release of DocBank and we annotate the latest version of the paper. This may result in changes to the content and layout of the paper.
- Changes in compilation environments and compiler versions may also have led to subtle differences in compiled PDF layout.

For tokens that could not be linked, we had to use matching of contexts and tokens, which may have caused misalignment. This in turn affects the evaluation.

[29] `https://github.com/pymupdf/PyMuPDF`

[30] `https://tei-c.org/release/doc/tei-p5-doc/it/html/NH.html`

The evaluation is available as a Jupyter notebook in the GitHub repository.

Leveraging the Fusion-in-Decoder for Label Classification

Azumi Okuda Hideya Mino Taro Miyazaki Jun Goto
NHK Science and Technology Research Laboratories
{okuda.a-gc, mino.h-gq, miyazaki.t-jw, goto.j-fw}@nhk.or.jp

Abstract

Text classification is an important technique in natural language processing for categorizing text into appropriate domains. With the increasing amount of textual data, robust text classification is in high demand. This paper focuses on single-label classification of text for scholarly articles, aiming to analyze a large number of papers. Inspired by the successful Fusion-in-Decoder method used in question-answering tasks, we propose an accurate method suitable for long articles. We evaluate the effectiveness of our method through experiments on single-label classification with scholarly articles, demonstrating its high F1 scores.

1 Introduction

Text classification plays a significant role in natural language processing, and several methods have been proposed (Kim, 2014; Zhang and LeCun, 2016; Zheng and Yang, 2019; Minaee et al., 2021). This paper focuses on a classification task for scholarly articles. The rapid growth of scholarly articles, for instance over 370,000 papers on COVID-19 published by 2022, necessitates efficient analysis. Pre-trained language models such as BERT (Devlin et al., 2019) face challenges in processing long texts such as scholarly articles. They are often limited by input length, leading to token overflow and utilization of only the initial part of the text. Additionally, these models do not consider the importance of each sentence in the full text for accurate label classification.

To address these limitations, we propose a method that leverages techniques from question answering (QA) tasks to enhance label classification accuracy for long texts. Specifically, we extract a set of sentences deemed informative based on the summary section, which represent a collection of important information in the paper. We combine the vector representations of these sentences using Fusion-in-Decoder (FiD) (Izacard and Grave, 2021b), a high-performing approach in QA tasks, to estimate the label. Although FiD was originally proposed for QA tasks, we applied it to paper analysis because it can extract important sentences from long documents and implement them in neural networks. We evaluate our proposed method using the CORD-19 dataset (Beltagy et al., 2020) of scientific papers on COVID-19. The results of our evaluation experiment demonstrate the effectiveness of our approach.

2 Related Work

Existing pre-trained language models generally used in text classification, such as BERT (Devlin et al., 2019), have limitations on the input length, preventing the utilization of all information in long documents during fine-tuning. While Longformer (Beltagy et al., 2020) and BigBird (Zaheer et al., 2021) are notable approaches for handling long documents, they still have limitations regarding input length.

When considering the handling of a large amount of data, QA tasks can provide valuable insights. Karpukhin et al. (2020) proposed Dense Passage Retriever (DPR), which retrieves relevant passages from a large number of documents, achieving high accuracy in an open-domain QA task.

Lee et al. (2019) introduced the Open-Retrieval Question Answering (ORQA) model for open-domain QA tasks. The ORQA model comprises a retriever that identifies relevant sentences from external knowledge and a reader that extracts answers from the retrieved sentences and questions. Building on the ORQA model, Izacard and Grave (2021b) proposed Fusion-in-Decoder (FiD) by improving the reader part. Additionally, Izacard and Grave (2021a) proposed a method to train the retriever using the knowledge from the reader, leading to improved accuracy in QA tasks. In this work, we adapt Izacard et al.'s FiD to the task of single-label classification.

Proceedings of the 2nd Workshop on Information Extraction from Scientific Publications, pages 68–73
Nov 1, 2023.

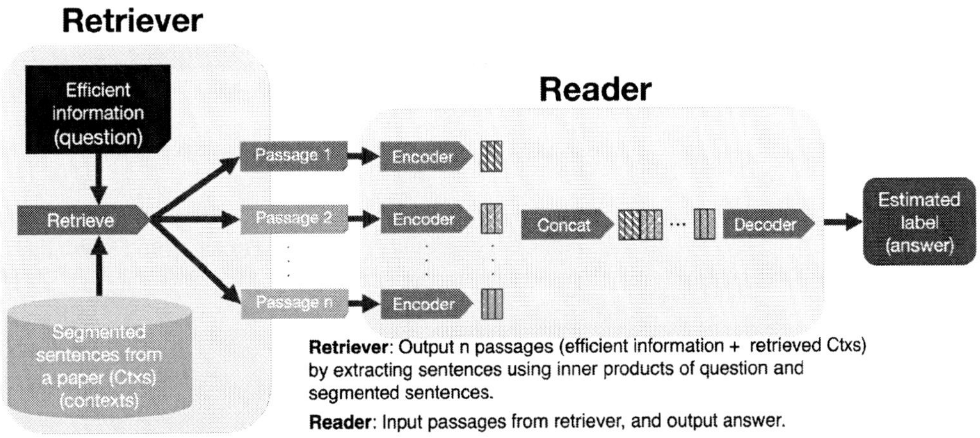

Figure 1: Overview of the proposed method.

3 Methodology

3.1 The Fusion-in-Decoder for Label Classification

The core idea of the proposed method involves incorporating the Fusion-in-Decoder (FiD) into a label classification task. Figure 1 shows a diagram of the proposed method with the inclusion of the FiD. The FiD comprises two components: the retriever and reader (Izacard and Grave, 2021b).

Retriever The retriever component requires *efficient information*, referred to as a question or query in the QA task, and segmented sentences of a paper (*Ctxs*), referred to as a context. The retriever is based on Dense Passage Retriever (DPR) (Karpukhin et al., 2020). In Figure 1, *efficient information* and *Ctxs* are embedded as dense vector representations by BERT (Devlin et al., 2019) networks. The retriever is trained to reflect the relevancy between representation vector of each sentence by the dot product. The objective of using dot product is to ensure that the inner product of the efficient information and the segmented sentences (*Ctxs*) produces appropriate value for retrieving relevant sentences from *Ctxs* with using efficient information as query. We take into consideration the cross-attention score in the reader, which we will be described in following section. This is because a sentence with several attentions in the previous reader, considered to be more useful for classification. Finally, the retriever outputs a set of sentences from *Ctxs*, which is referred to as passage retrieval. This component retrieves valuable *Ctxs* for label classification based on *efficient information*.

Reader The reader is based on a pretrained transformer-based sequence-to-sequence network. The reader component requires passages, which comprise both the *efficient information* and the retrieved *Ctxs*. More precisely, each sentence in *Ctxs* is concatenated with the *efficient information*, which is referred to as a passage. These passages are independently processed by each reader's encoder, which outputs an embedded expression for each passage. The encoded outputs are then concatenated and fed into the decoder. The decoder generates an *estimated label* for the paper as an answer in the QA task.

Repeated training During the process in the reader, the cross-attention scores are calculated between the *efficient information* and passage in the transformer model. Based on the assumption that passages with high cross-attention scores calculated by the reader contribute to accurate label estimation, the retriever calculates the inner product between the *efficient information* and segmented sentences within the passages and is trained to establish an association between them. During the process in the retriever, the passages used in the reader are updated. Due to their interdependence, the repeated training of the reader and retriever models leads to an improvement in the accuracy of each model.

Segmented sentences for retriever Izacard and Grave (2021b) incorporated external knowledge sources, such as Wikipedia, for the segmented sentences (*Ctxs*) in the QA task. In this paper, we utilize a scholarly article from the same domain that contains the entire paper as the *Ctxs*, which includes pertinent information for classifying papers. We assume that each scholarly article in training data comprises three components: an abstract, main text, and label that represent the genre of the article. Scholarly articles are often longer than typical model such as BERT can handle. FiD utilize shorter sentences that extracted using retriever, so it can handle such long articles.

3.2 Training Process

Based on Section 3.1, the proposed model is trained as follows:

1. Both the abstract and main text of an article are divided into sentences. During the initial training of the reader, the segmented abstracts which have correct labels, are utilized as the contexts. To simplify the training process, a fixed *efficient information* "What genre best describes this abstract?" is employed for all papers, instead of selecting essential information for label estimation as part of the question. A detailed analysis of appropriate *efficient information* is provided in Section 5.

2. The retriever is trained using the cross-attention scores calculated by the reader. The objective is to ensure that the inner product of the *efficient information* and the segmented sentences (*Ctxs*) produces an appropriate value. By optimizing this training objective, the retriever trains to select relevant *Ctxs* that align well with the given *efficient information*.

3. Using the retriever trained in step 2, the relevant sentences are retrieved from *Ctxs* using FAISS (Johnson et al., 2019). The objective is to extract highly relevant sentences as contexts and avoid extremely short sentences. This process, known as passage retrieval, helps identify and select the most informative and meaningful sentences from *Ctxs* for further analysis.

4. The *efficient information* and *Ctxs* extracted in step 3 are fed into the new reader model as a passage, and the reader is re-trained based on this input.

5. Steps 2 to 4 are repeated alternately to iteratively train the reader and the retriever.

4 Experiments

4.1 Experimental Settings

4.1.1 Dataset

We conducted experiments using the CORD-19, which is a collection of papers released by the Allen Institute for AI[1]. The dataset is open access and includes papers sourced from PubMed, PubMed Central, the World Health Organization's COVID-19 database, and preprint servers such as bioRxiv, medRxiv, and arXiv. Each paper in CORD-19 is accompanied by metadata, including author names, submission dates, and acquisition sources, along with the abstract. For our experiments, we used 7,127 papers extracted from CORD-19, specifically from the bioRxiv. Each paper is associated with 25 research field labels. The average number of sentences in the full text of the papers is approximately 154.

4.1.2 Training Setup

We implemented our approach with FiD (Izacard and Grave, 2021b) [2].

The reader was initialized with the pretrained text-to-text transfer transformer (T5) base model (Raffel et al., 2020) with 220 million paremeters, available in the HuggingFace Transformers library.

During the initial training of the reader, the contexts (*Ctxs*) cannot be used because the retriever is not yet trained. We assumed that the abstract of each paper would be effective for label classification and used it as the initial value of *Ctxs*. We trained the readers for 20K steps.

The retriever was initialized with pretrained BERT base model (Devlin et al., 2019). For the retriever's output, we selected the top 20 sentences, excluding those comprising 10 words or less, from the search results of the paper database. We trained the retriever for 50k steps.

We fine-tuned the reader and the retriever using Adam (Kingma and Ba, 2017) with a constant learning rate 10^{-4} and dropout rate of 10%. The loss function and other settings related to learning followed the original FiD settings.

4.1.3 Evaluation

For the baseline, we used T5 where the full text of each paper was treated as a single passage to simulate T5 embeddings of full texts.

[1] https://allenai.org/data/cord-19

[2] https://github.com/facebookresearch/FiD

	Ctxs	Iteration	Micro-F1	Macro-F1
T5(baseline)	-	-	0.552	0.366
Proposed Method	abstract	0	0.555	0.362
	retrieved	1	0.562	0.298
	retrieved	2	0.554	0.339
	retrieved	3	**0.575**	0.377
	retrieved	4	0.570	**0.386**
	retrieved	5	0.551	0.350
	retrieved	6	0.541	0.305
	retrieved	7	0.552	0.354
	retrieved	8	0.540	0.319

Table 1: Experimental results.

Efficient information	Ctxs	Iteration	Micro-F1	Macro-F1
fix	abstract	0	0.555	0.362
fix	full text	0	0.590	0.380
abstract	abstract	0	0.570	0.396

Table 2: Results of additional experiments for analyzing the effects of changing efficient information.

For the evaluation, we employed the widely used classification metrics, namely Micro-F1 and Macro-F1, which provide insights into the overall performance on the classification tasks. We used NVIDIA V100 for training.

4.2 Experimental Results

Table 1 shows the experimental results of the label classification task. The "Iteration" column indicates the number of iterations of the reader and retriever.

Our method outperformed T5 in both Micro-F1 and Macro-F1. This is because the proposed method takes each sentence into account by the reader, which distinguishes it from both baseline methods performed. In the T5 baseline, all sentences were inputted as a single sentence, whereas each sentence was inputted separately for the proposed method. Our proposed method improved the accuracy by learning long sentences that exceed the T5 token limit.

We show F1 scores of the proposed method for each iteration in Table 1. This sequential process would allow the model to improve and make more accurate predictions. Comparing the initial learned reader with the T5 baseline, we observed that both Micro-F1 and Macro-F1 achieved similar levels of accuracy. This suggests that the process of cutting off long full texts and utilizing segmented abstracts as *Ctxs* is sufficient for achieving comparable performance in using the entire text.

In the proposed method, we utilize the segmented abstract as *Ctxs* for the first reader. The output of the retriever, which is trained based on the reader's output, serves as the input for the subsequent reader in the pipeline. During the repeated iterations, we observed that the Micro-F1 score remained relatively unchanged until the fourth iteration, while the Macro-F1 showed improvement. At the fifth iteration, both the Micro-F1 and Macro-F1 scores decreased. Based on these observations, we decided to stop the iteration. It is inferred that the reason why the accuracy improved by continuing the iteration is that it became possible to retrieve further important information written in full text. Therefore, it is thought that the improvement in accuracy saturated after several iterations. This pattern aligns with findings from previous studies on QA tasks using Fusion-in-Decoder (FiD), where it was reported that performance tends to improve up to approximately the fourth iteration (Izacard and Grave, 2021a). Similarly, in our study, it appears that the performance improvement reached a point of saturation (3rd or 4th iteration), beyond which further iterations did not lead to significant gains.

5 Analysis

In Table 1, we used segmented abstracts as the initial contexts (*Ctxs*). To investigate the effect of using a larger amount of text, we replaced the abstracts with segmented full texts. The results (second row in Table 2) show that using full text yields higher Micro-F1 and Macro-F1 scores compared to using abstracts (first row in Table 2). This indicates that providing more context to the reader contributes to improved accuracy. However, it is important to note that increasing the context size also increases the computation time. In this study, training the reader with full text required approximately 9 hours, while training with abstracts only required approximately 3 hours.

In Table 2, we show the result of a supplementary experiment. In Table 1, our initial approach used a common phrase as *efficient information* in section 3.2. However, the original Fusion-in-Decoder (FiD) used a characteristic sentence for estimating the answer. The results without any iterations (second row in Table 1) estimate labels using abstracts without employing retrievers. The Micro-F1 score is similar to the baseline (first row in Table 1), indicating that abstracts contain useful information for label classification. Therefore, instead of using a common fixed phrase for efficient information, we experimented using abstract as *efficient information*.

Compared to the experiment described in Section 4 without any iteration (first row of Table 2), both the Micro-F1 and Macro-F1 have improved the accuracy. This suggests that the selection of *efficient information* is significant in improving the accuracy of label classification.

6 Conclusion

We extended the Fusion-in-Decoder (FiD) approach, originally designed for question answering, to a label classification task for scholarly papers. Through experiments using papers related to COVID-19, we validated the effectiveness of the proposed method.

For future work, we plan to improve the retriever's performance by refining the input selection. Since a retriever model is trained using only cross-attention scores of a reader model for references, we will find new additional criteria to get more effective passages. Also, we will conduct experiments on other such datasets to confirm the effectiveness of the proposed method.

Limitations

We have not conducted human evaluation to confirm whether the output passages generated by a retriever model are the most effective information for a reader model.

Acknowledgements

We would like to thank our colleagues, Ichiro Yamada, Yuki Yasuda, Taichi Ishiwatari and Kinugawa Kazutaka for useful discussions and advice. We also thank Simon Clippingdale for proofreading our English and the anonymous reviewers for their comments and suggestions.

References

Iz Beltagy, Matthew E. Peters, and Arman Cohan. 2020. Longformer: The long-document transformer. *arXiv preprint arXiv:2004.05150*.

Jacob Devlin, Ming-Wei Chang, Kenton Lee, and Kristina Toutanova. 2019. BERT: Pre-training of deep bidirectional transformers for language understanding. In *Proceedings of the 2019 Conference of the North American Chapter of the Association for Computational Linguistics: Human Language Technologies, Volume 1 (Long and Short Papers)*, pages 4171–4186, Minneapolis, Minnesota. Association for Computational Linguistics.

Gautier Izacard and Edouard Grave. 2021a. Distilling knowledge from reader to retriever for question answering. In *The International Conference on Learning Representations*.

Gautier Izacard and Edouard Grave. 2021b. Leveraging passage retrieval with generative models for open domain question answering. In *Proceedings of the 16th Conference of the European Chapter of the Association for Computational Linguistics*, pages 874–880.

Jeff Johnson, Matthijs Douze, and Hervé Jégou. 2019. Billion-scale similarity search with GPUs. *IEEE Transactions on Big Data*, 7(3):535–547.

Vladimir Karpukhin, Barlas Oguz, Sewon Min, Patrick Lewis, Ledell Wu, Sergey Edunov, Danqi Chen, and Wen-tau Yih. 2020. Dense passage retrieval for open-domain question answering. In *Proceedings of the 2020 Conference on Empirical Methods in Natural Language Processing (EMNLP)*, pages 6769–6781, Online. Association for Computational Linguistics.

Yoon Kim. 2014. Convolutional neural networks for sentence classification. In *Proceedings of the 2014 Conference on Empirical Methods in Natural Language Processing (EMNLP)*, pages 1746–1751, Doha, Qatar. Association for Computational Linguistics.

Diederik P. Kingma and Jimmy Ba. 2017. Adam: A method for stochastic optimization. In *Proceedings of the 3rd International Conference on Learning Representations*.

Kenton Lee, Ming-Wei Chang, and Kristina Toutanova. 2019. Latent retrieval for weakly supervised open domain question answering. In *Proceedings of the 57th Annual Meeting of the Association for Computational Linguistics*, pages 6086–6096, Florence, Italy. Association for Computational Linguistics.

Shervin Minaee, Nal Kalchbrenner, Erik Cambria, Narjes Nikzad, Meysam Chenaghlu, and Jianfeng Gao. 2021. Deep learning-based text classification: A comprehensive review. *ACM Comput. Surv.*, 54(3):62:1–62:40.

Colin Raffel, Noam Shazeer, Adam Roberts, Katherine Lee, Sharan Narang, Michael Matena, Yanqi Zhou, Wei Li, and Peter J. Liu. 2020. Exploring the limits of transfer learning with a unified text-to-text transformer. *Journal of Machine Learning Research*, 21(140):1–67.

Manzil Zaheer, Guru Guruganesh, Avinava Dubey, Joshua Ainslie, Chris Alberti, Santiago Ontanon, Philip Pham, Anirudh Ravula, Qifan Wang, Li Yang, and Amr Ahmed. 2021. Big bird: Transformers for longer sequences.

Xiang Zhang and Yann LeCun. 2016. Text understanding from scratch. *arXiv preprint arXiv:1502.01710*.

Shaomin Zheng and Meng Yang. 2019. A new method of improving bert for text classification. In *Intelligence Science and Big Data Engineering. Big Data and Machine Learning: 9th International Conference, IScIDE 2019, Nanjing, China, October 17–20, 2019, Proceedings, Part II 9*, pages 442–452. Springer.

Enhancing Academic Title Generation Using SciBERT and Linguistic Rules

Elena Callegari
University of Iceland
Reykjavík, Iceland
ecallegari@hi.is

Peter Vajdecka
Prague Univ. of Economics and Business
Prague, Czechia
vajp02@vse.cz

Desara Xhura
SageWrite ehf.
Reykjavík, Iceland
desara@sagewrite.com

Anton Karl Ingason
University of Iceland
Reykjavík, Iceland
antoni@hi.is

Abstract

This study tackles the challenge of generating appropriate academic titles based on the paper's abstract. We approach this task as a high-level text summarization problem and introduce an innovative post-processing method that combines a predictive model with a set of linguistic rules to enhance the quality of the title generation. We start by evaluating three Natural Language Generation models (BART, T5, Flan T5), by identifying the top-performing model and by configuring it to generate diverse titles. We then conduct experiments employing various post-processing strategies -using SciBERT and linguistic rules- to select the best title out of all machine-generated options. Finally, we assess our title selection methods in relation to human evaluations.

1 Introduction

Titles of academic articles are more than simple labels; they serve as a concise representation of the contents of the paper, providing a glimpse into its purpose. Since titles serve as an initial touchpoint, they play an indispensable role in piquing readers' interest, emphasizing the relevance of the research, and enhancing its visibility within the vast scholarly landscape. Crafting the right title can be difficult, as one must distill potentially very complex research into a single, concise statement. This can be particularly challenging as the title must reflect both the depth and breadth of the paper, while also appealing to a diverse academic audience. Selecting an appropriate title also holds significance in the context of citations: according to both Paiva et al. (2012) and Deng (2015), papers with titles that have specific characteristics, such as a certain maximum length, get cited more often than papers that do not meet such criteria.

Traditionally, researchers have relied on their own judgment and expertise to craft compelling titles that summarize the findings of their research articles. In this paper, we delve into the task of automatically generating stylistically and discipline-appropriate titles for academic articles. To do that, we thought of generating titles using an article's abstract as input, as abstracts capture key passages and findings of a paper. An alternative would be to use the full paper as input, but using only the abstract allows us to reduce run times and hence costs.

Generating a title on the basis of a paper's abstract can be thought of as a special kind of summarization process: the abstract must be condensed into a short "sentence" that is maximally descriptive of its contents. Accordingly, we approach the task of automatically generating titles for academic abstracts as a summarization task. This is in line with existing research on title generation or comparable tasks. Unlike existing methods, however, our key contribution lies in experimenting with different post-processing strategies to further refine the quality of automatically generated titles. A particularly novel approach is that of using linguistic-stylistic rules, which we use to automatically filter out generated titles that do not adhere to accepted conventions on what constitutes an optimal academic title.

1.1 Related Work

We will review the literature on both title generation itself as well as headline generation, which pertains to the automatic creation of news-article headlines and is thus a task similar to title generation.

In contemporary research, automatic title/headline generation is often approached as a text summarization problem. The field of text summarization is generally split into two primary categories: extractive and abstractive summariza-

Proceedings of the 2nd Workshop on Information Extraction from Scientific Publications, pages 74–83
Nov 1, 2023.

Model	Rouge-1 F-score	Rouge-2 F-score	Rouge-L F-score	Rouge-1 P	Rouge-2 P	Rouge-L P	Rouge-1 R	Rouge-2 R	Rouge-L R
BART Large	0.249	0.077	0.214	0.256	0.081	0.218	**0.267**	0.083	0.231
T5 Large	**0.255**	**0.094**	**0.231**	**0.270**	**0.100**	**0.244**	0.262	**0.097**	**0.237**
Flan T5 Large	0.242	0.073	0.213	0.259	0.078	0.227	0.245	0.074	0.215

Table 1: Initial title generation results

tion. Presently, both these categories are addressed using methodologies anchored in the Transformer architecture (Song et al., 2020; Bukhtiyarov and Gusev, 2020; Liu and Lapata, 2019). A prevalent strategy for both forms of summarization is the encoder-decoder language model, exemplified by models like BertSumExt (Liu and Lapata, 2019) and PEGASUS (Zhang et al., 2020). Viewing summarization as a seq2seq challenge aligns well with the encoder-decoder framework, given the presence of a source and target text, akin to NMT scenarios. In this configuration, the generative decoder section conducts abstractive summarization. For strictly extractive endeavors, decoders are typically substituted by a specific classifier determining which input tokens will appear in the final summary. Another strategy is to fine-tune a GPT-2 (Radford et al., 2019) style auto-regressive model for the summarization task; this approach was adopted by both Koppatz et al. (2022) for headline generation and Mishra et al. (2021) for title generation.

Many contemporary title and headline generation methods have adopted metrics like BLEU or ROUGE to assess model performance (Matsumaru et al., 2020; Bukhtiyarov and Gusev, 2020; Tilk and Alumäe, 2017; Mishra et al., 2021); these are also standard for summarization evaluation. An exception is Koppatz et al. (2022), who also rely on manual structured review by domain experts to assess the quality of their automatically generated headlines. While human evaluations (especially if by domain experts) represent a gold standard, they are both expensive and time-consuming to obtain. This is especially true for academic titles, as evaluating how well a title captures the essence of an academic paper means being able to make sense of potentially extremely technical, specialized information.

2 Title Generation

2.1 Dataset

We created an initial dataset containing 136,640 academic articles. We obtained this dataset by downloading the Huggingface ArXiv dataset (`https://huggingface.co/datasets/scientific_papers`) and the Kaggle ArXiv dataset (`https://www.kaggle.com/datasets/Cornell-University/arxiv`), by selecting those articles that appeared in both datasets (by cross-referencing article ids), and by extracting the following information for each article: title, abstract, category, and full article text. Merging the two datasets was necessary as the Huggingface ArXiv dataset does not contain the full text of a paper, nor its category. While we are not using the full text of articles for this specific study, we plan on doing so in the future for a follow-up study, hence it was important for us to have a dataset containing all parts of the articles we use.

2.2 Testing out Different Models

As we decided to treat title generation as a summarization task, we looked into models that could best handle summarization. We considered three different state-of-the-art language models: T5 Large (Raffel et al., 2020), Flan T5 Large (Chung et al., 2022) and BART Large (Lewis et al., 2019).

T5 treats every NLP task as a text-to-text problem, which suits title generation perfectly –the model reads in the abstract as text input and outputs the generated title as text. Flan T5 Large stands as an improved version of the T5 model, having undergone fine-tuning across a blend of tasks. Demonstrating superior performance, Flan T5 outperforms its predecessor by handling more ubiquitous tasks. However, we wanted to see how these models compare on a less common task such as summarizing academic abstracts to generate titles. On the other hand, BART, with its unique architecture that is both auto-regressive and auto-encoding, can also be used to input an abstract and output a short summary in the form of a title. BART's ability to consider the context from both directions enables the model to generate fluent and coherent titles that accurately represent the content of the abstracts.

As a first step, we tried generating titles using all three language models. To do that, we split our dataset into a training subset, a validation subset and a test subset (70:15:15 split), and trained

BART Large, T5 Large and Flan T5 Large. We employed PyTorch as the framework for training our generating models and utilized the same set of hyperparameters to train each generating model. We trained all models for 3 epochs with a learning rate of 1e-5, a batch size of 6, and using the Adam optimizer (Kingma and Ba, 2014). We set the maximum input sequence length to 512 tokens and the maximum output sequence length to 128 tokens. To promote diversity and exploration during training, we employed a sampling parameter set to true. To ensure reproducibility and control the randomization during training, we set the random seed to 42.

2.3 Final Model Selection

We evaluated the performance of our three models by comparing the title generated by each model to the original title of the paper, to determine how (dis)similar artificial titles were with respect to the original. While similarity to the original title is not in itself a measure of the quality of a machine-generated title (a maximally dissimilar title might still be an excellent title), we reasoned that computing similarity scores could be an at least partial indication of a machine-generated title being "human-like" (i.e. similar to what a human writer would come up with) and hence a good title. Considering that most of the evaluation mechanisms based on similarity scores are highly correlated (Fabbri et al., 2021), we decided to resort to ROUGE (Lin, 2004). The results are given in Table 1. T5 Large performed best on almost all ROUGE metrics except ROUGE 1 Recall, where BART Large performed better.

One of the goals of our study was to determine how much we could improve the performance of our best-performing model through further post-processing. Based on Table 1, we thus decided to settle on T5 Large as the model to use for all additional post-processing experiments.

Our post-processing consisted of two steps: refining title generation through SciBERT, and refining title generation through linguistic-stylistic rules.

3 Post-Processing, Step 1: SciBERT

For the first post-processing step, we wanted to determine whether we could obtain higher ROUGE scores by generating multiple titles for each abstract using T5 Large, selecting the most representative titles out of all those generated, and creating a synthetic dataset using these most representative titles.

3.1 Extraction of Oracles

Using T5 Large, we generated five titles for each of the abstracts in our training and validation subsets. Below we provide an example of the types of titles that were generated using T5 Large. Using the example abstract displayed in Fig.1, originally from a paper by Mallick et al. (2017) titled *"Energy-dependent variability of the bare Seyfert 1 galaxy Ark 120"*, we generated the following five titles:

1. *A long-period XMM-Newton observation of the bare Seyfert 1 galaxy Ark 120*
2. *Ark 120: spectral-timing analysis of XMM-Newton observance over four consecutive orbits in 2014*
3. *Ark 120: spectral-timing analysis and hardness-intensity diagram*
4. *Broad-band X-ray spectroscopy of Ark 120: A spectral-timing analysis of a long 486 ks XMM-Newton observation*
5. *A spectral-timing analysis of the long 486 ks XMM-Newton observation of the bare Seyfert 1 galaxy Ark 120*

For each of the titles generated by T5 Large, we computed a ROUGE score by comparing the generated title to the paper's original title. Following this, we created a synthetic dataset with a specific labeling scheme: the title with the top ROUGE score was labeled as "1" (we refer to this as the *oracle*), while the title with the lowest score received a "0" label. Note that titles with intermediate scores were neither labeled nor included in this dataset. The purpose of this was to focus on the two most distinct title generations for a given abstract.

3.2 Fine-tuning SciBERT on the Synthetic Dataset

We trained SciBERT (Beltagy et al., 2019) on the obtained synthetic dataset. We decided to use SciBERT as it outperforms BERT in a variety of tasks in the scientific domain (Beltagy et al., 2019) and achieves SOTA performance in multi-class text classification on the SciCite dataset (Cohan et al., 2019).

In our study, we used a modified version of SciBERT, which was previously pre-trained to optimize

Original Abstract (Mallick et al. 2017)

We present results from a detailed spectral-timing analysis of a long ~486 ks XMM-Newton observation of the bare Seyfert 1 galaxy Ark 120 which showed alternating diminution and increment in the 0.3-10 keV X-ray flux over four consecutive orbits in 2014. We study the energy-dependent variability of Ark 120 through broad-band X-ray spectroscopy, fractional root-mean-squared (rms) spectral modelling, hardness-intensity diagram and flux-flux analysis. The X-ray (0.3-10 keV) spectra are well fitted by a thermally Comptonized primary continuum with two (blurred and distant) reflection components and an optically thick, warm Comptonization component for the soft X-ray excess emission below ~2 keV. During the first and third observations, the fractional X-ray variability amplitude decreases with energy while for second and fourth observations, X-ray variability spectra are found to be inverted-crescent and crescent shaped, respectively. The rms variability spectra are well modelled by two constant reflection components, a soft excess component with variable luminosity and a variable intrinsic continuum with the normalization and spectral slope being correlated. The spectral softening of the source with both the soft excess and UV luminosities favours Comptonization models where the soft excess and primary X-ray emission are produced through Compton up-scattering of the UV and UV/soft X-ray seed photons in the putative warm and hot coronae, respectively. Our analyses imply that the observed energy-dependent variability of Ark 120 is most likely due to variations in the spectral shape and luminosity of the hot corona and to variations in the luminosity of the warm corona, both of which are driven by variations in the seed photon flux.

Figure 1: Abstract Example

the performance of the model for scientific text analysis. This prediction model is influenced by the success of using the transformer-model architecture for the classification of sentences in extractive summarization (Liu and Lapata, 2019) or later applied in fact-checking summarization (Atanasova et al., 2020). In our experiment, we fine-tune SciBERT model to generate a probability for each generated title. This probability interprets how similar the generated title is to the original (human) title, while the original title does not enter the model in the prediction. This model learns to distinguish the titles that are most and least similar to the original, human title. Our fine-tuned SciBERT model could be applied as a classifier as well, but we only wanted to rank our generated titles by assigning a SciBERT probability value to each generated title.

To fine-tune our SciBERT model, we followed the design and optimization decisions described in Beltagy et al. (2019) and Devlin et al. (2019). Our approach involved using a linear one-layer feed-forward classifier with the ReLu activation function. The classifier took the last hidden state of the [CLS] token as input, effectively using it as the sequence's features. We conducted extensive experiments to determine the optimal hyperparameters for fine-tuning SciBERT. This included varying the number of epochs (ranging from 2 to 5), batch sizes (16, 32, or 50), learning rates (5e-5, 5e-6, 1e-5, or 2e-5), and incorporating or excluding a dropout rate of 0.1. To optimize the training process, we utilized the AdamW optimizer and cross-entropy loss. Our best results were achieved by fine-tuning the models for 3 epochs, with a batch size of 32 samples, a learning rate of 5e-5, and no dropout applied. Following this, we applied a linear warmup and linear decay technique as described in Devlin et al. (2019). We employed the softmax function to determine probabilities for predictions, which served as the initial selection or ranking score for finding the best title candidate.

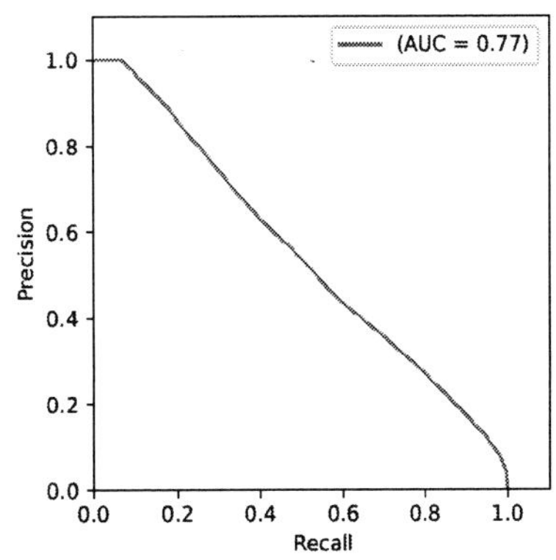

Figure 2: PR curve on testing dataset

3.3 Results

To evaluate the effectiveness of title generation selection, employing Precision-Recall (PR) curves and the corresponding Area Under Curve (AUC) (see Fig.2) provides comprehensive and robust testing (Boyd et al., 2013). This quality approach allows for an exhaustive evaluation of the model's performance across a broad spectrum of probability rankings.

The achieved performance of the model Area Under the Precision-Recall Curve (AUC-PR) 0.77 is particularly interesting because we always labeled the generated titles with the highest and lowest ROUGE scores in the synthetic training dataset.

In the initial row of Table 2, we consider the baseline model as a fine-tuned T5 Large, producing a single title for each abstract, identical to row 2 in Table 1. In the subsequent row of Table 2, we analyze the same fine-tuned T5 Large model, but this time generating five titles for each abstract. From this set of machine-generated titles, we select the machine-generated title with the highest SciBERT probability. Those selected titles for each

Model	Rouge-1 F-score	Rouge-2 F-score	Rouge-L F-score	Rouge-1 Precision	Rouge-2 Precision	Rouge-L Precision	Rouge-1 Recall	Rouge-2 Recall	Rouge-L Recall
T5 - Baseline	0.255	0.094	0.231	0.270	0.100	0.244	0.262	0.097	0.237
T5 + SciBERT	**0.281**	**0.103**	**0.253**	**0.295**	**0.109**	0.265	**0.291**	**0.107**	**0.262**
T5 + SciBERT + Linguistic rules	**0.281**	**0.103**	**0.253**	**0.295**	**0.109**	**0.266**	0.288	**0.107**	0.260
Oracles by Rouge 1 F-score	0.393	0.176	0.352	0.416	0.188	0.372	0.400	0.179	0.357

Table 2: Improved title generation results

abstract are compared to original human titles. Consequently, in Table 2, the ROUGE metric is consistently calculated based on the same original human titles, although the chosen artificial titles may differ across various models. When comparing the second row to the first row in the table, we observed a significant improvement in the overall title quality by utilizing SciBERT for title selection. This improvement is evident across all ROUGE metrics. However, when comparing the second row with the last row, where ROUGE utilized artificial titles for evaluation, it becomes evident that there is still considerable room for further improvement.

4 Post-Processing, Step 2: Linguistic Rules

To ensure the quality of artificially generated titles for academic papers, we also implemented a second post-processing step that involved evaluating each title against a set of linguistic-stylistic rules. These rules were designed to adhere to the conventions of academic titles while at the same time enhancing clarity, conciseness and outreach potential of the paper. We employed six distinct rules; titles that met all rules were assigned a score of 6, titles meeting only 5 rules were assigned a score of 5, and so on. The six rules we used are outlined below. We arrived at these rules after consulting several papers and online resources on how to write effective titles for academic papers.

I. *Title Length*: Titles should be concise, but also not so short that it is unclear what the paper is about, or how it differs from related articles discussing the same topic (Knight and Ingersoll, 1996; Paiva et al., 2012; SHU Library, 2020). Therefore, for this category, we gave a 0 score to titles longer than 16 words (Wordvice, 2023) or shorter than 5 words (USC Libraries, 2023), and a score of 1 otherwise.

II. *Geographical Locations*: Paiva et al. (2012) found a negative correlation between mentions of specific geographical locations (e.g. "Mortality Rates in Sub-Saharan Africa") in titles and number of citations per article. Accordingly, we gave a score of 0 to titles containing any reference to geographical locations, and a score of 1 otherwise.

III. *Forbidden Punctuation Marks*: Paiva et al. (2012) found a negative correlation between the number of citations and the presence of exclamation marks, question marks, and dashes in titles (see also USC Libraries (2023)). We thus gave a 0 score to titles containing these punctuation marks: '?', '-', '!'.

IV. *Suboptimal Nouns*: According to Knight and Ingersoll (1996), phrases such as "The Effects of," "A Comparison of," "The Treatment of," and "Reports of a Case of" should be avoided in titles (see also SHU Library (2020); USC Libraries (2023)). Accordingly, we gave a 0 score to titles containing the nouns "analysis," "effects," "comparison," "treatment," "report/reports".

V. *Passive Verbs*: Active voice should be preferred in academic titles (SciPress, 2017). We gave a 0 score to titles containing verbs in the passive voice, and a 1 score otherwise.

VI. *Abbreviations*: We gave a 0 score to titles that included abbreviations. This rule aimed to ensure that the titles are accessible to a wide range of readers without relying on specialized knowledge or acronyms (SHU Library, 2020; Wordvice, 2023).

To assign these linguistic scores, we wrote Python text-processing rules that would take generated titles as input and assign to each title a score from 0 to 6 based on how many of the above rules each title met. While there are many tips on how to write effective titles for scientific publications, we specifically chose the above-mentioned rules as it is easy to code text-processing scripts that check automatically whether these rules are met. The motivation for adding this additional post-processing step was thus to obtain a simple and computationally inexpensive way of further checking machine-generated titles for adherence to standard norms in academic writing. We reasoned in particular that adding this type of post-processing could partially eliminate/reduce the scope of work of any human evaluator who was to manually check each machine-generated title for quality, which can be a lengthy and costly process.

4.1 Linguistic Score Results

We normalized the linguistic scores using the following formula:

$$linguistic\ score = \frac{\sum(all_{scores})}{6}$$

where all_{scores} indicates the list of linguistic rules to be summed up in the equation.

This allowed us to obtain a total linguistic score ranging from 0.0 to 1 for each of the generated titles, 1 being a title that meets all six linguistic rules, 0.0 being a title that flouts all rules. For each title, we then multiplied this normalized linguistic score by the SciBERT probabilities obtained in the previous post-processing step to obtain a combined SciBERT*linguistic score. Titles with the highest SciBERT*linguistic score were chosen as the best titles out of all generated options.

We also calculated the number of times a title ranked first by the combined SciBERT*linguistic score would also be the title ranked first by SciBERT probability alone. We looked at the titles generated for 20,000 abstracts, and in this sample, the highest-ranked title was the same in 18,770 cases (= 1,230 differences). If we examine these discrepancies more closely, we find that the majority occur because some of the highest-ranked titles according to SciBERT probability exceed 16 words in length.

While the addition of a linguistic post-processing step has not yielded dramatically different results, it did have an effect. It is possible that if more stylistic rules were to be implemented, or if more restrictive rules were to be adopted (for example, maximum title length could be reduced to 13 words, as suggested by different academic style guides), this type of linguistic post-processing could be useful in automatically discarding a larger chunk of title generations that do not comply with academic guidelines.

In Table 2 (third row), we also see how ROUGE metrics on SciBERT probability ranking change if linguistic scores are considered as well. We see in particular that, if linguistic scores are also applied, ROUGE scores are almost comparable to T5 model with SciBERT probability ranking only (second row). Note however that this could also be due to the original title flouting one or more of the linguistic rules we selected for this post-processing step.

5 Human Evaluations

As a final step of this study, we sought to understand the nuances of human evaluations vis-à-vis machine-generated academic titles. To achieve this, we asked three human annotators to evaluate the titles that our model generated for a selection of 40 abstracts from our dataset. All three evaluators were academics themselves.

We decided to include a human evaluation step for several reasons. First of all, we wanted to determine whether title evaluation is a purely subjective matter, or whether there is some consensus among different individuals concerning what constitutes a good or a bad title. Secondly, we wanted to determine how feasible of a task it is to ask human annotators to evaluate the quality of titles of academic papers. In the specialized realm of academic articles, titles generally refer to highly technical information. This raised the question of the extent to which human evaluators could accurately judge if an academic title captures the essence of a paper's technical depth: even if one only selects evaluators who are at least familiar with the field of research of a particular set of abstracts, it is impossible to expect that each evaluator will be able to fully understand all of the abstracts they are asked to review. Finally, we were interested in determining whether the subtleties introduced by the linguistic improvements in our second post-processing step might resonate more profoundly with human evaluators.

Evaluators were presented with the original abstract, five machine-generated titles, and the original title of the paper from which the abstract was derived, resulting in a total of six titles to be evaluated. Note that we randomly selected 40 abstracts from the set of 1,230 abstracts for which SciBERT and SciBERT*linguistics outputted distinct highest-ranking titles (see again section 4.1).

The sequence in which the titles were presented was randomized. Furthermore, to prevent any attempt by the evaluators to evaluate the machine-generated titles by comparing them with the original title, evaluators were told that all titles, without exception, were machine-generated.

The evaluators were asked to read the abstract, read each of the six titles, and then pick i) what they thought was the 'best title'—that is, the title they perceived as the most fitting given the content of the abstract and the intrinsic qualities of the title itself, ii) what they thought was the second-best title, and iii) what they thought was the worst title out of all six title options. Our decision to request evaluators to pinpoint the best, second-best, and worst titles, rather than having them rank all six titles from best to worst, was twofold. Firstly, we anticipated that the deeply technical nature of some abstracts could pose challenges in the ranking process; we figured that simply selecting best, second-best and worst title would be a more feasible task. Secondly, we recognized that when presented with a set of titles potentially bearing very close similarities, distinguishing and ranking all six titles on a gradient scale might be problematic. The inclusion of the original title amidst the machine-generated ones also served a dual purpose. First of all, we wanted to assess if evaluators would rank the original title of the paper as 'best title'. Moreover, this approach also allowed us to determine how frequently machine-generated titles are perceived as superior to the original title of a given paper.

5.1 Inter-Annotator Agreement

In order to ascertain the inter-annotator agreement rate, we calculated Fleiss' kappa (Fleiss, 1971). The results are reported in Table 3:

Title	Fleiss' Kappa
Best Title	0.5805
Second Best Title	0.5195
Worst Title	0.5962

Table 3: Fleiss' Kappa Results

For the interpretation of Fleiss' kappa values, the following ranges are generally used:

Range	Interpretation
$\kappa > 0.75$	Excellent agreement
$0.40 < \kappa \leq 0.75$	Fair to good agreement
$\kappa \leq 0.40$	Poor agreement

Table 4: Interpretation of Fleiss' Kappa Values

We further investigated the degree of consensus among evaluators by calculating how many times out of 40 (i.e. the total number of abstracts evaluated by our annotators) at least two reviewers both picked the same title as best, second-best, or worst title:

- Number of times at least 2 reviewers agreed on best title: 31 times
- Number of times at least 2 reviewers agreed on second best title: 17 times
- Number of times at least 2 reviewers agreed on worst title: 29 times

Based on these results, we can conclude that evaluators seemed to frequently agree on what they deemed to be the best and worst titles, even despite the very technical nature of the abstracts and titles they were asked to evaluate. This challenges the notion that title evaluation is purely subjective, suggesting that consensus among different individuals is in fact quite attainable. Furthermore, these results also indicate that the evaluators' rankings were deliberate and informed, rather than random.

5.2 Human Evaluation vs. Different Methods

As a final step, we wanted to determine how human evaluations relate to the different title selection methods we explored in this paper. To do so, we went through the selections made by our three evaluators, and created a set of so-called *strong candidate* machine-generated titles. A machine-generated title was deemed to be a *strong candidate* if either of the following conditions were met:

i. At least two evaluators selected that specific machine-generated title as their "best title" or "second best title" choice.

ii. The machine-generated title was selected by an evaluator who also selected the original title for that abstract as their "best title" or "second-best title" selection. E.g. if an evaluator selected the original title as their "second-best" choice, the machine-generated title that they selected as their "best" choice was considered to be a *strong candidate*.

These two conditions rested on the following assumptions:

- Some machine-generated titles might be perceived by evaluators as being of higher quality than the original paper title.
- If an evaluator chooses the original title as their "best title" selection, we assume they understand the contents of the abstract well enough, and thus that any title that they rank as "second-best title" must also be a good title for that specific abstract.

- If an evaluator chooses the original title as their "second-best title" selection for a given article, we assume they understand the contents of the abstract well enough, and thus that any title that they rank as "best title" must also be both appropriate for that specific abstract, and possibly a better title than the original title.

- If at least two evaluators select a given machine-generated title as their "best" or "second-best" selection, the title must be a good title for that abstract.

Based on these criteria, we compiled a set of *strong candidate* machine-generated titles for each of the 40 abstracts evaluated by human evaluators. The set typically comprised a maximum of two candidate titles per abstract.

After identifying the *strong candidate* titles for each of the 40 abstracts, we compared how effective each of the three selection methods used in this paper (Rouge, SciBERT alone and SciBERT* Linguistics) was in capturing human rankings. Specifically, we checked if the title ranked as highest by each of these three methods was part of the *strong candidates* list. If the title ranked as highest by a given method was part of the *strong candidates* list, it was marked as a "correct selection".

Our aim was to ascertain the number of correct selections each method achieves out of 40 trials (i.e. our forty abstracts). The results are reported below:

- Rouge (Oracles) made a correct selection 8 times,

- SciBERT made a correct selection 7 times,

- SciBERT*Linguistics topped the list with 10 correct selections.

Although the frequency of correct selections is not particularly high, likely due to the challenging nature of the task, it is interesting to see that Rouge outperformed SciBERT, especially since we trained SciBERT using similarities identified by Rouge. Furthermore, it is noteworthy that the integration of linguistic principles with SciBERT elevated the number of correct selections from 7 to 10, making this the most successful method when considering human evaluations.

6 Concluding remarks

We hypothesized that automatically generating an adequate research paper title can be treated as a high-level text summarization problem: a title can be seen as a very condensed summary of the paper's abstract. In this context, we have presented a novel post-processing approach that combines a SciBERT prediction model enhanced with linguistic-stylistic rules to tackle the problem of finding adequate titles for research papers.

We started by considering three powerful NLG models (BART Large, T5 Large, FLAN T5 Large) and evaluating their text-generation results against the original titles. Out of these models, we chose the best-performing one: T5 Large. T5 Large was then set up to generate multiple diverse titles for the same abstract. For each abstract, we generated five different titles and again compared them against the original title of the paper using ROUGE. Subsequently, we created a synthetic dataset by labeling the title with the top ROUGE score as "1", and the title with the lowest ROUGE score as "0"; we then trained SciBERT on this synthetic dataset. In addition, we defined a set of linguistic rules a title should adhere to. Based on these rules, we calculated a normalized score between 0 and 1 for each generated title. We then multiplied this normalized linguistic score by the SciBERT probabilities obtained in the previous post-processing step.

We also assessed our title selection methods in relation to human evaluations. The human evaluations section was instrumental in providing insights into the nuances of human perspectives concerning machine-generated academic titles. Our findings revealed that while title evaluation can be subjective to some extent, there exists a noticeable degree of consensus among evaluators about what constitutes a quality title. The performance comparison between various methods, with the linguistics-enhanced SciBERT emerging as the most successful in capturing human evaluations, further underscores the effectiveness of our proposed approach.

In the future, we would like to experiment with generating titles using a paper's conclusion section rather than its abstract. Working with conclusions is more complicated than working with abstracts, as not all papers have a self-standing conclusion section, yet an improvement of our results might be obtained as conclusions often define in more detail what the key contributions of a paper are.

7 Acknowledgements

This study was partly supported by a grant from Rannís, the Icelandic Institute for Research, and a grant by the European Union (Women TechEU, European Innovation Ecosystems programme, Horizon Europe). Computational resources were provided by the e-INFRA CZ project (ID:90254), supported by the Ministry of Education, Youth and Sports of the Czech Republic. This work has been partially supported by CHIST-ERA within the CIMPLE project (CHIST-ERA-19-XAI-003).

References

Pepa Atanasova, Jakob Grue Simonsen, Christina Lioma, and Isabelle Augenstein. 2020. Generating fact checking explanations. In *Proceedings of the 58th Annual Meeting of the Association for Computational Linguistics*, pages 7352–7364.

Iz Beltagy, Kyle Lo, and Arman Cohan. 2019. SciBERT: A pretrained language model for scientific text. In *Proceedings of the 2019 Conference on Empirical Methods in Natural Language Processing and the 9th International Joint Conference on Natural Language Processing (EMNLP-IJCNLP)*, pages 3615–3620, Hong Kong, China. Association for Computational Linguistics.

Kendrick Boyd, Kevin H Eng, and C David Page. 2013. Area under the precision-recall curve: point estimates and confidence intervals. In *Machine Learning and Knowledge Discovery in Databases: European Conference, ECML PKDD 2013, Prague, Czech Republic, September 23-27, 2013, Proceedings, Part III 13*, pages 451–466. Springer.

Alexey Bukhtiyarov and Ilya Gusev. 2020. Advances of transformer-based models for news headline generation. In *Artificial Intelligence and Natural Language: 9th Conference, AINL 2020, Helsinki, Finland, October 7–9, 2020, Proceedings 9*, pages 54–61. Springer.

Hyung Won Chung, Le Hou, Shayne Longpre, Barret Zoph, Yi Tay, William Fedus, Eric Li, Xuezhi Wang, Mostafa Dehghani, Siddhartha Brahma, et al. 2022. Scaling instruction-finetuned language models. *arXiv preprint arXiv:2210.11416*.

Arman Cohan, Waleed Ammar, Madeleine Van Zuylen, and Field Cady. 2019. Structural scaffolds for citation intent classification in scientific publications. *arXiv preprint arXiv:1904.01608*.

Boer Deng. 2015. Papers with shorter titles get more citations. *Nature*, 2(8):150266.

Jacob Devlin, Ming-Wei Chang, Kenton Lee, and Kristina Toutanova. 2019. BERT: Pre-training of deep bidirectional transformers for language understanding. In *Proceedings of the 2019 Conference of the North American Chapter of the Association for Computational Linguistics: Human Language Technologies, Volume 1 (Long and Short Papers)*, pages 4171–4186, Minneapolis, Minnesota. Association for Computational Linguistics.

Alexander R. Fabbri, Wojciech Kryściński, Bryan McCann, Caiming Xiong, Richard Socher, and Dragomir Radev. 2021. SummEval: Re-evaluating Summarization Evaluation. *Transactions of the Association for Computational Linguistics*, 9:391–409.

Joseph L Fleiss. 1971. Measuring nominal scale agreement among many raters. *Psychological bulletin*, 76(5):378.

Diederik P Kingma and Jimmy Ba. 2014. Adam: A method for stochastic optimization. *arXiv preprint arXiv:1412.6980*.

Kenneth L Knight and Christopher D Ingersoll. 1996. Structure of a scholarly manuscript: 66 tips for what goes where. *Journal of Athletic Training*, 31(3):201.

Maximilian Koppatz, Khalid Alnajjar, Mika Hämäläinen, and Thierry Poibeau. 2022. Automatic generation of factual news headlines in finnish. *arXiv preprint arXiv:2212.02170*.

Mike Lewis, Yinhan Liu, Naman Goyal, Marjan Ghazvininejad, Abdelrahman Mohamed, Omer Levy, Ves Stoyanov, and Luke Zettlemoyer. 2019. Bart: Denoising sequence-to-sequence pre-training for natural language generation, translation, and comprehension. *arXiv preprint arXiv:1910.13461*.

Chin-Yew Lin. 2004. Rouge: A package for automatic evaluation of summaries. In *Text summarization branches out*, pages 74–81.

Yang Liu and Mirella Lapata. 2019. Text summarization with pretrained encoders. In *Proceedings of the 2019 Conference on Empirical Methods in Natural Language Processing and the 9th International Joint Conference on Natural Language Processing (EMNLP-IJCNLP)*, pages 3730–3740.

Labani Mallick, Gulab C Dewangan, IM McHardy, and Mayukh Pahari. 2017. Energy-dependent variability of the bare seyfert 1 galaxy ark 120. *Monthly Notices of the Royal Astronomical Society*, 472(1):174–188.

Kazuki Matsumaru, Sho Takase, and Naoaki Okazaki. 2020. Improving truthfulness of headline generation. *arXiv preprint arXiv:2005.00882*.

Prakhar Mishra, Chaitali Diwan, Srinath Srinivasa, and G Srinivasaraghavan. 2021. Automatic title generation for text with pre-trained transformer language model. In *2021 IEEE 15th International Conference on Semantic Computing (ICSC)*, pages 17–24. IEEE.

Carlos Eduardo Paiva, João Paulo da Silveira Nogueira Lima, and Bianca Sakamoto Ribeiro Paiva. 2012. Articles with short titles describing the results are cited more often. *Clinics*, 67:509–513.

Alec Radford, Jeffrey Wu, Rewon Child, David Luan, Dario Amodei, Ilya Sutskever, et al. 2019. Language models are unsupervised multitask learners. *OpenAI blog*, 1(8):9.

Colin Raffel, Noam Shazeer, Adam Roberts, Katherine Lee, Sharan Narang, Michael Matena, Yanqi Zhou, Wei Li, and Peter J Liu. 2020. Exploring the limits of transfer learning with a unified text-to-text transformer. *The Journal of Machine Learning Research*, 21(1):5485–5551.

SciPress. 2017. 12 key tips on how to write a good research paper title. `https://shorturl.at/cMQVW`. Last Accessed: 14th of October 2023.

SHU Library. 2020. Organizing academic research papers: Choosing a title. `https://library.sacredheart.edu/c.php?g=29803&p=185911`. Last Accessed: 14th of October 2023.

Kaiqiang Song, Bingqing Wang, Zhe Feng, Ren Liu, and Fei Liu. 2020. Controlling the amount of verbatim copying in abstractive summarization. In *Proceedings of the AAAI conference on artificial intelligence*, volume 34, pages 8902–8909.

Ottokar Tilk and Tanel Alumäe. 2017. Low-resource neural headline generation. *arXiv preprint arXiv:1707.09769*.

USC Libraries. 2023. Research guides: Organizing your social sciences research paper: Choosing a title. `https://libguides.usc.edu/writingguide/title`. Last Accessed: 14th of October 2023.

Wordvice. 2023. How to write a research paper title with examples. `https://blog.wordvice.com/how-to-write-the-perfect-title-for-your-\research-paper/`. Last Accessed: 14th of October 2023.

Jingqing Zhang, Yao Zhao, Mohammad Saleh, and Peter Liu. 2020. Pegasus: Pre-training with extracted gap-sentences for abstractive summarization. In *International Conference on Machine Learning*, pages 11328–11339. PMLR.

MuLMS: A Multi-Layer Annotated Text Corpus for Information Extraction in the Materials Science Domain

Timo Pierre Schrader[1,3] **Matteo Finco**[2] **Stefan Grünewald**[1,4]
Felix Hildebrand[2] **Annemarie Friedrich**[3]
[1]Bosch Center for Artificial Intelligence, Renningen, Germany
[2]Robert Bosch GmbH, Stuttgart, Germany
[3]University of Augsburg, Germany [4]University of Stuttgart, Germany
timo.schrader|matteo.finco|stefan.gruenewald@de.bosch.com
annemarie.friedrich@informatik.uni-augsburg.de

Abstract

Keeping track of all relevant recent publications and experimental results for a research area is a challenging task. Prior work has demonstrated the efficacy of information extraction models in various scientific areas. Recently, several datasets have been released for the yet understudied materials science domain. However, these datasets focus on sub-problems such as parsing synthesis procedures or on sub-domains, e.g., solid oxide fuel cells.

In this resource paper, we present MuLMS, a new dataset of 50 open-access articles, spanning seven sub-domains of materials science. The corpus has been annotated by domain experts with several layers ranging from named entities over relations to frame structures. We present competitive neural models for all tasks and demonstrate that multi-task training with existing related resources leads to benefits.

1 Introduction

Designing meaningful experiments in empirical sciences requires maintaining a detailed overview of the huge amounts of literature published every year. Applying natural language processing (NLP) in this context has risen to be an active research area (Chandrasekaran et al., 2020; Beltagy et al., 2021; Cohan et al., 2022). Besides the biomedical field, which has been studied extensively in the past decades (e.g., Collier et al., 2004; Cohen et al., 2012; Demner-Fushman et al., 2022), the less-studied materials science domain has recently received more attention (Mysore et al., 2019; Friedrich et al., 2020; O'Gorman et al., 2021).

Materials science research aims to design and discover new materials. Part of the papers is hence often dedicated to the *synthesis procedures*, the "recipe" for creating a material. Their extraction from papers has been covered by Mysore et al. (2019) and O'Gorman et al. (2021). Much materials science research develops materials in the context of creating a particular device, e.g., batteries or photovoltaic panels. The device is tested in various conditions and the literature needs to be analysed for identifying promising set-ups. Friedrich et al. (2020) address this for solid oxide fuel cells.

In this paper, we introduce **MuLMS** (the Multi-Layer Materials Science corpus), a new dataset of scientific publications annotated by domain experts with named entity (NE) mentions, relations, and frame structures corresponding to a broad notion of measurements (see Figure 1). In contrast to prior works, we include papers from a variety of materials science sub-domains. To the best of our knowledge, the existing datasets only annotate particular paragraphs or subsets of the sentences with NE mentions. Our dataset is the first to *exhaustively* annotate a large-scale collection of materials science articles with NEs and facilitates novel semantic search applications, e.g., answering search queries such as "find a passage within a paper reporting a measurement using material X, condition Y, and obtaining a value of at least Z."

The design of MuLMS' annotation scheme results from a collaboration of NLP and materials science experts. Our inter-annotator agreement study shows good agreement for most categories and decisions. We propose several machine learning tasks on the annotated data and present strong neural baselines for all tasks, which signals a high level of consistency across the annotations in our dataset. We cast detecting sentences describing measurements as a sentence classification task and provide a robust tagger for recognizing NEs. We propose to treat relation and semantic role extraction on MuLMS in a single step using a dependency parser that predicts relations between the NEs in a sentence. According to our multi-task experiments with related datasets, training jointly with MuLMS is beneficial for performance on those datasets.

Our contributions are as follows. (1) We publicly release a dataset of 50 open-access scientific publications *exhaustively* annotated by a domain

Proceedings of the 2nd Workshop on Information Extraction from Scientific Publications, pages 84–100
Nov 1, 2023. ©2023 Association for Computational Linguistics

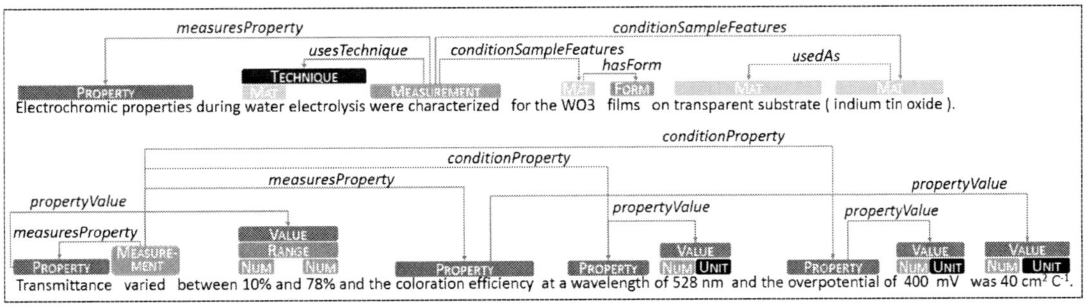

Figure 1: **Multi-Layer Materials Science Corpus**: named entity, relation and semantic role annotations.

expert with NE mentions, relations, and measurement frames.[1] (2) We define a set of NLP tasks on MuLMS and provide strong transformer-based baselines. Our code will be published. (3) We formulate the relation and frame-argument extraction as a single dependency parsing task, which extracts *all* relations in a sentence in one processing step. (4) We perform an extensive set of multi-task learning experiments with related corpora, showing that MuLMS is a useful auxiliary task for two other materials science NLP datasets.

2 Related Work

Several **materials science NLP datasets** have recently been released, e.g., targeting NE recognition (Yamaguchi et al., 2020; O'Gorman et al., 2021). The Materials Science Procedural Text (MSPT) corpus (Mysore et al., 2019) consists of paragraphs describing synthesis procedures annotated with graph structures capturing relations and typed arguments. SOFC-Exp (Friedrich et al., 2020) marks similar graph structures describing experiments.

In this paper, we compare two state-of-the-art approaches to **Named Entity Recognition** (NER). Huang et al. (2015) use a CRF layer (Lafferty et al., 2001) on top of a neural language model (in their case a BiLSTM) for sequence-tagging related tasks. Yu et al. (2020) treat NER as a graph-based dependency parsing task by representing NEs as spans between the first and last token of an entity. In the materials science domain, Friedrich et al. (2020) test a variety of embedding combinations in a CRF-based tagger. O'Gorman et al. (2021) compare different pre-trained transformers for token classification. Both studies find SciBERT (Beltagy et al., 2019), a BERT-style model pre-trained on scientific documents, to be very effective.

Relation and Event Extraction. Friedrich et al. (2020) treat their slot filling task in the SOFC subdomain as a sequence tagging task, assuming that each sentence represents at most one experiment. To predict a possible relation between two entities, Swarup et al. (2020) retrieve a set of sentences similar to the input sentence, and learn to copy relations from these sentences. Mysore et al. (2017) experiment with unsupervised methods for extracting action graphs for synthesis procedures.

An exhaustive overview of the literature on biomedical relation extraction is out of the scope of this paper. Recent works have used graph-neural networks (Huang et al., 2020), or convolutional neural networks (Ramponi et al., 2020). Sarrouti et al. (2022) compare various pre-trained transformer models. Semantic parsing of frame structures (Fillmore and Baker, 2001) has been addressed using graph-convolutional networks (Marcheggiani and Titov, 2020), BiLSTMs (He et al., 2018), and recently by generating structured output using encoder-decoder models (Hsu et al., 2022; Lu et al., 2021). Tackling semantic dependency parsing with a biaffine classifier architecture was first proposed by Dozat and Manning (2018).

3 MuLMS Corpus

In this section, we present our new corpus.

3.1 Source of Texts and Preprocessing

We select 50 scientific articles licensed under CC BY from seven popular sub-areas of materials science: electrolysis, graphene, polymer electrolyte fuel cell (PEMFC), solid oxide fuel cell (SOFC), polymers, semiconductors, and steel. The four SOFC papers were selected from the SOFC-Exp corpus (Friedrich et al., 2020). 11 papers were selected from the OA-STM corpus[2] and classified into the above subject areas by a domain ex-

[1] https://github.com/boschresearch/mulms-wiesp2023

[2] https://github.com/elsevierlabs/OA-STM-Corpus

pert. The majority of the papers were found via PubMed[3] and DOAJ[4] using queries prepared by a domain expert. For the OA-STM data, we use the sentence segmentation provided with the corpus, which has been created using GENIA tools (Tsuruoka and Tsujii, 2005). For the remaining texts, we rely on the sentence segmentation provided by INCEpTION (Klie et al., 2018) with some manual fixes. As shown in Table 1, documents are rather long with a tendency to long sentences (but with high variation due to, i.a., short headings).

3.2 Annotation Scheme

We annotate various layers: NEs, relations, and frame structures representing measurements.

3.2.1 Named Entities

We annotate the following materials-science specific NE mentions and assign the following NE types to these mentions:

MAT: mentions of materials described by their chemical formula (*WO_3*) or its chemical name (*indium tin oxide*).

FORM: mentions of the form or morphology of the material, e.g., *thin film, gas, liquid, cubic.*

INSTRUMENT: mentions of devices used to perform a materials-science-related measurement, e.g., *Olympus BX52 microscope.*

DEVICE: mentions of devices (target products) whose construction or improvement is the aim of the research (e.g., *photodetector, transistor, supercapacitor*). DEVICE is not used for instrumentation devices that are only used as a tool.

NUM: mentions of numbers such as *0.46*.

UNIT: mentions of units such as *nm* or *V*.

RANGE: mentions of numeric expressions indicating ranges, e.g., *0.46±.11*

VALUE: nested type capturing expressions of values usually composed of a NUM, RANGE and a UNIT, e.g., *~5 x 3mm2*

CITE: citations, e.g., *Setman et al.* or *[13]*.

PROPERTY: expressions referring to properties of materials or conditions in experiments, e.g., *stress rate* or *electron conductivity*.

TECHNIQUE: mentions of experimental techniques used in the characterization steps, e.g., *Scanning electron microscopy (SEM)*.

SAMPLE: mention of the material or a component made of materials studied in a measurement, either referred to by a particular name or its composition, its batch name (*Aq-825*) or by referring to the whole component (*MEA-Pt/C*) or to part of the material's structure (*ionomer patches*). In simulation papers, the SAMPLE may also be the computational model under study (*RBF-ANN*).

#Documents	50
#Documents train / dev / test	36 / 7 / 7
#Sentences	10186
#Sentences/Document	203.7±73.2
#Tokens/Sentence	28.7±17.9

Table 1: Basic **corpus statistics** for MuLMS.

3.2.2 Relations and Measurement Frame

We treat measurement annotation in a frame-like (Fillmore and Baker, 2001) fashion, using the span type MEASUREMENT to mark the triggers (e.g., *was measured, is plotted*) that introduce the *Measurement* frame to the discourse. About 88% of the triggers are verbs. The remaining 12% occur in figure captions without verb phrases and are annotated either on nouns (*Comparison*) or, in absence of more suitable phrases, on figure labels such as *Figure 17*. The trigger annotations of these sentences serve as the root of the tree/graph annotations as illustrated in Figure 1.

There are also cases in which the *Measurement* frame is evoked, but there are no technical details or results that we can extract about the measurement. We mark the triggers of these sentences with the tag QUAL_MEAS (qualitative mention of a measurement). An example of such a sentence is "*We compare a critical volume to be detached from the different nanostructures.*"

Measurement-related Relations. We annotate several relations that start at a MEASUREMENT tag and that end at the annotations of the corresponding slot fillers within the sentence. Consider the following sentence: "*To characterize the ORR activity of the catalyst, linear scan voltammetry (LSV) was tested from 0 to 1.2 V on an RDE with a scan rate of 50 mV/s in O2-saturated HClO4 solution.*"

***measuresProperty*:** indicates the PROPERTY (e.g., *ORR activity*) that is measured.

***conditionSampleFeatures*:** indicates the SAMPLE or MATERIAL whose property is measured. In the above example, the sample is the *catalyst*.

***usesTechnique*:** relates to the TECHNIQUE (e.g., *linear scan voltammetry*) used in a measurement.

***conditionInstrument*:** refers to the INSTRUMENT used to make a measurement, e.g., *RDE/rotating*

[3] https://pubmed.ncbi.nlm.nih.gov

[4] https://doaj.org

Relation	Example
hasForm	silicon$_{MAT}$–*hasForm*→ hexagonal$_{FORM}$
usedIn	Sic$_{MAT}$ –*usedIn*→ MOSFET$_{DEVICE}$
usedAs	PtNi3M$_{MAT}$ –*usedAs*→ catalysts
dopedBy	chlorinated$_{Material}$–*dopedBy*→SiC$_{MAT}$

Table 2: Measurement-independent **relations** annotated in MuLMS. MAT is short for MATERIAL.

Label	Count	%	Label	Count	%
MAT	15596	33.6	CITE	1709	3.7
NUM	6081	13.1	SAMPLE	1461	3.2
VALUE	4852	10.5	TECHNIQUE	1036	2.2
UNIT	4330	9.3	DEV	808	1.7
PROPERTY	3925	8.5	RANGE	736	1.6
FORM	3568	7.7	INSTRUMENT	378	0.8
MEASUREMENT	2171	4.7	*total*	46,351	-

Table 3: Corpus counts for **named entity** annotations.

Label	Count	%	Label	Count	%
hasForm	2910	17.3	*meas.Prop.Val.*	751	4.5
measuresProperty	2080	12.4	*usedTogether*	672	4.0
usedAs	1839	11.0	*conditionEnv.*	549	3.3
propertyValue	1794	10.7	*usedIn*	434	2.6
conditionProperty	1648	9.8	*conditionInstr.*	357	2.2
conditionSample	1434	8.5	*takenFrom*	118	0.7
cond.Prop.Value	1158	6.9	*dopedBy*	65	0.4
usesTechnique	985	5.9	*total*	16,794	

Table 4: Corpus counts for **measurement relations**.

	MEAS	QUAL_MEAS	OTHER
MEAS	48	6	6
QUAL_MEAS	12	37	11
OTHER	10	17	92

Table 5: Inter-annotator agreement for **identifying measurement sentences**: confusion matrix.

disk electrode.

***conditionProperty*:** a property that is a condition in the experiment, e.g., *scan rate* (which in turn has the *propertyValue* of *50 mv/s*).

***propertyValue*:** connects the mention of a PROPERTY and that of its corresponding VALUE. This relation may also occur if a mention of a PROPERTY occurs independently of a measurement.

***conditionEnvironment*:** identifies the MATERIALS (e.g., *O2* and *HClO4*) and VALUEs (e.g., an operating temperature of *30°C*) that provide the environment of the measurement.

***takenFrom*:** connects the MEASUREMENT with the bibliographic reference CITE from which the setup has been inspired or taken over.

In most cases, a *conditionProperty* or a *measuresProperty* connects the MEASUREMENT annotation to a PROPERTY node, at which a *propertyValue* relation starts that ends at the respective VALUE. However, in some cases, the condition or measured property is not mentioned explicitly. In this case, we link the VALUE directly to the MEASUREMENT node via a *conditionPropertyValue* or a *measuresPropertyValue* link. For consistency reasons, we also add these links in cases that mention the property explicitly, turning the trees into graph structures. Out of the added *conditionPropertyValue* links, 967 are for such explicit cases, while the other 206 describe implicit cases. In the case of *measuresPropertyValue*, 722 links are for explicit cases and 36 for implicit cases.

Further Relations. In the following, we explain relations that can appear independently of measurements. Examples are shown in Table 2.

***hasForm*:** connects mention of MATERIAL and the corresponding FORM annotation.

***usedIn*:** connects MATERIAL and the DEVICE it is used in. In Table 2, *MOSFET* stands for *Metal Oxide Semiconductor Field-Effect Transistors.*

***usedAs*:** links a specific MATERIAL mention with a more generic one such as *catalyst*, a material class defined by its function.

***dopedBy*:** indicates dopants (e.g., *chlorine*), i.e., impurities added to a main material (e.g., *SiC*).

***usedTogether*:** connects two MATERIALs if they are used together in an experiment, i.e., if the materials are part of an assembly or a mixture.

3.3 Corpus Statistics

We now analyze our corpus and provide detailed corpus statistics. In total, there are 46,351 NE annotations. Table 3 shows the counts by NE label. There are roughly 1.5 MAT annotations per sentence as these are nested and occurrences of composite materials often result in many combined MAT tags. Table 4 reports the counts of annotated relations (16,794 in total), with *hasForm* as the most frequent relation with 2910 instances and *dopedBy* the least frequent with only 65 instances.

Out of all 10186 sentences, 2111 (20.7%) describe a measurement (i.e., they contain at least one MEASUREMENT annotation). On average, each document contains 43.4 MEASUREMENT annotations. In addition, there are 1476 sentences (14.5%) marked as containing a QUAL_MEAS, with 40 sentences of these also containing a MEASUREMENT annotation.

Label	P	R	F1	Label	P	R	F1
MAT	96.7	91.2	93.9	CITE	97.4	97.4	97.4
NUM	98.9	100.0	99.4	SAMPLE	3.1	12.5	4.7
VALUE	100	100	100.0	TECHN.	77.5	59.6	67.4
UNIT	97.9	100.0	98.9	DEVICE	96.0	82.8	88.9
PROPERTY	42.6	37.7	40.0	RANGE	100.0	100.0	100.0
FORM	95.7	86.3	90.8	INSTR.	80.0	76.9	78.4
MEAS.	44.6	51.0	47.6	*average*	*79.3*	*76.6*	*77.9*

Table 6: Inter-annotator agreement: **named entities.**

3.4 Inter-Annotator Agreement (IAA)

Our entire dataset has been annotated by a graduate student of materials science, who was also involved in the design of the annotation scheme. We perform two agreement studies, comparing to the annotations of a second annotator with a PhD degree in environment engineering and several years of experience in materials science research.

Agreement on identifying Measurement sentences. In this agreement study, we estimate the degree of agreement whether a sentence expresses a MEASUREMENT, a QUAL_MEAS, or whether it does not express a measurement at all. We sample 60 sentences marked with MEASUREMENT, 60 sentences marked with QUAL_MEAS, and 120 sentences not marked as either by the first annotator. Table 5 shows the confusion matrix for the 239 sentences for which both annotators provided a label. One automatically selected sentence was not labeled by one of the annotators due to incomprehensibility. In terms of Cohen's κ (Cohen, 1960), agreement amounts to 59.2, indicating moderate to substantial agreement (Landis and Koch, 1977). When collapsing MEASUREMENT and QUAL_MEAS, κ is 63.4 (substantial).

Agreement on named entities. We next compute agreement for NE and relation annotations. IAA on "easy" types such as MAT, NUM, UNIT, VALUE and RANGE has been shown to be very high in prior work (Friedrich et al., 2020). Hence, as our resources are limited, we provide annotations of these types for correction to the second annotator. We sample 134 sentences such that each entity type occurs at least 25 times in the annotations of the first annotator and have the second annotator correct or add entity annotations. We then compare the annotated sets of NE mentions using precision and recall (for a justification of this choice of agreement metrics, see Appendix C). Results using relaxed matching (containment) are shown in Table 6 (detailed counts in Appendix C).

Label	P	R	F1	κ	matches
propertyValue	81.2	81.2	81.2	0.88	26
condSampleFeat.	43.1	40.0	41.5	0.23	22
usedIn	40.0	52.2	45.3	0.55	12
usesTechnique	72.9	67.3	70.0	0.86	35
hasForm	54.7	71.4	61.9	0.64	35
takenFrom	33.3	63.6	43.7	0.57	7
measuresProp.	80.5	72.9	76.5	0.80	70
dopedBy	35.3	50.0	41.4	0.25	6
conditionProp.	27.7	59.1	37.7	0.31	13
conditionInstr.	24.0	60.0	34.3	0.44	6
conditionEnv.	0.0	0.0	0.0	0.00	0
usedAs	23.5	85.7	36.9	0.37	12
usedTogether	13.8	28.6	18.6	0.20	4

Table 7: Inter-annotator agreement: **relations.**

For most types, scores are in the expected range of difficult semantic annotation tasks. Agreement on identifying Measurement sentences is good; the decision of where exactly to place the MEASUREMENT annotation differs between annotators.

Agreement on relations. We sample 178 sentences in which each relation occurs at least 25 times according to the first annotator. We keep NE annotations and ask the second annotator to add relations. Table 7 shows the results in terms of precision, recall, and κ per relation type. The latter has been computed by treating all pairs of NE annotations as potential relations, using NO_REL if no relation has been annotated. Overall κ on relations is 0.61 (substantial). For each relation label, we can map all other relation types to $OTHER$ and compute agreement for the binary decision whether the label is present or not (analysis suggested by Krippendorff (1989)). κ aims to quantify the degree of agreement *above* chance. Interpreting our κ scores according to the scale of Landis and Koch (1977), we reach at **fair** agreement for *conditionPropertyValue*, *usedTogether*, *conditionSampleFeatures*, *dopedBy*, and *usedAs*. We reach **moderate** agreement for *usedIn*, *takenFrom*, and *conditionInstrument.* For the practically important relations *propertyValue*, *measuresProperty*, and *usesTechnique*, we even reach **almost perfect** agreement.

For the non-easily identifiable types, post-hoc discussion with the second annotator (who did not receive an extensive training on the task) concluded it was not always clear to them when using related labels (e.g., *conditionProperty* and *conditionEnvironment*). Yet, these labels can be learned with good or acceptable accuracy (see Appendix E), indicating that the primary annotator has used the labels consistently.

4 Task Definitions and Modeling

In this section, we define several NLP tasks for MuLMS and describe our computational models.

4.1 Pre-trained Models

We use BERT (Devlin et al., 2019) as the underlying text encoder for all of our models. We also use variants of BERT, namely SciBERT (Beltagy et al., 2019), which has been pre-trained on articles in the scientific domain, and MatSciBERT (Gupta et al., 2022), a version of SciBERT further pre-trained on materials science articles. We use the uncased, 768-dimensional variant of each model, which we fine-tune.

4.2 Detecting Measurements

We model the task of classifying whether a sentence contains a MEASUREMENT or a QUAL_MEAS annotation as a ternary sentence classification task, i.e., it is also possible that a sentence does not refer to any measurement. As we are primarily interested in detecting MEASUREMENT, we map the few multi-label cases carrying both positive labels to MEASUREMENT. We use a linear layer plus softmax with the CLS token embedding as input. For training, we downsample the amount of non-measurement sentences.

4.3 Named Entity Recognition (NER)

We compare two state-of-the-art models for NER, (a) a sequence tagger and (b) a dependency parser. For the **sequence tagger**, we encode the NE labels using the nested BILOU scheme (Alex et al., 2007), which leverages a label set of combined types constructed from the training set for nested NEs. As there are only very few cases (about 0.65% of all NE annotations) where a token receives more than three stacked NE labels, in order to avoid sparsity issues, we consider only the "bottom" three layers of stacked entities. We feed the contextualized embeddings of the last transformer layer of the respective first wordpiece token of each "real" token into a linear layer and then use a CRF (Lafferty et al., 2001) to optimize predictions for the entire sequence.

Modeling NER as a **dependency parsing** task (Yu et al., 2020) can easily account for nested NEs. The main idea is to predict edges reaching from the end token of an NE to its start token as depicted in Figure 2. We adapt the STEPS parsing pipeline (Grünewald et al., 2021a) to the task. There are three combinations of tags in our dataset that occasionally cover the exact same span and that occur more than 20 times: VALUE+NUM, VALUE+RANGE and MAT+FORM. We hence introduce the above combined labels. For any other infrequent conflicting labels, we do not add extra tags, i.e., the model can never catch these cases. We decide on this slight restriction of the model capabilities in order to avoid sparsity issues. In the evaluation, we do not filter for these cases but of course use all nested NEs as annotated.

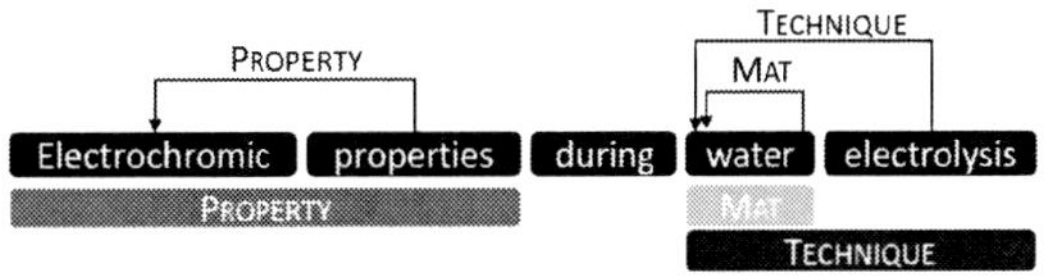

Figure 2: NER as dependency parsing (Yu et al., 2020).

4.4 Relation Extraction

Given an input sentence along with all named entities within it, as well as their types (either gold or predicted depending on the experimental setting), we predict which (if any) relation is present between them. We treat all relations in a single model and predict all relations of a sentence simultaneously by modeling relation extraction as a graph parsing task. Following Toshniwal et al. (2020), we first create an embedding $\mathbf{e}_i$ for the ith NE in the sentence by concatenating the token embeddings of its first and last token ($\mathbf{e}_{i,\text{START}}$, $\mathbf{e}_{i,\text{END}}$). We also concatenate a learned embedding for the NE's label ($\mathbf{e}_{i,\text{LABEL}}$): $\mathbf{e}_i = \mathbf{e}_{i,\text{START}} \oplus \mathbf{e}_{i,\text{END}} \oplus \mathbf{e}_{i,\text{LABEL}}$

Considering NEs as nodes in a graph, we use a biaffine classifier architecture (Dozat and Manning, 2017) using the implementation of Grünewald et al. (2021a,b) to predict the relation between each pair. The non-existence of a relation is encoded as simply another label ($\varnothing$). For details on the parser architecture, see Appendix B.

5 Experiments

We now detail our experimental results.

Experimental Settings. We split our corpus into train, dev, and test sets on a per-document basis. Within the train set, we provide five distinct tune splits (*train1* to *train5*). For all experiments and for hyperparameter tuning, we always train five models. Similar to cross-validation, we train on four folds and use the fifth "training fold" for model selection (cf. van der Goot (2021) for details). Hy-

LM (sampling)	MEASUREMENT P	R	F1	QUAL_MEAS P	R	F1
Random baseline	24.7	19.7	21.9$\pm$2.4	15.1	14.4	14.7$\pm$1.5
BERT(0.7)	**74.1**	71.4	72.5$\pm$2.1	49.9	51.6	50.6$\pm$0.7
SciBERT(0.7)	71.1	79.5	**75.0**$\pm$0.7	52.7	52.8	52.7$\pm$1.4
MatSciBERT(0.85)	70.6	**80.1**	74.9$\pm$1.3	**52.8**	**56.9**	**54.7**$\pm$1.0
*human agreement**	*68.6*	*80.9*	*73.8*	*61.7*	*61.7*	*61.7*

Table 8: Ternary sentence classification results for **identifying measurement sentences** on test set. "Sampling" indicates amount of OTHER sentences used for training. **estimated on subset of data.*

Model	LM	Micro F1	Macro F1
Dependency Parser	BERT	73.0$\pm$0.7	61.7$\pm$2.3
	SciBERT	76.5$\pm$0.3	65.8$\pm$0.9
	MatSciBERT	**77.3**$\pm$0.3	**67.6**$\pm$1.4
CRF Tagger	BERT	75.3$\pm$0.6	63.2$\pm$0.7
	SciBERT	78.7$\pm$0.4	69.3$\pm$1.0
	MatSciBERT	**79.6**$\pm$0.4	**70.7**$\pm$0.7

Table 9: **Named entity recognition** results on test set.

perparameters are chosen based on the best dev results, and we finally report results for the test set. The splits are the same across all tasks. Because the training data varies across the five runs for which we report results, standard deviations are usually larger than when using the same training data. For hyperparameter settings, see Appendix A.

5.1 Identifying Measurement Sentences

Table 8 reports the results for identifying sentences that contain a MEASUREMENT or a QUAL_MEAS annotation. In each experiment, we tune the down-sampling rate for the majority class OTHER and the learning rate (using grid search from 1e-4 to 1e-7). The *random baseline* assigns labels according to the percentage of instances in the (full) training set carrying a particular label. The average overall accuracy of the MatSciBERT classifier is 78.2%. SciBERT and MatSciBERT perform similarly, with MatSciBERT having a small edge. Identification of MEASUREMENT is comparable to our estimate of human agreement. For identifying QUAL_MEAS, there is headroom.

5.2 Named Entity Recognition Results

Table 9 shows the results for named entity recognition. Again, MatSciBERT performs best with Micro F1 scores approaching 80, which indicates that NE mentions are consistently annotated in MuLMS. The CRF-based tagger outperforms the dependency-parser-based NER model by a considerable margin. For detailed per-label statistics, see Appendix E. Precision and recall are approximately balanced for all labels. An exception is SAMPLE, which is both infrequent in the dataset and hard to identify for humans. Both models suffer from low recall for this tag.

LM	dev Micro F1	dev Macro F1	test Micro F1	test Macro F1
Maj. basel.	38.3	29.4	37.2	27.4
BERT	69.5$\pm$0.5	63.4$\pm$1.0	63.5$\pm$0.6	57.7$\pm$1.1
SciBERT	72.5$\pm$0.8	65.7$\pm$0.6	67.5$\pm$0.9	**62.0**$\pm$2.2
MatSciBERT	**73.2**$\pm$1.0	**66.5**$\pm$1.1	**67.6**$\pm$1.0	**62.0**$\pm$1.0

Table 10: **Relation extraction** results: gold entities.

5.3 Relation Extraction Results

Table 10 shows the results for relation extraction on gold entities. A predicted relation is counted as correct if and only if there is a relation with the same start span, end span, and relation label in the set of gold relations for the sentence. The majority baseline assigns to each pair of entities the relation that is most common in the training set for the respective entity types of the governing and dependent spans (see Appendix E).

The results demonstrate that a biaffine dependency parsing approach achieves robust performance overall and outperforms the baseline by a substantial margin. The two models trained on scientific text outperform BERT. Their results are similar, with MatSciBERT having a slight edge.

Analysis of per-label scores (see Appendix E) for MatSciBERT) shows that the highest scores are achieved for *conditionInstrument* (92.2 F1), *usesTechnique* (91.0 F1), and *takenFrom* (84.7). This is somewhat surprising especially for *conditionInstrument* and *takenFrom*, as these are among the rarest relation types in the corpus (see Table 4). However, our majority baseline achieves high accuracies on these relation types as well (>90 F1 for *conditionInstrument* and *usesTechnique*), i.e., they are easily inferable from entity types. The worst performance is observed on the relation types *usedTogether* (4.0 F1), *dopedBy* (22.7 F1), and *usedIn* (37.9 F1). These relations occur relatively rarely and also cannot be inferred from entity types.

Relation extraction on predicted entities. Finally, we also run our relation extraction module on predicted named entities using the respective best-performing models (both based on MatSciBERT). Models are evaluated as above, with the additional

Dataset	LR	Micro F1	Macro F1
MuLMS	1e-4/7e-3	**79.6**$_{\pm 0.4}$	**70.7**$_{\pm 0.7}$
+ SOFC-Exp		79.5$_{\pm 0.4}$	70.4$_{\pm 1.3}$
+ MSPT		79.2$_{\pm 0.6}$	69.9$_{\pm 0.8}$
SOFC-Exp	3e-4/7e-3	**83.4**$_{\pm 0.9}$	**81.0**$_{\pm 1.0}$
+ MuLMS		81.9$_{\pm 1.7}$	79.6$_{\pm 1.7}$
MSPT	5e-5/9e-3	**81.6**$_{\pm 0.4}$	**57.8**$_{\pm 0.6}$
+ MuLMS		80.4$_{\pm 0.4}$	56.4$_{\pm 0.8}$

Table 11: **NER MTL** results: MatSciBERT tagger.

	dev		test	
Dataset	Micro F1	Macro F1	Micro F1	Macro F1
MuLMS	73.2$_{\pm 1.0}$	66.5$_{\pm 1.1}$	67.6$_{\pm 1.0}$	62.0$_{\pm 1.0}$
+ SOFC	72.5$_{\pm 0.9}$	65.8$_{\pm 0.7}$	68.1$_{\pm 0.7}$	61.1$_{\pm 0.7}$
+ MSPT	**73.9**$_{\pm 0.4}$	**67.4**$_{\pm 0.4}$	**68.7**$_{\pm 0.7}$	**63.7**$_{\pm 0.7}$
SOFC-Exp	71.3$_{\pm 0.6}$	62.8$_{\pm 2.1}$	66.9$_{\pm 1.6}$	59.8$_{\pm 1.5}$
+ MuLMS	**72.3**$_{\pm 0.5}$	**64.3**$_{\pm 3.7}$	**68.7**$_{\pm 1.5}$	**60.9**$_{\pm 3.6}$
+ MSPT	**72.3**$_{\pm 0.9}$	63.1$_{\pm 2.6}$	67.6$_{\pm 2.0}$	60.8$_{\pm 4.3}$
MSPT	84.2$_{\pm 0.6}$	82.5$_{\pm 0.7}$	84.6$_{\pm 0.8}$	83.0$_{\pm 0.8}$
+ MuLMS	**85.3**$_{\pm 0.2}$	**83.4**$_{\pm 0.8}$	**85.6**$_{\pm 0.4}$	**84.1**$_{\pm 0.6}$
+ SOFC	83.7$_{\pm 1.4}$	81.8$_{\pm 1.4}$	84.7$_{\pm 1.1}$	83.2$_{\pm 1.4}$

Table 12: Relation extraction multi-tasking results using MatSciBERT-based parser.

requirement that the boundaries of start/end spans of a predicted relation must also exactly match those of the respective gold spans. Prediction accuracy drops substantially: to micro-F1 scores of 42.5 and 36.5 on dev and test, respectively, corresponding to macro-F1 scores of 37.9 and 32.8. The reason for this is error propagation as relations can only be retrieved if the entities are predicted correctly, and as incorrectly labeled entities can mislead the relation classifier.

5.4 Multi-Task Learning Across Datasets

To find out whether information extraction accuracy can be increased by employing multi-task learning (MTL), we perform a series of experiments in which we combine MuLMS training data with NE and relation data from other materials science datasets, namely the SOFC-Exp and MSPT corpora (see Sec. 2).[5] In all experiments, we use a shared MatSciBERT and one classification head for each task (dataset). When reporting results on MuLMS, we use the same setup as before, but add the complete training sets of SOFC-Exp or MSPT during training. When reporting results on SOFC and MSPT, we train on all of their training data and the complete training data of MuLMS and perform early stopping on dev. For these experiments, reported scores are averages over 5 runs with different random seeds.

For **NER** (Table 11), we do not observe overall improvements. We hypothesize that this is because in SOFC-Exp, NE types are much coarser-grained, and in MSPT, NE annotations are focused on synthesis procedure paragraphs only. Nevertheless, as can be seen by the per-label scores in Appendix E, average scores on MuLMS are mainly hurt by decreases on SAMPLE, while scores for RANGE increase considerably by up to 3.9%.

[5]We removed one document from the test split of the SOFC-Exp corpus that is also part of the train set of MuLMS.

Results for MTL for **relations** are shown in Table 12. We observe that adding MuLMS to the training data of both SOFC-Exp and MSPT results in improvements. Incorporating SOFC-Exp instances in the training does not meaningfully increase prediction accuracy on MuLMS, whereas incorporating instances from MSPT leads to modest improvements. Intuitively, this makes sense: relations in SOFC-Exp focus on a specific type of experiment, while MuLMS covers a broader range of measurements. Similarly, some MuLMS relations bear resemblance to MSPT relations (e.g., those dealing with instruments or apparatus), which explains why training jointly is beneficial.

6 Conclusion and Outlook

In this resource paper, we have presented a new large-scale dataset of 50 scientific articles in the domain of materials science *exhaustively* annotated with named entity mentions, relations, and measurement-related frames. Our inter-annotator agreement study shows good agreement for most decisions. Our experiments with state-of-the-art neural models highlight that most distinctions can be learned with good accuracy, and that synergies can be achieved by training jointly with existing more specific materials-science NLP datasets.

Future work is needed to improve on end-to-end or joint models of NER and relation extraction as our experiments showed that a pipeline-based setting suffers from error propagation. A potential next step is to adapt sequence-to-sequence models to the structure induction tasks of MuLMS, following ideas of (Hsu et al., 2022; Lu et al., 2021). Finally, employing data augmentation techniques in particular for the less frequent relation types is a viable path for future work.

Limitations

As discussed in Sec. 3.4, we expect our inter-annotator agreement scores to underestimate the reproducibility of the task. It is, unfortunately, not trivial to find annotators with the required background knowledge. Hence, scores reflect agreement after only an initial very brief training phase, but nevertheless (in our opinion) give useful insights on the relative difficulty of the labeling decisions.

In our relation extraction experiments, we use label embeddings based on either gold or predicted entity labels (depending on the experimental setup) as an input to our system. Providing gold entity label information in particular constitutes a setting that is considerably easier for a relation classifier than providing no label information. Using predicted entity mention and labels showed to suffer from error propagation. In future work, it may be interesting to evaluate the performance of a relation extraction system that is not given label information, or that predicts entity labels jointly with relations.

Ethical Considerations

The annotators participating in our project were completely aware of the goal of the annotations and even helped designing the annotation scheme. They gave explicit consent to the publication of their annotations. The main annotator was paid considerably above our country's minimum wage.

References

Beatrice Alex, Barry Haddow, and Claire Grover. 2007. Recognising nested named entities in biomedical text. In *Biological, translational, and clinical language processing*, pages 65–72, Prague, Czech Republic. Association for Computational Linguistics.

Iz Beltagy, Arman Cohan, Guy Feigenblat, Dayne Freitag, Tirthankar Ghosal, Keith Hall, Drahomira Herrmannova, Petr Knoth, Kyle Lo, Philipp Mayr, Robert M. Patton, Michal Shmueli-Scheuer, Anita de Waard, Kuansan Wang, and Lucy Lu Wang, editors. 2021. *Proceedings of the Second Workshop on Scholarly Document Processing*. Association for Computational Linguistics, Online.

Iz Beltagy, Kyle Lo, and Arman Cohan. 2019. SciBERT: A pretrained language model for scientific text. In *Proceedings of the 2019 Conference on Empirical Methods in Natural Language Processing and the 9th International Joint Conference on Natural Language Processing (EMNLP-IJCNLP)*, pages 3615–3620, Hong Kong, China. Association for Computational Linguistics.

Alex Brandsen, Suzan Verberne, Milco Wansleeben, and Karsten Lambers. 2020. Creating a dataset for named entity recognition in the archaeology domain. In *Proceedings of the Twelfth Language Resources and Evaluation Conference*, pages 4573–4577, Marseille, France. European Language Resources Association.

Muthu Kumar Chandrasekaran, Anita de Waard, Guy Feigenblat, Dayne Freitag, Tirthankar Ghosal, Eduard Hovy, Petr Knoth, David Konopnicki, Philipp Mayr, Robert M. Patton, and Michal Shmueli-Scheuer, editors. 2020. *Proceedings of the First Workshop on Scholarly Document Processing*. Association for Computational Linguistics, Online.

Arman Cohan, Guy Feigenblat, Dayne Freitag, Tirthankar Ghosal, Drahomira Herrmannova, Petr Knoth, Kyle Lo, Philipp Mayr, Michal Shmueli-Scheuer, Anita de Waard, and Lucy Lu Wang, editors. 2022. *Proceedings of the Third Workshop on Scholarly Document Processing*. Association for Computational Linguistics, Gyeongju, Republic of Korea.

Jacob Cohen. 1960. A coefficient of agreement for nominal scales. *Educational and Psychological Measurement*, 20(1):37–46.

Kevin B. Cohen, Dina Demner-Fushman, Sophia Ananiadou, Bonnie Webber, Jun'ichi Tsujii, and John Pestian, editors. 2012. *BioNLP: Proceedings of the 2012 Workshop on Biomedical Natural Language Processing*. Association for Computational Linguistics, Montréal, Canada.

Nigel Collier, Patrick Ruch, and Adeline Nazarenko, editors. 2004. *Proceedings of the International Joint Workshop on Natural Language Processing in Biomedicine and its Applications, NLPBA/BioNLP 2004, Geneva, Switzerland, August 28-29, 2004.*

Dina Demner-Fushman, Kevin Bretonnel Cohen, Sophia Ananiadou, and Junichi Tsujii, editors. 2022. *Proceedings of the 21st Workshop on Biomedical Language Processing*. Association for Computational Linguistics, Dublin, Ireland.

Jacob Devlin, Ming-Wei Chang, Kenton Lee, and Kristina Toutanova. 2019. BERT: Pre-training of deep bidirectional transformers for language understanding. In *Proceedings of the 2019 Conference of the North American Chapter of the Association for Computational Linguistics: Human Language Technologies, Volume 1 (Long and Short Papers)*, pages 4171–4186, Minneapolis, Minnesota. Association for Computational Linguistics.

Timothy Dozat and Christopher D. Manning. 2017. Deep biaffine attention for neural dependency parsing. In *International Conference on Learning Representations*.

Timothy Dozat and Christopher D. Manning. 2018. Simpler but more accurate semantic dependency parsing. In *Proceedings of the 56th Annual Meeting of the Association for Computational Linguistics (Volume 2: Short Papers)*, pages 484–490, Melbourne, Australia. Association for Computational Linguistics.

Charles J Fillmore and Collin F Baker. 2001. Frame semantics for text understanding. In *Proceedings of WordNet and Other Lexical Resources Workshop, NAACL*, volume 6.

Annemarie Friedrich, Heike Adel, Federico Tomazic, Johannes Hingerl, Renou Benteau, Anika Marusczyk, and Lukas Lange. 2020. The SOFC-exp corpus and neural approaches to information extraction in the materials science domain. In *Proceedings of the 58th Annual Meeting of the Association for Computational Linguistics*, pages 1255–1268, Online. Association for Computational Linguistics.

Stefan Grünewald, Annemarie Friedrich, and Jonas Kuhn. 2021a. Applying occam's razor to transformer-based dependency parsing: What works, what doesn't, and what is really necessary. In *Proceedings of the 17th International Conference on Parsing Technologies and the IWPT 2021 Shared Task on Parsing into Enhanced Universal Dependencies (IWPT 2021)*, pages 131–144, Online. Association for Computational Linguistics.

Stefan Grünewald, Frederik Tobias Oertel, and Annemarie Friedrich. 2021b. RobertNLP at the IWPT 2021 shared task: Simple enhanced UD parsing for 17 languages. In *Proceedings of the 17th International Conference on Parsing Technologies and the IWPT 2021 Shared Task on Parsing into Enhanced Universal Dependencies (IWPT 2021)*, pages 196–203, Online. Association for Computational Linguistics.

Tanishq Gupta, Mohd Zaki, N. M. Anoop Krishnan, and Mausam. 2022. MatSciBERT: A materials domain language model for text mining and information extraction. *npj Computational Materials*, 8(1):102.

Luheng He, Kenton Lee, Omer Levy, and Luke Zettlemoyer. 2018. Jointly predicting predicates and arguments in neural semantic role labeling. In *Proceedings of the 56th Annual Meeting of the Association for Computational Linguistics (Volume 2: Short Papers)*, pages 364–369, Melbourne, Australia. Association for Computational Linguistics.

George Hripcsak and Adam S Rothschild. 2005. Agreement, the f-measure, and reliability in information retrieval. *Journal of the American medical informatics association*, 12(3):296–298.

I-Hung Hsu, Kuan-Hao Huang, Elizabeth Boschee, Scott Miller, Prem Natarajan, Kai-Wei Chang, and Nanyun Peng. 2022. DEGREE: A data-efficient generation-based event extraction model. In *Proceedings of the 2022 Conference of the North American Chapter of the Association for Computational Linguistics: Human Language Technologies*, pages 1890–1908, Seattle, United States. Association for Computational Linguistics.

Kung-Hsiang Huang, Mu Yang, and Nanyun Peng. 2020. Biomedical event extraction with hierarchical knowledge graphs. In *Findings of the Association for Computational Linguistics: EMNLP 2020*, pages 1277–1285, Online. Association for Computational Linguistics.

Zhiheng Huang, Wei Xu, and Kai Yu. 2015. Bidirectional LSTM-CRF models for sequence tagging. In *CorRR*, volume abs/1508.01991.

Jan-Christoph Klie, Michael Bugert, Beto Boullosa, Richard Eckart de Castilho, and Iryna Gurevych. 2018. The INCEpTION platform: Machine-assisted and knowledge-oriented interactive annotation. In *Proceedings of the 27th International Conference on Computational Linguistics: System Demonstrations*, pages 5–9, Santa Fe, New Mexico. Association for Computational Linguistics.

Dan Kondratyuk and Milan Straka. 2019. 75 languages, 1 model: Parsing Universal Dependencies universally. In *Proceedings of the 2019 Conference on Empirical Methods in Natural Language Processing and the 9th International Joint Conference on Natural Language Processing (EMNLP-IJCNLP)*, pages 2779–2795, Hong Kong, China. Association for Computational Linguistics.

Klaus Krippendorff. 1989. Content analysis.

John D. Lafferty, Andrew McCallum, and Fernando C. N. Pereira. 2001. Conditional random fields: Probabilistic models for segmenting and labeling sequence data. In *Proceedings of the Eighteenth International Conference on Machine Learning (ICML 2001), Williams College, Williamstown, MA, USA, June 28 - July 1, 2001*, pages 282–289. Morgan Kaufmann.

J Richard Landis and Gary G Koch. 1977. An application of hierarchical kappa-type statistics in the assessment of majority agreement among multiple observers. *Biometrics*, pages 363–374.

Ilya Loshchilov and Frank Hutter. 2019. Decoupled weight decay regularization.

Yaojie Lu, Hongyu Lin, Jin Xu, Xianpei Han, Jialong Tang, Annan Li, Le Sun, Meng Liao, and Shaoyi Chen. 2021. Text2Event: Controllable sequence-to-structure generation for end-to-end event extraction. In *Proceedings of the 59th Annual Meeting of the Association for Computational Linguistics and the 11th International Joint Conference on Natural Language Processing (Volume 1: Long Papers)*, pages 2795–2806, Online. Association for Computational Linguistics.

Diego Marcheggiani and Ivan Titov. 2020. Graph convolutions over constituent trees for syntax-aware semantic role labeling. In *Proceedings of the 2020 Conference on Empirical Methods in Natural Language*

Processing (EMNLP), pages 3915–3928, Online. Association for Computational Linguistics.

Sheshera Mysore, Zachary Jensen, Edward Kim, Kevin Huang, Haw-Shiuan Chang, Emma Strubell, Jeffrey Flanigan, Andrew McCallum, and Elsa Olivetti. 2019. The materials science procedural text corpus: Annotating materials synthesis procedures with shallow semantic structures. In *Proceedings of the 13th Linguistic Annotation Workshop*, pages 56–64, Florence, Italy. Association for Computational Linguistics.

Sheshera Mysore, Edward Kim, Emma Strubell, Ao Liu, Haw-Shiuan Chang, Srikrishna Kompella, Kevin Huang, Andrew McCallum, and Elsa Olivetti. 2017. Automatically extracting action graphs from materials science synthesis procedures. *NIPS Workshop on Machine Learning for Molecules and Materials.*

Tim O'Gorman, Zach Jensen, Sheshera Mysore, Kevin Huang, Rubayyat Mahbub, Elsa Olivetti, and Andrew McCallum. 2021. MS-mentions: Consistently annotating entity mentions in materials science procedural text. In *Proceedings of the 2021 Conference on Empirical Methods in Natural Language Processing*, pages 1337–1352, Online and Punta Cana, Dominican Republic. Association for Computational Linguistics.

Alan Ramponi, Barbara Plank, and Rosario Lombardo. 2020. Cross-domain evaluation of edge detection for biomedical event extraction. In *Proceedings of the Twelfth Language Resources and Evaluation Conference*, pages 1982–1989, Marseille, France. European Language Resources Association.

Mourad Sarrouti, Carson Tao, and Yoann Mamy Randriamihaja. 2022. Comparing encoder-only and encoder-decoder transformers for relation extraction from biomedical texts: An empirical study on ten benchmark datasets. In *Proceedings of the 21st Workshop on Biomedical Language Processing*, pages 376–382, Dublin, Ireland. Association for Computational Linguistics.

Daivik Swarup, Ahsaas Bajaj, Sheshera Mysore, Tim O'Gorman, Rajarshi Das, and Andrew McCallum. 2020. An Instance Level Approach for Shallow Semantic Parsing in Scientific Procedural Text. In *Findings of the Association for Computational Linguistics: EMNLP 2020*, pages 3010–3017, Online. Association for Computational Linguistics.

Shubham Toshniwal, Haoyue Shi, Bowen Shi, Lingyu Gao, Karen Livescu, and Kevin Gimpel. 2020. A cross-task analysis of text span representations. In *Proceedings of the 5th Workshop on Representation Learning for NLP*, pages 166–176, Online. Association for Computational Linguistics.

Yoshimasa Tsuruoka and Jun'ichi Tsujii. 2005. Bidirectional inference with the easiest-first strategy for tagging sequence data. In *Proceedings of Human Language Technology Conference and Conference on Empirical Methods in Natural Language Processing*, pages 467–474, Vancouver, British Columbia, Canada. Association for Computational Linguistics.

Rob van der Goot. 2021. We need to talk about train-dev-test splits. In *Proceedings of the 2021 Conference on Empirical Methods in Natural Language Processing*, pages 4485–4494, Online and Punta Cana, Dominican Republic. Association for Computational Linguistics.

Ashish Vaswani, Noam Shazeer, Niki Parmar, Jakob Uszkoreit, Llion Jones, Aidan N. Gomez, Lukasz Kaiser, and Illia Polosukhin. 2017. Attention is all you need.

Kyosuke Yamaguchi, Ryoji Asahi, and Yutaka Sasaki. 2020. SC-CoMIcs: A superconductivity corpus for materials informatics. In *Proceedings of the Twelfth Language Resources and Evaluation Conference*, pages 6753–6760, Marseille, France. European Language Resources Association.

Juntao Yu, Bernd Bohnet, and Massimo Poesio. 2020. Named entity recognition as dependency parsing. In *Proceedings of the 58th Annual Meeting of the Association for Computational Linguistics*, pages 6470–6476, Online. Association for Computational Linguistics.

Appendix

A Hyperparameters

We use AdamW (Loshchilov and Hutter, 2019) as optimizer for all our models. We use an inverse square-root learning rate scheduler similar to the one used by Vaswani et al. (2017) where ws refers to the number of warmup steps:

$$lr = \sqrt{ws} \cdot \min(\frac{1}{\sqrt{step\_num}}, step\_num \cdot ws^{-1.5})$$

For our measurement identification experiments, we downsample the amount of non-measurement sentences since they represent the majority in the training data. We tune this downsampling rate per model since each BERT variant has been shown to prefer a slightly different one. We apply early stopping after 3 epochs without improvement in terms of F1.

Our NER sequence tagging models are trained with two separate learning rates; one for BERT + linear output layer and another one for the CRF output layer. Both learning rates are reported in the respective column of Table 13. We train for 60-100 epochs, depending on the size of the combined dataset, and take the model with the best evaluation score during this period.

For relation extraction, we use a base learning rate of 4e-5 for all experiments, which we found

Model	LM	LR
CRF	BERT	1e-4/7e-3
	SciBERT	5e-5/7e-3
	MatSciBERT	1e-4/7e-3
Dep. Pars.	BERT	2e-4
	SciBERT	9e-5
	MatSciBERT	3e-4

Table 13: **Hyperparameters:** Learning rates for NER models.

to perform best in preliminary experiments. We employ early stopping with a patience of 15 epochs for all experiments.

Our models are trained with Nvidia A100 and V100 GPUs using the PyTorch framework.

B Details on Biaffine Parser Architecture

We here describe the biaffine parser architecture used to predict relations between named entities. Taking as input the NE embeddings described in Sec. 4.4, head and dependent representations for the i'th NE are computed via two single-layer feed-forward neural networks:

$$\mathbf{h}_i^{head} = \text{FNN}^{head}(\mathbf{e}_i)$$
$$\mathbf{h}_i^{dep} = \text{FNN}^{dep}(\mathbf{e}_i)$$

These representations are then fed to a biaffine classifier that maps head–dependent pairs onto logit vectors $s_{i,j}$ whose dimensionality corresponds to the inventory of relation labels. Using the softmax operation, these scores are transformed into probability distributions $P(y_{i,j})$ over relation labels:

$$\text{Biaff}(\mathbf{x}_1, \mathbf{x}_2) = \mathbf{x}_1^\top \mathbf{U}\mathbf{x}_2 + W(\mathbf{x}_1 \oplus \mathbf{x}_2) + \mathbf{b}$$
$$\mathbf{s}_{i,j} = \text{Biaff}(\mathbf{h}_i^{head}, \mathbf{h}_j^{dep})$$
$$P(y_{i,j}) = \text{softmax}(\mathbf{s}_{i,j})$$

The predicted relation for a pair of named entities is the one receiving the highest probability (which may be $\varnothing$, i.e., no relation).

Token embeddings. The token embeddings $\mathbf{e}_{i,\text{START}}$ and $\mathbf{e}_{i,\text{END}}$, which form part of the NE embeddings $\mathbf{e}_i$, are computed as a learned scalar mixture of BERT layers as described by Kondratyuk and Straka (2019).

C Detailed Corpus Statistics

Table 14 shows the NE counts in MuLMS by datasplit.

Table 15 and Table 16 show the detailed counts for our inter-annotator agreement study.

Choice of agreement metrics for evaluating agreement on named entity annotations. The task of identifying and labeling NE mentions is a sequence labeling task, hence, κ is not applicable. Brandsen et al. (2020) provide a good explanation of why this is the case in their section 5.1. Using unitizing α_U is an option, but there is no standard implementation or interpretation for NE annotations in the NLP community, and it does not work for overlapping annotations (which we have in our dataset). We opted for using precision and recall, which are intuitively interpretable (*How many of the instances of one type marked by one annotator have also been marked by the respective other annotator?*). Hripcsak and Rothschild (2005) convincingly argue (with a very simple proof) that for sequence labeling tasks such as NEs, F1 actually approaches κ.

Label	total	train	dev	test
MAT	15596	10875	2318	2403
NUM	6081	4142	1077	862
VALUE	4852	3266	895	691
UNIT	4330	2880	789	661
PROPERTY	3925	2867	598	460
FORM	3568	2716	345	507
MEASUREMENT	2171	1531	345	295
CITE	1709	1280	274	155
SAMPLE	1461	1031	249	181
TECHNIQUE	1036	755	146	135
DEV	808	459	235	114
RANGE	736	546	105	85
INSTRUMENT	378	278	50	50

Table 14: Label counts for **named entities** in MuLMS.

D SOFC-Exp and MSPT Corpora

In Sec. 5.4, we perform several multi-task learning (MTL) experiments with MuLMS and two additional NLP datasets in the materials science domain, SOFC-Exp (Friedrich et al., 2020) and MSTP (Mysore et al., 2019). We here describe them briefly.

There are 4 named entities in the SOFC-Exp corpus: MATERIAL, which refers to mentions of materials or chemical formulas, VALUE, which denotes numerical values and their corresponding physical unit, DEVICE, which marks device types used in an experiment, and EXPERIMENT, which indicates frame evoking words. Furthermore, there are 16 distinct slots that are modeled as relations between experiment frame evoking word and cor-

Label	P	R	matches exact	matches relaxed	# A1	# A2
MAT	96.7	91.2	144	145	150	159
NUM	98.9	100.0	86	86	87	86
VALUE	100.0	100.0	53	54	54	54
UNIT	97.9	100.0	47	47	48	47
PROPERTY	42.6	37.7	21	29	68	77
FORM	95.7	86.3	44	44	46	51
MEAS.	44.6	51.0	17	25	56	49
CITE	97.4	97.4	38	38	39	39
SAMPLE	3.1	12.5	1	1	32	8
TECHNIQUE	77.5	59.6	25	31	40	52
DEV	96.0	82.8	18	24	25	29
RANGE	100.0	100.0	24	25	25	25
INSTRUMENT	80.0	76.9	18	20	25	26

Table 15: Inter-annotator agreement: **named entities**. Precision and recall computed from relaxed matches.

Label	P	R	matches	# A1	# A2
propertyValue	81.2	81.2	26	32	32
usedIn	40.0	52.2	12	30	23
hasForm	54.7	71.4	35	64	49
measuresProperty	80.5	72.9	70	87	96
conditionProperty	27.7	59.1	13	47	22
conditionEnvironment	0.0	0.0	0	19	4
usedTogether	13.8	28.6	4	29	14
conditionSampleFeatures	43.1	40.0	22	51	55
usesTechnique	72.9	67.3	35	48	52
takenFrom	33.3	63.6	7	21	11
dopedBy	35.3	50.0	6	17	12
conditionInstrument	24.0	60.0	6	25	10
usedAs	23.5	85.7	12	51	14

Table 16: Inter-annotator agreement for **relations**.

responding entity. Table 17 shows the counts for these relations. These counts are not equal to the ones reported by Friedrich et al. (2020) since we have to remove relations that span across multiple sentences as this case cannot be handled by our relation extraction pipeline.

The MSPT corpus introduces additional the 21 entities:

- PROPERTY-MISC
- PROPERTY-UNIT
- NUMBER
- CHARACTERIZATION-APPARATUS
- APPARATUS-UNIT
- CONDITION-MISC
- META
- SYNTHESIS-APPARATUS
- OPERATION
- AMOUNT-MISC

Label	train	dev	test
AnodeMaterial	220	32	26
CathodeMaterial	173	71	37
Conductivity	36	19	23
CurrentDensity	59	6	17
DegradationRate	15	4	1
Device	311	59	109
ElectrolyteMaterial	187	22	120
FuelUsed	124	28	40
InterlayerMaterial	34	17	6
OpenCircuitVoltage	41	3	25
PowerDensity	138	24	70
Resistance	118	15	57
SupportMaterial	88	13	2
TimeOfOperation	42	3	12
Voltage	30	3	14
WorkingTemperature	330	63	138

Table 17: SOFC-Exp relation counts in our setup.

- AMOUNT-UNIT
- REFERENCE
- PROPERTY-TYPE
- MATERIAL
- MATERIAL-DESCRIPTOR
- APPARATUS-DESCRIPTOR
- APPARATUS-PROPERTY-TYPE
- CONDITION-UNIT
- NONRECIPE-MATERIAL
- CONDITION-TYPE
- BRAND

Table 18 lists the counts of the 14 relations of the MSPT dataset that we use in our MTL experiments.

Label	train	dev	test
Recipe-target	270	53	92
Solvent-material	352	61	107
Atmospheric-material	144	25	35
Recipe-precursor	654	152	199
Participant-material	1315	236	400
Apparatus-of	358	56	93
Condition-of	1378	232	415
Descriptor-of	1157	193	333
Number-of	2114	422	663
Amount-of	1099	244	376
Apparatus-attr-of	66	56	24
Brand-of	326	83	91
Core-of	177	23	89
Next-operation	1311	233	391

Table 18: MSPT relation counts in our setup.

E Detailed Experimental Results

This appendix provides further details on our experimental results. Table 26 depicts the results for identifying sentences containing MEASUREMENT or QUAL_MEAS annotations.

NER. Table 19 and Table 20 report F1 for NER on MuLMS per label. Table 21 gives per-label scores for NER in our MTL experiments. Table 22 and Table 23 provide per-label scores for the SOFC-Exp corpus and MSPT corpus in a single-task setting as well as in a multi-task setting with MuLMS added to the training.

Relation extraction. Table 27 lists per-relation scores when using gold NEs or when using predicted NEs for relation extraction, as well as per-relation scores for the majority baseline. Table 25 shows relation extraction scores per label for both dev and test. Table 24 shows overall results for predicted entities on dev and test.

Label	P	R	F1
MAT	83.6 ±1.3	82.2 ±1.2	82.8 ±0.8
NUM	94.9 ±0.6	94.8 ±1.0	94.9 ±0.7
VALUE	89.4 ±0.6	87.0 ±1.2	88.2 ±0.9
UNIT	94.2 ±0.4	90.4 ±1.1	92.3 ±0.6
PROPERTY	49.8 ±3.0	53.0 ±4.5	51.1 ±1.4
CITE	88.6 ±0.8	87.7 ±2.0	88.2 ±1.3
TECHNIQUE	49.6 ±3.4	51.1 ±5.6	50.1 ±2.9
RANGE	70.3 ±5.8	74.8 ±3.5	72.3 ±3.0
INSTRUMENT	46.7 ±2.7	44.8 ±3.5	45.6 ±2.0
SAMPLE	72.5 ±10.2	36.7 ±6.2	47.9 ±4.1
FORM	66.5 ±3.0	71.4 ±1.9	68.9 ±2.5
DEVICE	82.6 ±2.0	74.9 ±2.5	78.6 ±1.9
MEASUREMENT	61.6 ±2.1	55.3 ±3.0	58.2 ±0.8

Table 19: Per label scores for NER using BILOU tagging and MatSciBERT.

Label	CRF-Tagger	Dep. Parser
MAT	**82.8**$\pm$0.8	80.0$\pm$0.4
NUM	**94.9**$\pm$0.7	94.2$\pm$0.4
VALUE	**88.2**$\pm$0.9	82.7$\pm$1.1
UNIT	**92.3**$\pm$0.6	90.8$\pm$0.7
PROPERTY	51.1$\pm$1.4	**51.7**$\pm$2.0
CITE	**88.2**$\pm$1.3	85.7$\pm$1.5
TECHNIQUE	50.1$\pm$2.9	**51.4**$\pm$2.4
RANGE	**72.3**$\pm$3.0	66.4$\pm$4.0
INSTRUMENT	**45.6**$\pm$2.0	44.1$\pm$3.3
SAMPLE	**47.9**$\pm$4.1	29.4$\pm$18.1
FORM	**68.9**$\pm$2.5	67.6$\pm$1.1
DEVICE	**78.6**$\pm$1.9	76.4$\pm$2.2
MEASUREMENT	58.2$\pm$0.8	**58.7**$\pm$0.7

Table 20: **Per-Label NER** results on test in terms of **F1** (using MatSciBERT).

Label	Single-Task	+ SOFC	+ MSPT
MAT	**82.8**	82.3	82.3
NUM	94.9	**95.6**	**95.6**
VALUE	**88.2**	88.1	**88.2**
UNIT	92.3	92.1	**92.6**
PROPERTY	**51.1**	49.4	50.8
CITE	**88.2**	88.1	87.8
TECHNIQUE	50.1	**52.9**	50.0
RANGE	72.3	**76.2**	75.2
INSTRUMENT	45.6	**45.9**	42.8
SAMPLE	**47.9**	38.3	45.8
FORM	68.9	**69.9**	64.9
DEVICE	**78.6**	77.9	76.3
MEASUREMENT	**58.2**	57.8	56.9

Table 21: **Per-Label NER** results for MuLMS on test in terms of **F1** for single-task and multi-task MatSciBERT taggers.

Label	Single-Task	+ MuLMS
MATERIAL	**75.8**	73.2
EXPERIMENT	**81.7**	81.2
VALUE	**93.9**	92.0
DEVICE	**72.6**	72.0

Table 22: **Per-Label Named Entity Recognition** results for SOFC-Exp on test in terms of **F1** using single-task and multi-task MatSciBERT taggers.

Label	ST	+ MuLMS
META	**47.5**	46.3
PROPERTY-MISC	32.8	**34.7**
SYNTHESIS-APPARATUS	**68.7**	66.7
OPERATION	**85.0**	84.9
PROPERTY-UNIT	42.3	**44.5**
AMOUNT-MISC	**41.4**	26.0
NUMBER	94.8	**95.5**
AMOUNT-UNIT	**95.5**	95.0
REFERENCE	**70.9**	67.7
PROPERTY-TYPE	**24.6**	19.0
MATERIAL	**84.1**	81.6
MATERIAL-DESCRIPTOR	**67.8**	63.7
CHARACTERIZATION-APPARATUS	16.2	**28.8**
APPARATUS-UNIT	57.8	**61.5**
APPARATUS-DESCRIPTOR	**67.0**	65.1
APPARATUS-PROPERTY-TYPE	0.0	0.0
CONDITION-MISC	72.3	**73.5**
CONDITION-UNIT	**95.2**	94.3
NONRECIPE-MATERIAL	**62.3**	59.6
CONDITION-TYPE	**15.7**	12.8
BRAND	**71.1**	64.0

Table 23: **Per-Label Named Entity Recognition** results for MSPT on test in terms of **F1** using single-task (ST) and multi-task MatSciBERT taggers.

	micro F1	macro F1
dev	$42.5_{\pm 1.0}$	$37.9_{\pm 1.7}$
test	$36.5_{\pm 0.9}$	$32.8_{\pm 1.2}$

Table 24: Relation extraction results in terms of **F1**, predicted named entities (including standard deviation over five folds).

Label	dev	test
hasForm	$71.3_{\pm 0.8}$	$76.1_{\pm 0.5}$
measuresProperty	$88.0_{\pm 1.0}$	$83.1_{\pm 0.8}$
measuresPropertyValue	$84.1_{\pm 2.2}$	$73.8_{\pm 1.0}$
usedAs	$50.2_{\pm 2.3}$	$41.8_{\pm 1.9}$
conditionProperty	$83.0_{\pm 1.3}$	$72.3_{\pm 1.0}$
conditionPropertyValue	$74.7_{\pm 2.5}$	$63.2_{\pm 2.5}$
conditionSampleFeatures	$67.6_{\pm 0.9}$	$66.0_{\pm 2.1}$
usesTechnique	$94.6_{\pm 0.6}$	$91.0_{\pm 0.9}$
conditionEnvironment	$57.1_{\pm 6.2}$	$39.0_{\pm 3.0}$
propertyValue	$86.7_{\pm 1.3}$	$82.5_{\pm 2.1}$
usedIn	$49.3_{\pm 5.6}$	$37.9_{\pm 3.7}$
conditionInstrument	$98.2_{\pm 0.8}$	$92.2_{\pm 0.9}$
dopedBy	$0.0_{\pm 0.0}$	$22.7_{\pm 18.7}$
takenFrom	$85.5_{\pm 3.7}$	$84.7_{\pm 3.6}$
usedTogether	$7.5_{\pm 2.0}$	$4.0_{\pm 1.7}$
Macro-avg.	$66.5_{\pm 1.1}$	$62.0_{\pm 1.0}$
Micro-avg.	$73.2_{\pm 1.0}$	$67.6_{\pm 1.0}$

Table 25: Per-label F1 scores for relation extraction using MatSciBERT (gold named entities).

LM	Label	dev P	dev R	dev F1	test P	test R	test F1
BERT	MEASUREMENT	**71.5**±1.9	67.1±3.0	69.2±1.3	**74.1**±3.1	71.4±5.6	72.5±2.1
	QUAL_MEAS	45.6±2.8	61.4±3.7	52.2±2.1	49.9±3.1	51.6±3.2	50.6±0.7
	2-Class Macro Avg.	58.5±2.0	64.3±2.8	60.7±1.3	**62.0**±3.0	61.5±3.7	61.5±1.2
SciBERT	MEASUREMENT	69.1±1.9	77.6±1.5	73.1±0.4	71.1±2.0	79.5±1.6	**75.0**±0.7
	QUAL_MEAS	**54.0**±1.7	66.3±5.0	**59.4**±1.9	52.7±0.5	52.8±3.2	52.7±1.4
	2-Class Macro Avg.	**61.5**±1.2	72.0±2.8	**66.2**±1.0	61.9±0.9	66.2±1.8	63.9±0.6
MatSciBERT	MEASUREMENT	69.4±2.6	**77.9**±4.0	**73.2**±0.7	70.6±2.2	**80.1**±3.5	74.9±0.6
	QUAL_MEAS	51.4±1.4	**67.0**±1.6	58.2±1.1	**52.8**±0.8	**56.9**±2.6	**54.7**±1.0
	2-Class Macro Avg.	60.4±1.9	**72.4**±2.0	65.7±0.4	61.7±1.0	**68.5**±2.4	**64.8**±0.7
human agreement	MEASUREMENT			*74.2*			*74.2*
	QUAL_MEAS			*61.7*			*61.7*

Table 26: Ternary sentence classification results for identifying sentences containing MEASUREMENT or QUAL_MEAS annotations vs. NONE. Human agreement is only suitable for a rough comparison because it is estimated on a subset of the data.

Label	Gold Entities P	Gold Entities R	Gold Entities F1	Predicted Entities P	Predicted Entities R	Predicted Entities F1	Majority Baseline P	Majority Baseline R	Majority Baseline F1
hasForm	74.0 ±1.8	78.5 ±1.1	76.1 ±0.5	54.2 ±3.6	55.5 ±1.6	54.8 ±2.3	0.0	0.0	0.0
measuresProperty	80.2 ±1.1	86.3 ±2.2	83.1 ±0.8	39.3 ±2.8	36.6 ±2.2	37.8 ±1.4	50.5	99.6	67.0
measuresPropertyValue	68.6 ±1.9	80.0 ±1.5	73.8 ±1.0	41.5 ±4.1	38.3 ±4.8	39.7 ±3.6	0.0	0.0	0.0
usedAs	49.2 ±2.8	36.5 ±2.2	41.8 ±1.9	30.1 ±4.6	19.1 ±3.0	23.2 ±3.4	0.0	0.0	0.0
conditionProperty	65.3 ±2.1	81.2 ±2.5	72.3 ±1.0	29.0 ±3.6	27.4 ±2.6	27.9 ±1.8	0.0	0.0	0.0
conditionPropertyValue	51.3 ±3.0	82.4 ±3.3	63.2 ±2.5	26.7 ±2.8	42.5 ±2.7	32.7 ±2.4	27.2	100.0	42.7
conditionSampleFeatures	60.7 ±2.8	72.3 ±1.3	66.0 ±2.1	34.4 ±4.6	28.4 ±3.1	31.0 ±3.3	70.4	42.8	53.2
usesTechnique	87.1 ±1.1	95.2 ±1.3	91.0 ±0.9	44.7 ±1.6	37.9 ±2.7	41.0 ±1.8	81.8	100.0	90.0
conditionEnvironment	40.4 ±2.6	37.9 ±4.1	39.0 ±3.0	32.2 ±4.1	27.0 ±3.8	29.2 ±3.1	0.0	0.0	0.0
propertyValue	78.7 ±3.1	86.8 ±2.7	82.5 ±2.1	40.9 ±2.6	46.7 ±5.1	43.4 ±2.0	0.0	0.0	0.0
usedIn	42.5 ±4.9	35.6 ±7.6	37.9 ±3.7	18.6 ±7.1	14.2 ±3.6	15.9 ±4.8	0.0	0.0	0.0
conditionInstrument	93.4 ±0.1	91.1 ±1.6	92.2 ±0.9	38.6 ±1.9	36.6 ±3.7	37.5 ±2.5	90.4	100.0	94.9
dopedBy	26.7 ±22.6	20.0 ±16.3	22.7 ±18.7	20.0 ±40.0	6.7 ±13.3	10.0 ±20.0	0.0	0.0	0.0
takenFrom	75.3 ±5.1	96.9 ±3.8	84.7 ±3.6	67.8 ±7.8	61.5 ±6.9	64.0 ±4.6	46.4	100.0	63.4
usedTogether	9.6 ±3.5	2.5 ±1.1	4.0 ±1.7	9.6 ±4.0	2.4 ±1.1	3.8 ±1.7	0.0	0.0	0.0
Macro-avg.	60.2 ±0.8	65.5 ±1.6	62.0 ±1.0	35.2 ±2.7	32.0 ±1.6	32.8 ±1.2	24.4	36.1	27.4
Micro-avg.	66.8 ±1.7	68.4 ±0.4	67.6 ±1.0	38.6 ±2.3	34.7 ±1.3	36.5 ±0.9	50.5	29.5	37.2

Table 27: Per-label scores (MuLMS test set) for **relation extraction** using MatSciBERT. Majority baseline is computed on gold entities.

Label	MuLMS only			MuLMS + SOFC-Exp			MuLMS + MSPT		
	P	**R**	**F1**	**P**	**R**	**F1**	**P**	**R**	**F1**
hasForm	74.0 ±1.8	78.5 ±1.1	76.1 ±0.5	78.0 ±2.9	78.8 ±1.8	78.3 ±0.9	74.2 ±0.7	79.6 ±1.3	76.8 ±0.9
measuresProperty	80.2 ±1.1	86.3 ±2.2	83.1 ±0.8	79.0 ±1.1	87.1 ±0.9	82.8 ±0.4	78.8 ±1.2	86.6 ±1.3	82.5 ±0.3
measuresPropertyValue	68.6 ±1.9	80.0 ±1.5	73.8 ±1.0	68.9 ±3.5	82.7 ±2.2	75.1 ±2.0	70.3 ±0.7	82.1 ±3.1	75.7 ±1.5
usedAs	49.2 ±2.8	36.5 ±2.2	41.8 ±1.9	47.9 ±2.6	35.7 ±2.0	40.8 ±1.3	51.9 ±1.3	37.5 ±1.8	43.5 ±1.4
conditionProperty	65.3 ±2.1	81.2 ±2.5	72.3 ±1.0	67.4 ±2.5	82.1 ±2.5	73.9 ±0.8	66.1 ±1.9	80.3 ±2.2	72.5 ±1.6
conditionPropertyValue	51.3 ±3.0	82.4 ±3.3	63.2 ±2.5	53.7 ±4.2	77.8 ±4.3	63.3 ±2.0	51.1 ±2.6	78.5 ±3.1	61.8 ±2.1
conditionSampleFeatures	60.7 ±2.8	72.3 ±1.3	66.0 ±2.1	61.1 ±3.7	71.4 ±3.8	65.7 ±1.4	62.8 ±3.4	72.2 ±2.5	67.1 ±2.6
usesTechnique	87.1 ±1.1	95.2 ±1.3	91.0 ±0.9	85.6 ±0.8	97.1 ±1.0	91.0 ±0.3	87.2 ±1.1	95.7 ±0.8	91.2 ±0.6
conditionEnvironment	40.4 ±2.6	37.9 ±4.1	39.0 ±3.0	46.3 ±3.5	46.2 ±4.6	46.0 ±2.7	47.2 ±6.3	49.8 ±4.7	48.3 ±5.2
propertyValue	78.7 ±3.1	86.8 ±2.7	82.5 ±2.1	76.2 ±2.7	85.5 ±1.7	80.5 ±1.2	81.4 ±1.7	88.7 ±1.7	84.8 ±1.1
usedIn	42.5 ±4.9	35.6 ±7.6	37.9 ±3.7	45.5 ±7.0	47.6 ±5.7	45.9 ±3.7	41.8 ±4.9	40.4 ±5.5	40.5 ±1.4
conditionInstrument	93.4 ±0.1	91.1 ±1.6	92.2 ±0.9	93.6 ±0.1	93.2 ±0.9	93.4 ±0.5	93.5 ±0.1	91.9 ±1.6	92.7 ±0.9
dopedBy	26.7 ±22.6	20.0 ±16.3	22.7 ±18.7	0.0 ±0.0	0.0 ±0.0	0.0 ±0.0	28.3 ±16.3	26.7 ±13.3	27.0 ±14.0
takenFrom	75.3 ±5.1	96.9 ±3.8	84.7 ±3.6	61.7 ±7.5	98.5 ±3.1	75.6 ±5.7	77.0 ±8.6	98.5 ±3.1	86.2 ±6.2
usedTogether	9.6 ±3.5	2.5 ±1.1	4.0 ±1.7	8.8 ±3.3	2.2 ±0.8	3.5 ±1.2	12.0 ±7.2	3.6 ±3.4	5.4 ±4.8
Macro-avg.	60.2 ±0.8	65.5 ±1.6	62.0 ±1.0	58.2 ±1.5	65.7 ±1.1	61.1 ±0.7	61.6 ±0.9	67.5 ±1.0	63.7 ±0.7
Micro-avg.	66.8 ±1.7	68.4 ±0.4	67.6 ±1.0	67.4 ±1.9	68.9 ±1.2	68.1 ±0.7	68.0 ±1.1	69.5 ±0.5	68.7 ±0.7

Table 28: Per-label scores (MuLMS test set, gold entities) for **multi-task relation extraction**.

An End-to-End Pipeline for Bibliography Extraction from Scientific Articles

Bikash Joshi, Anthi Symeonidou, Syed Mazin Danish, Floris Hermsen
Elsevier

Abstract

We introduce a comprehensive end-to-end pipeline designed to extract complete bibliography section from English scientific articles in digital-born PDF format and further split them into individual citations. At the heart of our pipeline lies the utilization of Language-independent Layout Transformer (LiLT), a multimodal model that combines text and layout features to enhance the accuracy and robustness of bibliography extraction. By considering both text and visual structure, LiLT significantly improves the identification of bibliographic sections within scientific articles. To split the extracted full bibliography into individual citations, we employ a custom fine-tuned version of SciBERT, a Transformer-based model that excels at handling complex formatting variations common in scholarly bibliography.

Having such end-to-end pipeline in-house allows us to bypass reliance on third-party black box tools, such as GROBID, offering greater control and transparency in the bibliography extraction process. Another highlight of our pipeline is its extensibility, as it can be seamlessly adapted to multilingual and image-based PDFs, hence allowing its utility across a wide range of scholarly content. When evaluated on an in-house dataset of digital-born English PDF articles published at Elsevier, we achieved an F1-score of 94.6%, a notable 3.1% improvement over GROBID, which is a well-regarded tool for bibliography parsing in the industry.

1 Introduction

Scientific articles are an essential part of the scientific community. In the digital age, where millions of scientific articles are published every year, efficient extraction of header (title, author names, affiliations, abstract) and bibliography entities from unstructured data, can facilitate not only the searchability and discoverability of scientific work, which is beneficial for the researchers, but it also plays a role in the automation of academic workflows.

Although most scientific articles received by scientific publishers come in semi-structured format (MS Word), a significant proportion of scholarly articles still reside in PDF-based documents. The diverse formatting, layouts, and font styles found in PDF articles demand sophisticated techniques to accurately extract bibliographic information, such as citation details, from these unstructured documents.

By facilitating precise referencing and citation tracking, bibliography extraction aids in the credibility and impact assessment of published research, a critical aspect for publishing companies as they endeavor to maintain the integrity and relevance of the scientific literature they curate. Mature tools such as GROBID (GRO, 2008–2023), Cermine (Tkaczyk et al., 2015) and Neural ParsCit (Prasad et al., 2018a), provide various APIs for header and bibliography entities extraction with good results (Romary and Lopez, 2015; Lo et al., 2020). However, these tools face limitations in coping with scanned documents or multilingual content. Addressing these challenges requires a more tailored and fine-tuned solution.

Most traditional approaches to information extraction from PDF documents have primarily relied on text-based methods as evidenced in (Cioffi and Peroni, 2022; Matsuoka et al., 2016; Prasad et al., 2018b). Document layout analysis with Convolutional Neural Networks (CNNs), visual information extraction with Graph Neural Networks (GNNs) and the emergence of Transformer architecture, have shifted the necessity of many annotated data and improved the accuracy of document layout analysis tasks (Zhong et al., 2019; Qasim et al., 2019). However, with the advent of Document AI, there has been a notable shift towards multimodal approaches that seamlessly integrate both textual and layout features (Cui et al., 2021). One prominent example of such a multimodal approach is LayoutLM, along with its subsequent

Proceedings of the 2nd Workshop on Information Extraction from Scientific Publications, pages 101–106
Nov 1, 2023. ©2023 Association for Computational Linguistics

versions, LayoutLMv2 and LayoutLMv3. These models represent pre-trained Document Foundation Models that effectively merge Natural Language Processing (NLP) and Computer Vision (CV) technologies and substantially outperform several text-based SOTA pre-trained models such as BERT and RoBERTa (Xu et al., 2020, 2022; Huang et al., 2022). Li et al also showed that the LayoutLM model shows better detection accuracy on the DocBank, a benchmark dataset for document layout analysis when compared with other transformer-based or R-CNN models (Li et al., 2020). However, the license of the LayoutLMv3 prohibits it from being used in industry. A good alternative for industrial use cases instead, is the Language-independent Layout Transformer (LiLT), a multimodal model, which overcomes the language barrier and decouples and learns the layout knowledge from the monolingual structured documents before generalizing it to the multilingual (Wang et al., 2022).

Our approach focuses on employing a multimodal approach to navigate the complexities of PDF articles and extract bibliographic data with precision, without depending on external tools for which we don't have the ability to alter their behavior, with the additional opportunity to expand to multilingual content.

2 Grobid Pipeline

GeneRation Of Bibliographic Data (GROBID) (GRO, 2008–2023) is a machine learning library for extracting, parsing and re-structuring raw documents such as PDF into structured XML/TEI encoded documents with a particular focus on technical and scientific publications. GROBID provides APIs for extraction of entities from both Head and Tail (bibliography) sections of PDF manuscripts. GROBID is popularly used for entity extraction from scientific articles and serves as a strong baseline for entity extraction from both header and bibliography. This tool has been around for more than a decade and considered a standard tool in both academia and industry (Lipinski et al., 2013).

3 In-house Bibliography Extraction Pipeline

In this work, we developed an in-house pipeline for extracting citations from PDF articles. This pipeline takes PDF articles as input and gives a list of citations as the final output. Figure 2 depicts the details of this pipeline. This pipeline is composed of the following main components:

3.1 PDF Parser

This component enables the extraction of text and layout information from the input PDFs. As shown in Figure 2, we also have a rule-based candidate selection logic, which helps us to select a few candidate pages containing bibliography. We experimented with various tools for parsing the selected PDF pages, two of which seemed particularly promising:

- PyMuPDF[1] is a Python-based PDF parser, which is actively maintained and enhanced with over 30 million downloads. This ease of use makes this tool quite popular across several entity extraction applications.
- PDFlib TET (Text and Image Extraction Toolkit)[2] is a library written in C/C++. It provides bindings for various programming languages, including Python. Also, it provides a binary executable, which can be invoked from various computational environments.

3.2 Bibliography Detector

The next module in our pipeline is the bibliography detection model, which takes the text and layout extracted by the PDF parser as input and performs token classification for each token, classifying them as either bibliography or non-bibliography. As the multimodal token classification model, we use the Language-independent Layout Transformer (LiLT).

LiLT (Wang et al., 2022) is a multimodal model which takes both text and bounding boxes as input. The entire framework represents a parallel dual-stream Transformer that concurrently processes two streams of information: one for text and the other for layout.

LiLT can be pre-trained on the structured documents of a single language and then directly fine-tuned on other languages with the corresponding off-the-shelf monolingual/multilingual pre-trained textual models. This transfer learning enables multimodal document understanding for many languages, potentially very useful in the context of applications that require multilingual capability. The LiLT architecture is shown in Figure 3.

[1]https://pymupdf.readthedocs.io
[2]https://www.pdflib.com/products/tet/

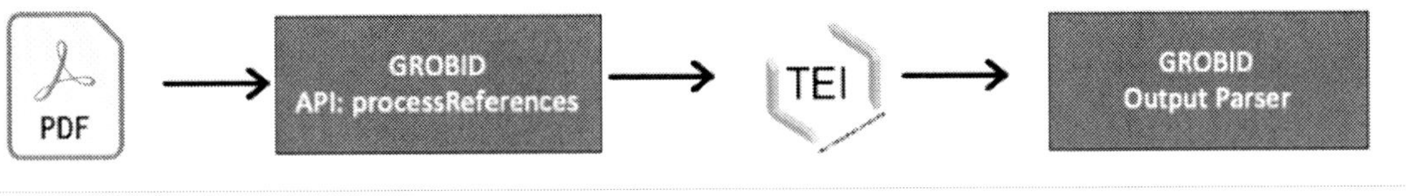

Figure 1: Grobid bibliography extraction pipeline

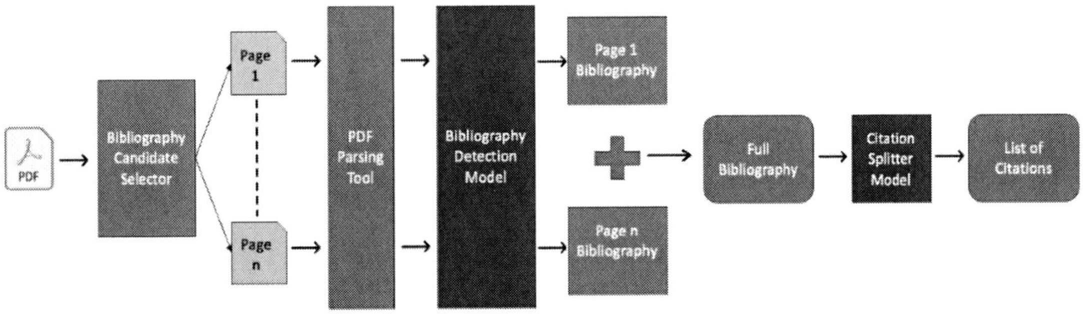

Figure 2: In-house bibliography extraction pipeline

3.3 Citation Splitter

The last component of this pipeline is a citation splitting model, designed to divide the full bibliography into separate citations. While this might seem a straightforward task, it presents a formidable challenge for machine learning algorithms due to the considerable diversity in citation formats.

In this work we fine-tune SciBERT (Beltagy et al., 2019), a BERT-like, transformer-based model trained on scientific content. We trained this customized SciBERT model as a token classifier, employing an in-house dataset of bibliographies for supervised learning. This approach enabled the model to learn to accurately detect the starting point of each citation within the bibliography. As new citations consistently commence after a newline in scientific articles, we made an additional effort to simplify the task for the model by retaining the newline information within the complete bibliography text as an extra clue for the model.

4 Experiments

4.1 Datasets

For training the bibliography detection model, we conducted experiments using two publicly available datasets: DocBank (Li et al., 2020) and GROTOAP2 (Tkaczyk et al., 2014). Our preliminary analysis and experimentation demonstrated the superiority of GROTOAP2 dataset over DocBank dataset in terms of its annotation quality.

To train the citation splitter model, we used an in-house dataset of bibliographies, by annotating the starting point of each citation within the bibliography.

For the final evaluation, we used scientific PDF articles in English from Elsevier's internal scientific articles database published after 2020. All experimental results reported in this article were conducted on this in-house dataset.

4.2 Compared Methods

We compare the following approaches:

- GROBID-CRF: GROBID with CRF-based models.
- GROBID-DL: GROBID with Deep Learning based models. As recommended in the documentation, we use BiLSTM-CRF model.
- In-house pipelines: A proposed stack of in-house models, with PyMuPDF and PDFlib as PDF parsing tools, LiLT as a bibliography detection model and a SciBERT-based citation splitter model.

4.3 Experimental Results

Table 1 shows the final results obtained in our experiments. We evaluated the extraction of the full bibliography section and the extraction of each citation in the bibliography.

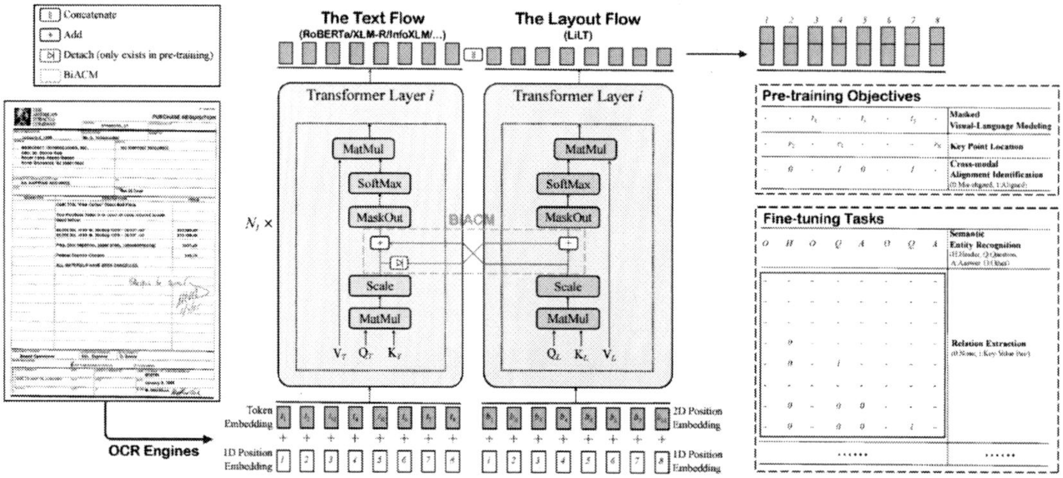

Figure 3: Language-Independent Layout Transformer (LiLT)

Pipeline	PDF Parsing Tool	Bibliography	Citations		
		Accuracy	Precision	Recall	F1
GROBID-CRF	pdfalto	50.2	90.8	89.8	90.3
GROBID-DL	pdfalto	50.9	92.2	90.8	91.5
In-house	PyMuPDF	66.7	92.4	93.2	92.8
In-house	PDFlib	**72.8**	**94.9**	**94.3**	**94.6**

Table 1: Comparison of different methods for extracting bibliography and citations

Full bibliography detection is evaluated in terms of accuracy, calculated as the ratio of the number of correctly detected bibliographies to the total number of bibliographies present in the evaluation dataset (GRO, 2008–2023; Ohta et al., 2014). The correctness of the bibliography is measured in terms of a relaxed edit distance (Levenshtein), keeping a tolerance of up to 10 consecutive mistakes and 10% total mistakes in terms of normalized edit distance). Evaluation at the citation-level is performed in terms of precision, recall and F1-score (GRO, 2008–2023). The metrics are defined as follows:

- Precision: Ratio of the number of correctly extracted citations to the total number of citations extracted by the system.
- Recall: Ratio of the number of correctly extracted citations to the number of all citations in the ground truth.
- F1 Score: 2* Precision * Recall / (Precision + Recall)

In the experimental results, we observed that GROBID is a strong baseline for this task. It is a very robust tool for performing entity extraction from PDF articles, especially the bibliography. Out of the two variants of GROBID, Grobid-DL was found superior. The proposed in-house pipeline with PDFlib PDF parser, LiLT based bibliography detection model and SciBERT based citation splitter is the best performing pipeline, outperforming Grobid baseline by a large margin of 3.1%. Among the two PDF parsing tools, PDFlib resulted in superior performance especially in terms of reading order detection and extraction of line and paragraph level information, which further allowed us to correct some of the prediction mistakes made at the token level.

5 Conclusion and Future Work

We have presented an end-to-end pipeline for the extraction of bibliographic information from scientific articles in digital-born PDF format. Our pipeline is designed to address the challenges posed by the diverse formatting, layouts, and font styles found in PDF articles. We have leveraged cutting-edge techniques and models, including LiLT and SciBERT, to achieve accurate and robust bibliography extraction. We achieved a significant improvement in accuracy over existing tools like GROBID, showcasing the potential of our approach in advancing the task of bibliography parsing.

We see several avenues for future research. One potential direction would be to integrate generative AI based Large Language Models (LLM) into the pipeline. The versatility of LLMs would increase the adaptability of our pipeline to a wider range of scholarly content, encompassing diverse research domains, languages, and publication formats. Alternatively, our LiLT-based pipeline could be adapted to handle languages other than English through transfer learning, which would be valuable as scientific research is conducted globally.

References

2008–2023. Grobid. `https://github.com/kermitt2/grobid`.

Iz Beltagy, Kyle Lo, and Arman Cohan. 2019. Scibert: A pretrained language model for scientific text. *arXiv preprint arXiv:1903.10676*.

Alessia Cioffi and Silvio Peroni. 2022. Structured references from pdf articles: assessing the tools for bibliographic reference extraction and parsing.

Lei Cui, Yiheng Xu, Tengchao Lv, and Furu Wei. 2021. Document ai: Benchmarks, models and applications.

Yupan Huang, Tengchao Lv, Lei Cui, Yutong Lu, and Furu Wei. 2022. Layoutlmv3: Pre-training for document ai with unified text and image masking.

Minghao Li, Yiheng Xu, Lei Cui, Shaohan Huang, Furu Wei, Zhoujun Li, and Ming Zhou. 2020. Docbank: A benchmark dataset for document layout analysis. *arXiv preprint arXiv:2006.01038*.

Mario Lipinski, Kevin Yao, Corinna Breitinger, Joeran Beel, and Bela Gipp. 2013. Evaluation of header metadata extraction approaches and tools for scientific pdf documents. In *Proceedings of the 13th ACM/IEEE-CS joint conference on Digital libraries*, pages 385–386.

Kyle Lo, Lucy Lu Wang, Mark Neumann, Rodney Kinney, and Dan S. Weld. 2020. S2orc: The semantic scholar open research corpus.

Daiki Matsuoka, Manabu Ohta, Atsuhiro Takasu, and Jun Adachi. 2016. Examination of effective features for crf-based bibliography extraction from reference strings. In *2016 eleventh international conference on digital information management (ICDIM)*, pages 243–248. IEEE.

Manabu Ohta, Daiki Arauchi, Atsuhiro Takasu, and Jun Adachi. 2014. Empirical evaluation of crf-based bibliography extraction from reference strings. pages 287–292.

Animesh Prasad, Manpreet Kaur, and Min-Yen Kan. 2018a. Neural parscit: A deep learning based reference string parser. *International Journal on Digital Libraries*, 19:323–337.

Animesh Prasad, Manpreet Kaur, and Min-Yen Kan. 2018b. Neural parscit: a deep learning-based reference string parser. *International journal on digital libraries*, 19:323–337.

Shah Rukh Qasim, Hassan Mahmood, and Faisal Shafait. 2019. Rethinking table recognition using graph neural networks. pages 142–147.

Laurent Romary and Patrice Lopez. 2015. Grobid-information extraction from scientific publications. *ERCIM News*, 100.

Dominika Tkaczyk, Pawel Szostek, and Lukasz Bolikowski. 2014. Grotoap2-the methodology of creating a large ground truth dataset of scientific articles. *D-Lib Magazine*, 20(11/12).

Dominika Tkaczyk, Pawel Szostek, Mateusz Fedoryszak, Piotr Jan Dendek, and Lukasz Bolikowski. 2015. Cermine: automatic extraction of structured metadata from scientific literature. *International Journal on Document Analysis and Recognition (IJDAR)*, 18(4):317–335.

Jiapeng Wang, Lianwen Jin, and Kai Ding. 2022. Lilt: A simple yet effective language-independent layout transformer for structured document understanding. *arXiv preprint arXiv:2202.13669*.

Yang Xu, Yiheng Xu, Tengchao Lv, Lei Cui, Furu Wei, Guoxin Wang, Yijuan Lu, Dinei Florencio, Cha Zhang, Wanxiang Che, Min Zhang, and Lidong Zhou. 2022. Layoutlmv2: Multi-modal pre-training for visually-rich document understanding.

Yiheng Xu, Minghao Li, Lei Cui, Shaohan Huang, Furu Wei, and Ming Zhou. 2020. LayoutLM: Pre-training of text and layout for document image understanding. In *Proceedings of the 26th ACM SIGKDD International Conference on Knowledge Discovery &amp Data Mining*. ACM.

Xu Zhong, Jianbin Tang, and Antonio Jimeno Yepes. 2019. Publaynet: largest dataset ever for document layout analysis.

Factored Verification: Detecting and Reducing Hallucination in Summaries of Academic Papers

Charlie George
Elicit
charlie@elicit.com

Andreas Stuhlmüller
Elicit
andreas@elicit.com

Abstract

Hallucination plagues even frontier LLMs—but how bad is it really for summarizing academic papers? We evaluate *Factored Verification*, a simple automated method for detecting hallucinations in abstractive summaries. This method sets a new SotA on hallucination detection in the summarization task of the HaluEval benchmark, achieving 76.2% accuracy. We then use this method to estimate how often language models hallucinate when summarizing across multiple academic papers and find 0.62 hallucinations in the average ChatGPT (16k) summary, 0.84 for GPT-4, and 1.55 for Claude 2. We ask models to self-correct using *factored critiques* and find that this lowers the number of hallucinations to 0.49 for ChatGPT, 0.46 for GPT-4, and 0.95 for Claude 2. The hallucinations we find are often subtle, so we advise caution when using models to synthesize academic papers.

1 Introduction

Hallucination—the generation of inaccurate or ungrounded information—is a largely unsolved problem for LLMs (Kryściński et al., 2019; Maynez et al., 2020; Ji et al., 2023). This is acceptable for creative use cases such as story generation and brainstorming, but would be highly problematic if common for academic summarization and Q&A where factual accuracy is key. How common is hallucination for SotA models when answering questions given the abstracts of multiple scientific papers?

To answer this question, we first construct a simple method for checking hallucination inspired by Kadavath et al. (2022) and Lightman et al. (2023): Given a summary, we automatically decompose it into key claims, assign a model-generated probability to each of the claims given the relevant sources, and combine these into an overall correctness probability. We validate this method on the hallucination detection benchmark HaluEval and

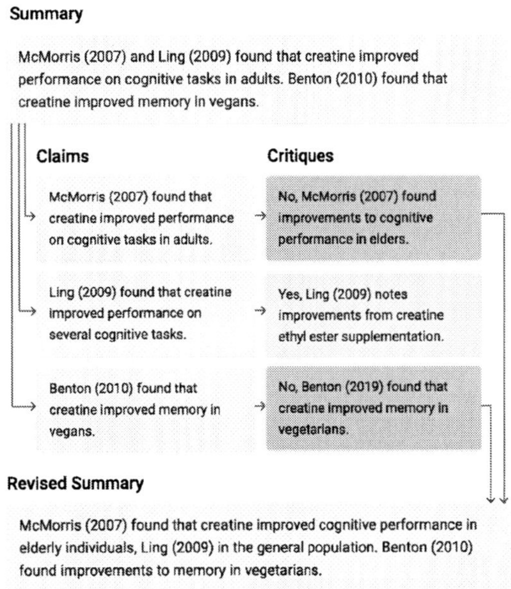

Figure 1: Factored Verification splits a summary into claims, checks each claim, and then optionally revises the summary to address the claim critiques. Each step is a language model task.

set a new SotA, exceeding the previous chain-of-thought-based method by 10 absolute percentage points using the same language model.

We then apply Factored Verification to detecting hallucination in a real-world scientific summarization task. Given the abstracts of eight papers and a question, the task is to provide a question-relevant summary. We measure hallucination for SotA models including GPT-4 (OpenAI, 2023) and Claude 2 (Bai et al., 2022a), and estimate that the average summary has between 0.62 and 1.57 hallucinations.

Given that we can automatically detect some hallucinations, can we use this knowledge to reduce them? We treat the claim-wise critiques generated by Factored Verification as model-generated advice (Saunders et al., 2022a) and show that we can reduce detected hallucinations for every model we study, but that significant hallucination remains.

Proceedings of the 2nd Workshop on Information Extraction from Scientific Publications, pages 107–116
Nov 1, 2023. ©2023 Association for Computational Linguistics

2 Detecting hallucination with Factored Verification

We first develop and validate Factored Verification, a simple method for using LLMs to detect hallucinations in settings where the relevant source material is provided.

2.1 Defining "hallucination"

We call a claim "hallucinated" if it is not backed by the source material provided in context, even if it could be supported with other sources. For example, if the source material discusses the implementation of a public transport policy and the model-generated summary infers that the policy was aimed at addressing sustainability challenges, this is a hallucination unless the source explicitly talked about this as the goal of the policy.

2.2 Method

Following Lightman et al. (2023), we break each summary into a list of claims and then assign each claim a probability of being correct, both using LLM prompting. The claim decomposition prompt is in Appendix A.1.1.

To compute the likelihood that a single claim is correct we use a few-shot prompt with GPT-4 base (OpenAI, 2023) and look up the probability of the final `Yes` token (Appendix A.1.2). For ChatGPT, which doesn't provide access to token probabilities, we ask the model to verify that each claim is supported using few-shot chain-of-thought (Jason Wei et al.), interpreting the resulting Yes/No answer as a 0/1 probability (Appendix A.1.3).

Assuming independence of the correctness of claims for simplicity, the probability that the summary is correct is the product of the probabilities of each of the individual claims:

$$P_{\text{summary}} = \prod_{i=1}^{n} P_{\text{claim}_i} \tag{1}$$

We classify a summary as hallucinated if P_{summary} is greater than a threshold θ.

2.3 Dataset

To measure how well Factored Verification works, we use the summarization task of HaluEval, a hallucination benchmark (Li et al., 2023). Each item in this task consists of a document and two summaries, one of which contains a subtle hallucination.

Due to cost constraints, we randomly sample 5% of the dataset as a "training" set, and 20% as a test set (1000 and 4000 items respectively). The training set is only used to set the decision threshold θ by running GPT-4 with the aforementioned claim likelihood prompt on the training set examples and calculating the average of P_{summary} for both faithful and hallucinated summaries.

2.4 Results

Factored Verification is SotA for hallucination detection, exceeding prior few-shot and chain-of-thought approaches for both ChatGPT and GPT-4 (Table 1).

Model	Few-shot	CoT	Factored
GPT-4	30.9%	75.5%	**76.2%**
ChatGPT (3.5)	58.5%*	61.2%*	**71.2%**

Table 1: HaluEval summarization results, showing % accuracy, $n = 4000$, * from Li et al. (2023).

For comparison, we also tested a single-prompt equivalent of Factored Verification, asking ChatGPT to write out each claim and verify it in one go. This achieved an accuracy of 63.3%, which is below the multi-prompt factored method (71.2%) and comparable to standard CoT results (61.2%).

We were surprised by GPT-4's low 30.9% accuracy when using the exact few-shot prompt from Li et al. (2023). To check our implementation, we ran the same code with ChatGPT and found an accuracy 59.9% on our sample, roughly matching the 58.5% from Li et al. (2023). Given that GPT-4 is much more competitive in the CoT and Factored Verification settings, we suspect that the Li et al. (2023) few-shot prompt has idiosyncratic limitations.

3 How often do models hallucinate in scientific summaries?

We now turn to our task of interest, generating summaries based on the abstracts of scientific papers. We will apply Factored Verification to estimate how frequently models hallucinate in this context.

3.1 Task

Given a question and eight abstracts, the task is to generate a question-relevant summary where each claim is cited with the paper that backs it up. Figure 2 shows a simplified example with only two papers.

> **Query:** What is the impact of creatine on cognition?
> **Summary:** The papers suggest that creatine supplementation may have a positive impact on cognition. Ling (2009) found that creatine ethyl ester supplementation improved performance on several cognitive tasks, although the results require replication using objective measures of compliance. Benton (2010) found that creatine supplementation improved memory in vegetarians, but not in those who consume meat.

Figure 2: Example of the scientific summarization task, simplified from eight to two papers.

The dataset of queries and abstracts[1] is generated by using 200 anonymized search queries and their associated top results from Elicit (Stuhlmüller and Byun, 2023).

3.2 Method

We follow the hallucination detection strategy outlined in Section 2.2, with the following modifications to reduce compute cost:

1. We directly treat sentences as claims.
2. We only check claims that have associated citations.
3. When checking each claim, we provide only the abstracts of the cited papers as sources.

We expect that these modifications lead to little degradation given that almost all sentences have citations and the simplification step from sentence to claim is not doing much work.

3.3 Results

We run Factored Verification with ChatGPT, GPT-4, Claude 2, and Claude Instant (OpenAI, 2023; Bai et al., 2022a). Table 2 shows that for all models, our method reports at least one hallucination in the majority of summaries.

We include additional results that show interactions between ChatGPT and GPT-4 when used as generation, criticism, and judge models in Table 3 in the Appendix.

3.4 Interpretation

Based on the 76% accuracy of Factored Verification on HaluEval, we know that there are likely false positives and/or false negatives, so we can't take the reported hallucination rates literally.

We manually inspected about a hundred claims evaluated by GPT-4. When GPT-4 said that a claim is supported, we agreed in all cases. When GPT-4 reported an unsupported claim, we agreed 66% of the time. So, our best guess for the true hallucination rate is 2/3 of the reported hallucination rate.

Many of the claims we encountered were wrong in subtle ways that we would likely have missed without seeing the GPT-4 critiques, and would expect non-expert evaluators to miss, including:

- Stating that a claim is supported by two abstracts when it is only supported by one
- Slightly exaggerating the findings of a paper
- Conflating the purpose of the study with the outcome
- Implying that two independent findings are linked

This augmentation of human evaluation is consistent with prior work by Saunders et al. (2022b) which found that model-generated critiques help humans find flaws in summaries.

4 Reducing hallucination in scientific summaries with Factored Verification

It is common for LLMs to apparently fail at a task, only to then succeed with better prompting. Can we prompt models using the detected inaccuracies to automatically reduce hallucination in scientific summaries?

4.1 Baseline

We ask GPT-4 to self-correct by first identifying false claims in its initial summary, then revising the summary given this correction (prompts in Appendix A.4.1 and A.5). This *increased* the average number of detected hallucinations from 1.55 to 2.13. Huang et al. (2023a) similarly found that the GPT-4 generation of LLMs struggles to directly self-correct across a variety of reasoning datasets.

4.2 Method

To improve on the baseline, we propose to reduce hallucination with Factored Verification in three steps, as illustrated in Figure 1 and shown in Algorithm 1.

[1] `https://github.com/elicit/fave-dataset`

Model	Hallucinations per summary (reported)	Hallucinations per summary (adjusted)	% of summaries with reported hallucinations
GPT-4	$1.26 \rightarrow 0.69$	$0.84 \rightarrow 0.46$	$63.25\% \rightarrow 40\%$
ChatGPT (3.5, 16k)	$0.93 \rightarrow 0.735$	$0.62 \rightarrow 0.49$	$54\% \rightarrow 41.63\%$
Claude 2	$2.32 \rightarrow 1.43$	$1.55 \rightarrow 0.95$	$83.0\% \rightarrow 71.50\%$
Claude instant	$2.35 \rightarrow 1.86$	$1.57 \rightarrow 1.24$	$87.0\% \rightarrow 81.50\%$

Table 2: Prevalence of hallucination for models when generating summaries of academic papers, before and after revision with factored critiques. Based on manual inspection of approximately 100 data points our best guess is that the true prevalence of hallucination ("adjusted") is 2/3 of the reports from automated evaluation.

First, we create claim-wise critiques (true/false judgments and supporting reasoning) analogous to the hallucination detection method above: We ask the model to evaluate the supportedness of each sentence based on the cited abstracts. We then concatenate the critiques of the unsupported claims to form the *factored critique*. Finally we ask the model to revise the summary given that critique.

Algorithm 1 Factored Verification: Revising a summary by generating sentence-wise critiques

```
Initialize empty list for critiques
for each sentence in the summary do
    Critique ← LLM.critique(sentence, cited abstracts)
    if sentence is unsupported then
        Add Critique to the list of critiques
    end if
end for
FactoredCritique ← concat(critiques)
RevisedSummary ← LLM.revise(FactoredCritique)
return RevisedSummary
```

Figure 3 shows an example critique.

4.3 Results

Table 2 shows that Factord Verification reduces the number of summaries with reported hallucination by 5.50% to 23.25% (absolute) depending on the model, with ChatGPT being the lowest-hallucination model before critique (0.62 estimated hallucinations per summary), and GPT-4 being the lowest-hallucination model after critique and across all settings (0.46 estimated hallucinations per summary).

5 Related work

Hallucination is widely known to be a significant problem for LLMs (Luo et al., 2023; Peng et al., 2023; Ji et al., 2023), although to a much lesser extent for abstractive summarization where the information needed to answer is fully provided (Cao et al., 2022; Huang et al., 2023c).

Various strategies have been proposed to mitigate hallucination. Some strategies aim to prevent their occurrence by checking how familiar models are with instructions (Luo et al., 2023). Others, including our proposed method, focus on the detection and correction of hallucinations post-generation (Cao et al., 2022; Huang et al., 2023b).

Of these, notable strategies are the use of external knowledge and retrieval augmentation, and automated feedback (Shuster et al., 2021; Peng et al., 2023; Zhang et al., 2023). While external knowledge is less relevant here, Factored Verification can be viewed as a kind of automated feedback.

In simultaneous work, Dhuliawala et al. (2023) propose an automated feedback method called Chain-of-Verification, which is effectively the same as ours: (i) Draft an initial response, (ii) plan fact-checking questions, (iii) answer the questions independently, and (iv) generate a final revised response. Their evaluation focuses on out-of-context fact checking. Consistent with our results, they find that the factored version of their approach reduces hallucination for question-answering and text generation tasks.

6 Relevance to AI alignment

To align powerful AI systems, we need to be able to provide accurate feedback and supervision even when systems surpass human-level performance, a property known as scalable oversight (Amodei et al., 2016).

Today, reinforcement learning from human feedback (RLHF) is often used to align LLMs (Christiano et al., 2023; Bai et al., 2022b; Ouyang et al., 2022). However, GPT-4 already surpasses the performance of the average human on many academic tasks (OpenAI, 2023), making it difficult for non-experts to provide effective reward signals. In our

Critique:
- For the sentence *"Giuntella (2015) found that immigration reduced waiting times for outpatient referrals, suggesting that policies affecting population dynamics can indirectly impact waiting times and thus healthcare costs."* in the summary: The claim accurately reflects the findings of Giuntella (2015) that immigration reduced waiting times for outpatient referrals. However, the claim extends the findings of the study to suggest that policies affecting population dynamics can indirectly impact waiting times and thus healthcare costs. While this may be a reasonable inference, it is not directly supported by the abstract.
- For the sentence *"Propper (2002) found that GP fundholders were able to secure shorter waiting times for their patients, suggesting that giving family doctors the ability to choose the hospital where their patients are treated and the means to pay for some services can reduce waiting times."* in the summary: The claim is not directly supported by the abstract. The abstract states that the study investigates whether GP fundholders were able to secure shorter waiting times for their patients, but it does not provide the results of this investigation. Therefore, the claim that Propper (2002) found that GP fundholders were able to secure shorter waiting times for their patients is not supported by the abstract.

Figure 3: Example of a factored critique generated with GPT-4

attempts to delegate evaluation of academic claims to non-expert contractors, we observed only 38% inter-rater agreement for unsupported claims, a sign of similar difficulties. In the short term this can be solved by using contractors with specialized domain knowledge. However, this won't work if models surpass the capabilities of the best humans.

We have shown that factored critiques let models correct some of their own mistakes without need for human supervision. If similar approaches can be extended beyond hallucination reduction to richer tasks, they could help us scale supervision in lockstep with future model capabilities.

7 Discussion

Our main finding is that the absolute rate of hallucination of SotA models like ChatGPT, Claude 2, and GPT-4 is surprisingly high for academic summarization. This is true even with revision using factored critiques, which results in 0.46 to to 1.24 estimated hallucinations per summary.

A natural question to ask in this context is whether we can finetune on model-revised summaries, incrementally bootstraping to more and more accurate summaries, initially detecting and eliminating the most egregious failure modes, then more subtle ones with each training iteration.

Overall, despite incredible advances, language models still struggle with accurate summarization in academic contexts. Many mistakes are only clear upon careful inspection of the sources and look identical to genuine answers otherwise. For now, we advise caution in situations where accuracy matters, as we would for human summaries as well.

8 Acknowledgments

We thank Noah Goodman, William Saunders, Jungwon Byun and James Brady for helpful early discussions. We would also like to thank Owain Evans and Justin Reppert for their feedback on early drafts. In addition, we are grateful to Ben Rachbach for help with human labeling and the rest of the Elicit team for supporting this work.

References

Dario Amodei, Chris Olah, Jacob Steinhardt, Paul Christiano, John Schulman, and Dan Mané. 2016. Concrete Problems in AI Safety. ArXiv:1606.06565 [cs].

Yuntao Bai, Andy Jones, Kamal Ndousse, Amanda Askell, Anna Chen, Nova DasSarma, Dawn Drain, Stanislav Fort, Deep Ganguli, Tom Henighan, Nicholas Joseph, Saurav Kadavath, Jackson Kernion, Tom Conerly, Sheer El-Showk, Nelson Elhage, Zac Hatfield-Dodds, Danny Hernandez, Tristan Hume, Scott Johnston, Shauna Kravec, Liane Lovitt, Neel Nanda, Catherine Olsson, Dario Amodei, Tom Brown, Jack Clark, Sam McCandlish, Chris Olah, Ben Mann, and Jared Kaplan. 2022a. Training a Helpful and Harmless Assistant with Reinforcement Learning from Human Feedback. *arXiv:2204.05862 [cs]*.

Yuntao Bai, Andy Jones, Kamal Ndousse, Amanda Askell, Anna Chen, Nova DasSarma, Dawn Drain, Stanislav Fort, Deep Ganguli, Tom Henighan, Nicholas Joseph, Saurav Kadavath, Jackson Kernion, Tom Conerly, Sheer El-Showk, Nelson Elhage, Zac Hatfield-Dodds, Danny Hernandez, Tristan Hume, Scott Johnston, Shauna Kravec, Liane Lovitt, Neel Nanda, Catherine Olsson, Dario Amodei, Tom Brown, Jack Clark, Sam McCandlish, Chris Olah, Ben Mann, and Jared Kaplan. 2022b. Training a Helpful and Harmless Assistant with Reinforcement Learning from Human Feedback. ArXiv:2204.05862 [cs].

Meng Cao, Yue Dong, and Jackie Cheung. 2022. Hallucinated but Factual! Inspecting the Factuality of Hallucinations in Abstractive Summarization. In *Proceedings of the 60th Annual Meeting of the Association for Computational Linguistics (Volume 1: Long Papers)*, pages 3340–3354, Dublin, Ireland. Association for Computational Linguistics.

Paul Christiano, Jan Leike, Tom B. Brown, Miljan Martic, Shane Legg, and Dario Amodei. 2023. Deep reinforcement learning from human preferences. ArXiv:1706.03741 [cs, stat].

Shehzaad Dhuliawala, Mojtaba Komeili, Jing Xu, Roberta Raileanu, Xian Li, Asli Celikyilmaz, and Jason Weston. 2023. Chain-of-Verification Reduces Hallucination in Large Language Models.

Jie Huang, Xinyun Chen, Swaroop Mishra, Huaixiu Steven Zheng, Adams Wei Yu, Xinying Song, and Denny Zhou. 2023a. Large Language Models Cannot Self-Correct Reasoning Yet. ArXiv:2310.01798 [cs].

Kung-Hsiang Huang, Hou Pong Chan, and Heng Ji. 2023b. Zero-shot Faithful Factual Error Correction. In *Proceedings of the 61st Annual Meeting of the Association for Computational Linguistics (Volume 1: Long Papers)*, pages 5660–5676, Toronto, Canada. Association for Computational Linguistics.

Yichong Huang, Xiachong Feng, Xiaocheng Feng, and Bing Qin. 2023c. The Factual Inconsistency Problem in Abstractive Text Summarization: A Survey.

Jason Wei, Xuezhi Wang, Dale Schuurmans, Maarten Bosma, Ed Chi, Quoc Le, and Denny Zhou. Chain of Thought Prompting Elicits Reasoning in Large Language Models.

Ziwei Ji, Nayeon Lee, Rita Frieske, Tiezheng Yu, Dan Su, Yan Xu, Etsuko Ishii, Yejin Bang, Wenliang Dai, Andrea Madotto, and Pascale Fung. 2023. Survey of Hallucination in Natural Language Generation. *ACM Computing Surveys*, 55(12):1–38.

Saurav Kadavath, Tom Conerly, Amanda Askell, Tom Henighan, Dawn Drain, Ethan Perez, Nicholas Schiefer, Zac Hatfield-Dodds, Nova DasSarma, Eli Tran-Johnson, Scott Johnston, Sheer El-Showk, Andy Jones, Nelson Elhage, Tristan Hume, Anna Chen, Yuntao Bai, Sam Bowman, Stanislav Fort, Deep Ganguli, Danny Hernandez, Josh Jacobson, Jackson Kernion, Shauna Kravec, Liane Lovitt, Kamal Ndousse, Catherine Olsson, Sam Ringer, Dario Amodei, Tom Brown, Jack Clark, Nicholas Joseph, Ben Mann, Sam McCandlish, Chris Olah, and Jared Kaplan. 2022. Language Models (Mostly) Know What They Know.

Wojciech Kryściński, Bryan McCann, Caiming Xiong, and Richard Socher. 2019. Evaluating the Factual Consistency of Abstractive Text Summarization.

Junyi Li, Xiaoxue Cheng, Wayne Xin Zhao, Jian-Yun Nie, and Ji-Rong Wen. 2023. HaluEval: A Large-Scale Hallucination Evaluation Benchmark for Large Language Models.

Hunter Lightman, Vineet Kosaraju, Yura Burda, Harri Edwards, Bowen Baker, Teddy Lee, Jan Leike, John Schulman, Karl Cobbe, and Ilya Sutskever. 2023. Let's Verify Step by Step.

Junyu Luo, Cao Xiao, and Fenglong Ma. 2023. Zero-Resource Hallucination Prevention for Large Language Models.

Joshua Maynez, Shashi Narayan, Bernd Bohnet, and Ryan McDonald. 2020. On Faithfulness and Factuality in Abstractive Summarization. In *Proceedings of the 58th Annual Meeting of the Association for Computational Linguistics*, pages 1906–1919, Online. Association for Computational Linguistics.

OpenAI. 2023. GPT-4 Technical Report.

Long Ouyang, Jeff Wu, Xu Jiang, Diogo Almeida, Carroll L. Wainwright, Pamela Mishkin, Chong Zhang, Sandhini Agarwal, Katarina Slama, Alex Ray, John Schulman, Jacob Hilton, Fraser Kelton, Luke Miller, Maddie Simens, Amanda Askell, Peter Welinder, Paul Christiano, Jan Leike, and Ryan Lowe. 2022. Training language models to follow instructions with human feedback. ArXiv:2203.02155 [cs].

Baolin Peng, Michel Galley, Pengcheng He, Hao Cheng, Yujia Xie, Yu Hu, Qiuyuan Huang, Lars Liden, Zhou Yu, Weizhu Chen, and Jianfeng Gao. 2023. Check Your Facts and Try Again: Improving Large Language Models with External Knowledge and Automated Feedback.

William Saunders, Catherine Yeh, Jeff Wu, Steven Bills, Long Ouyang, Jonathan Ward, and Jan Leike. 2022a. Self-critiquing models for assisting human evaluators. https://arxiv.org/abs/2206.05802v2.

William Saunders, Catherine Yeh, Jeff Wu, Steven Bills, Long Ouyang, Jonathan Ward, and Jan Leike. 2022b. Self-critiquing models for assisting human evaluators. ArXiv:2206.05802 [cs].

Kurt Shuster, Spencer Poff, Moya Chen, Douwe Kiela, and Jason Weston. 2021. Retrieval Augmentation Reduces Hallucination in Conversation.

Andreas Stuhlmüller and Jungwon Byun. 2023. Elicit: The AI Research Assistant. https://elicit.org/.

Shuo Zhang, Liangming Pan, Junzhou Zhao, and William Yang Wang. 2023. Mitigating Language Model Hallucination with Interactive Question-Knowledge Alignment.

A Appendix

A.1 Factored Verification prompts (HaluEval)

A.1.1 Decomposing a summary into claims

```
Below is a summary of a document.
Please extract ALL the claims from the
document. You should give your answer
as a list separated by "-" and start by
saying "The claims are:"

[summary].
```

A.1.2 Verifying the correctness of a claim with GPT-4 base

```
Below are a set of documents and claims.
We will check if the document that the
claim is supported by the document or
otherwise inaccurate. Below are some
examples. It can sometimes be the case
that a claim is very subtly wrong.

[Few-shot examples]

Example 5:

Document: [Document]

Claim: [Claim]

Supported: Yes
```

A.1.3 Verifying the correctness of a claim with ChatGPT

```
Below is a claim and a document. Check
that the claim is supported by the
document. If it is, say "Yes". If
it is not, say "No".

Document: [document]

Claim: [claim]

Give your answer in the following
format:

Reasoning: [give your reasoning
(including quotes) here]
Supported: [Yes/No]

Remember you MUST include quotes in
your reasoning.
```

A.2 Prompt template for generating summaries of academic papers

```
I now need you to help me summarize many
more papers in the same way as above.
Our research question is "[question]".

I've collected many papers that might
address this research question.

Paper [number]: [reference]

Title: [title]

Abstract: [abstract]

Write a summary of what the papers
collectively say about the research
question. Use the same format as the
summary above.

You must cite the papers in your summary.
You can use the following format:
Author (year)

You will only include the findings that
directly answer our research question,
ignoring other findings that are only
loosely relevant. Remember to include
citations in the final summary. Your
final summary should use varied and
engaging language.
```

A.3 Prompt templates for Factored Verification (academic papers)

A.3.1 Generating claim-wise critiques

```
I need some more help verifying some
claims from scientific papers.

The claim is from [paper references]:

[reference]:

Title: [title]

Abstract: [abstract]

==

Claim: [claim]

First give a critique of the claim.
Then, say whether it is supported by
the abstract["s" if we have multiple
abstracts]. Finally, if claim is not
supported give a revised claim that is
supported by the abstract["s" if we have
multiple abstracts].

If the claim is partially supported say
"No" for the "Supported" field and give
a revised claim that is fully supported
by the abstract.

Format:

Critique: [critique]
Supported: "Yes" or "No"
Revised Claim: [revised claim] or "N/A"
if claim is supported.
```

A.3.2 Revision based on claim-wise critiques

As a follow-up to the papers and model-provided summary:

```
  Ok, after reading your summary, I have
some feedback:

Feedback:

I have some concerns about the factual
accuracy of the summary:

- For the sentence "[original false
claim]" in the summary: [critique]

===

Can you correct your summary
incorporating each piece of my feedback?
The concerns are MOST important to
address. Start by writing "Corrected
summary:" and then your corrected
summary. Keep everything not mentioned
in my feedback the same.
```

A.4 Prompt templates for self-correction baseline (academic papers)

A.4.1 Generating self-correction feedback

```
Below is a list of academic papers.

[Papers]

This is a summary of the papers:
```

```
[summary]

Please read the papers and the summary
and give feedback. The feedback should
ONLY look the at factual accuracy of the
summary and make sure that any claims
made are FULLY supported by the relevant
papers. Write "Feedback:" and then your
feedback. You should give a VERY harsh
long and detailed piece of feedback.
```

A.5 Revision based on self-generated feedback

```
Ok, after reading your summary, I have
some feedback:

Feedback:

[Model feedback from prompt above]

Can you correct your summary
incorporating each piece of my feedback?
The concerns are MOST important to
address. Start by writing "Corrected
summary:" and then your corrected
summary. Keep everything not mentioned
in my feedback the same.
```

A.6 Additional results

See Table 3.

Summary model	Critique model	Judge	Hallucinations per summary (reported)	% of summaries with reported hallucinations
ChatGPT	-	GPT-4	0.89	51.00%
ChatGPT	ChatGPT	GPT-4	0.98	52.00%
ChatGPT	GPT-4	GPT-4	0.45	28.00%
GPT-4	-	GPT-4	1.55	69.50%
GPT-4	ChatGPT	GPT-4	1.19	67.00%
GPT-4	GPT-4	GPT-4	0.51	29.50%
GPT-4	-	ChatGPT	0.84	48.00%
GPT-4	ChatGPT	ChatGPT	0.37	23.50%
ChatGPT	-	ChatGPT	0.97	57.00%
ChatGPT	GPT-4	ChatGPT	0.85	49.50%
ChatGPT	ChatGPT	ChatGPT	0.66	37.00%

Table 3: Interaction effects between ChatGPT and GPT-4 as summary, critique, and judge models. ChatGPT refers to the GPT-3.5 series with 16k context. Dashes indicate that no revision was used. In the main paper, for ChatGPT and GPT-4, we average over { ChatGPT, GPT-4 } as critique generation and evaluation models to reduce interaction effects. For Claude models, we use ChatGPT as a judge.

APCS: Towards Argument based Pros and Cons Summarization of Peer Reviews

Sandeep Kumar†, Tirthankar Ghosal*, Asif Ekbal†
†Indian Institute of Technology Patna, India
∗National Center for Computational Sciences, Oak Ridge National Laboratory, USA
†(sandeep_2121cs29,asif)@iitp.ac.in
∗ghosalt@ornl.gov

Abstract

Peer review is an evaluation process where experts in a particular field assess the quality and credibility of a research paper or manuscript prior to its publication. Utilizing Artificial Intelligence (AI) in the peer review process has the potential to enhance the review process by providing more objective, efficient and accurate evaluations. Summarizing the pros and cons of peer reviews will be valuable for editors/area chairs to provide constructive feedback to authors, make informed decisions about manuscript publication and identify potential issues in the field. It will also assist them in understanding which areas of their work need improvement and which do not. In this research, we propose a novel architecture that uses a supervised method to generate generic pros and cons summaries to assist editors and authors in analyzing the feedback from peer reviews. Additionally, we propose an unsupervised method for generating aspect-based pros and cons summaries. Our proposed method achieves an average Rouge-1 F1 Score of 31.61 in generating generic pros and cons summaries and 32.62 in generating aspect-based summaries.

1 Introduction

Peer review, a process in which experts in a specific field assess the quality of research work, is a vital aspect of scientific discovery. It is well-known that peer reviews are controversial due to their quality, randomness, bias, and inconsistencies (Bornmann and Daniel, 2010). Additionally, there have been concerns about alleged reviewer bias in "single-blind" peer reviews (Tomkins et al., 2017) and arbitrariness between different reviewer groups (Langford and Guzdial, 2015). Despite these criticisms, within the scientific community, peer review is considered as an essential component of the academic writing process as it helps ensure that the papers published in scientific journals are of high quality and based on accurate experimentation. However, despite its significance, there is a lack of analysis and evaluation of the content and structure of reviews and their quality. According to a study by Kovanis et al. (Kovanis et al., 2016), approximately 63.4 million hours were spent on peer reviews in 2015 alone. The rapid increase in the number of publications in scientific fields motivates the development of automatic summarization tools for scientific articles. The number of scientific articles published per year has been growing at a rate of about 8% per year since the mid-17th century (Kovanis et al., 2016). The number of scientific papers indexed in the Web of Science database has been increasing at a rate of about 3% per year since the 1970s.

Investigating the inner workings of the peer review system can be challenging due to the need to protect publishers' privacy and intellectual property rights. However, OpenReview[1] provides a way to examine how the process is evolving in some areas, such as how authors are given opportunities to respond to feedback and how communication between authors and reviewers is being strengthened.

Argument mining in peer-review text is an important tool in the scientific publication process as it enables the automated analysis and extraction of key claims, evidence, and reasoning presented in a manuscript. This improves the efficiency, consistency, and fairness of the review process, detects potential biases, and assists authors in identifying areas for improvement, ultimately leading to a higher-quality manuscript and aiding in the advancement of scientific knowledge. Argument Mining can be used to efficiently extract the most relevant parts from reviews, which are paramount for the publication decision. Fromm et al. (Fromm et al., 2020) propose a simple argumentation scheme that distinguishes between non-arguments, supporting arguments, and attacking

[1]https://openreview.net/

Proceedings of the 2nd Workshop on Information Extraction from Scientific Publications, pages 117–129
Nov 1, 2023.

	Summary
Pros:	The paper introduces a novel approach for sentence representation by using multiple attentional vectors to extract multiple representations for a sentence. The authors have demonstrated consistent gains across three different tasks, providing evidence of the effectiveness of the model. The paper is reasonably clear, with no major technical issues, and the new model lends itself to more informative visualizations than could be obtained otherwise. The model also beats reasonable baselines on three datasets. The architecture is interesting and can be used within larger text understanding models. The approach is different from prior work, which is a positive aspect of the paper.
Cons:	a lack of analysis on the 2D representations, concerns about the value of r when applied to short sentences, a need for performance evaluations on dev sets or learning curves, and a lack of transparency in reporting model sizes. The paper also has a problem in its presentation, with no training objective defined, and there is a lack of appropriate addressing of prior work. The visualizations provided do not offer compelling evidence for the use of multiple attention vectors, and further experiments are needed to demonstrate the effectiveness of the 2D structure of the embedding matrix. Overall, there is a lack of convincing evidence that the 2D structure of the embedding matrix provides any meaningful advantage over similar attentive embedding models.

Table 1: Pros and Cons summary output of paper (ICLR 2017); `https://openreview.net/forum?id=BJC_jUqxe`

Aspects	Summary
Substance	Pros: The paper introduces a novel approach for sentence representation using 2D structure of embeddings, which produces more informative visualizations and beats reasonable baselines on three datasets. Cons: the reviewer would like to see more analysis on the 2D representations in order to be convinced of its effectiveness ablation studies?
Clarity	Pros: The paper is reasonably clear and there are no major technical issues. Cons: there are issues with the penalization term section and the paper's focus on unsupervised learning in the abstract, introduction and related work sections, and with the lack of clear definition of the training objective.
Meaningful Comparison	Cons: There is a substantial amount of prior work which the authors do not appropriately address , some of which is listed in previous comments .
Originality	Pros: the main innovation of this paper is the 2D structure of the embedding matrix Cons: 2D structure of the embedding matrix is not clearly shown to provide significant advantages over similar attentive embedding models already present in the literature.
No-aspect	Pros: This paper presents a method for sentence representation using a 2D matrix and self-attentive mechanism on LSTM encoder. It produces heat-map visualizations and good performance on downstream tasks. The model extracts matrix-valued sentence representation and could be used for tasks beyond NLP. The authors have shown consistent gains across multiple datasets. Cons: Some important experiments are missing, visualizations lack support for multiple attention vectors, main claims require more experimentation, unclear usage and conversion of embedding for downstream tasks, better model structure explanation needed, no comparison with similar works, minor issues like typos present.

Table 2: Aspect wise Pros and Cons summary output

arguments (NON/PRO/CON) as outlined in (Stab et al., 2018). This scheme can also be interpreted as a simplified version of the claim-premise model, where if there is a single claim, "The paper should be accepted," and arguments that either support or attack this claim.

An editor or chair writes a meta-review evaluating and summarizing the strengths and weaknesses of a peer review process as it pertains to a specific research or manuscript. Classification of meta-review is important because it allows readers to evaluate the quality and reliability of the research presented in the text and make informed decisions about its validity and usefulness. Additionally, it is important for researchers as it allows them to identify areas of improvement in their own research and writing process. Furthermore, it is essential for editors as it enables them to provide constructive feedback to authors, make informed decisions about the publication of a manuscript, and identify potential issues in the field. Thus, meta-review and its classification play a vital role in the scientific publication process. MReD dataset (Shen et al., 2022) consists of 7,089 meta-reviews and all its 45k meta-review sentences. Each sentence in a meta-review is classified into one of the 9 pre-defined intent categories: abstract, strength, weakness, rating summary, area chair (AC) disagreement, rebuttal process, suggestion, decision, and miscellaneous(misc).

Summarizing the pros and cons of a peer review text is crucial as it provides readers with a comprehensive understanding of the strengths and weaknesses of the peer review process as it pertains to a specific research or manuscript. This enables them to evaluate the quality and reliability of the research presented in the text, and make informed decisions about its validity and usefulness. Moreover, summarizing the pros and cons of a peer review text is of great importance for researchers, as it allows them to identify areas of improvement in their own research and writing process. For example, if a manuscript is rejected due to poor methodology, researchers can focus on addressing and improving that aspect of their work in future submissions. Furthermore, summarizing the pros and cons of a peer review text is essential for editors/area chair, as it enables them to provide constructive feedback and to make informed decisions about the publication of a manuscript, and identify potential issues in it, which can lead to taking appropriate steps to address them. Review text also contains aspects associated with it, such as novelty and motivation. Editors would benefit from knowing the specific pros and cons that reviewers have written about each aspect. In this research, we propose a way to generate both a generic pros and cons summary, as well as an aspect-wise pros and cons summary. This information can assist editors/area chair in quickly understanding which aspects of the paper need improvement and which do not, and can be beneficial for author as well to get a quick overview of the reviews. To demonstrate this, we present output from our proposed architecture in Table 1 and Table 2.

There exist reference summary for pro and con summary. Also the generation of human based summaries is expensive and require domain experts to summary. The meta reviewer usually mentions opinions about the submission's strengths and weakness as opinions about the submission's weaknesses. As strength mentioned in the meta review is mostly the summary of the pro argument and strength mentioned in the meta review is mostly the summary of the con argument of a paper. We used this idea and used the strength and weakness mentioned in the meta review as the reference summary.

We summarize our contributions as follows :-

- We propose an effective architecture that utilizes a supervised method for generating generic pros and cons summaries, to assist the editors and authors in analyzing peer reviews.
- We investigate the utilization of meta-reviews for this task without the availability of a reference summary for training.
- We propose a novel architecture that utilizes an unsupervised method for generating aspect-based pros and cons summaries for the same task.
- We have annotated 150 papers with aspect-based summaries to evaluate the generated aspect-based summary.

We make our code public[2].

2 Related Work

2.1 AI in Peer Reviews

The use of artificial intelligence in peer review has been garnering attention due to recent advancements in AI research. A dataset of scientific peer reviews was made available to facilitate research in this domain(Kang et al., 2018). Additionally, various studies have explored the correlation between overall recommendation scores and individual aspect scores. The CiteTracked dataset was introduced to ascertain the impact of citations from peer reviews(Plank and van Dalen, 2019). Furthermore, tools have been developed to analyze the quality, tone, and quantity of peer review comments, such as those mentioned in(Wicherts, 2016). The ASAP-Review dataset was formulated with the objective of automating scientific peer review(Yuan et al., 2021). Recently, a novel multitasking system was proposed, which leverages inter-dependency by sharing representations between two related tasks, such as aspect categorization and sentiment classification(Kumar et al., 2021). Shallow linguistic features, for instance, sentiment words, have been studied by Bornmann et al. to analyze language use in peer reviews(Bornmann et al., 2012).

2.2 Abstractive and Extractive Summarization

Extractive summarization involves creating summaries by selecting key sentences or phrases directly from the source text, retaining the original content's phrasing(Collins et al., 2017). Initially, extractive methods relied on simple statistical measures such as word frequency(Luhn, 1958b) and document location(Baxendale, 1958). As research evolved, classifiers using supervised learning identified potential summary sentences(Kupiec et al., 1995). Factors like sentence position, length, title words, and the presence of proper nouns became crucial cues(Yang et al., 2017; Nenkova et al., 2006). Modern extractive summarization predominantly employs neural models, integrating embeddings, CNNs, and RNNs(Kobayashi et al., 2015; Cheng and Lapata, 2016), and these systems often rank sentence salience before summarization(Erkan and Radev, 2004; Parveen et al., 2016).

Conversely, abstractive summarization crafts novel sentences and may use words not found in the source text(Widyassari et al., 2022). Although it offers more flexible summaries, the complexity of generating new content requires advanced natural language processing(Gambhir and Gupta, 2017). The encoder-decoder paradigm has emerged as a prominent technique in abstractive summarization(Xu et al., 2020; Lee et al., 2020; Yao et al., 2020), enabling efficient parameter optimization

[2]https://github.com/sandeep82945/Pros-Cons-Summarization-of-peer-reviews

and smoother summary generation.

2.3 Review Summarization

Several studies have explored the summarization of product reviews(Li et al., 2010; Gerani et al., 2014, 2019; Mason et al., 2016). For instance, Gerani et al.(Gerani et al., 2014) proposed an abstractive summarization system for product reviews, utilizing a template-based Natural Language Generation (NLG) framework and leveraging the discourse structure of reviews.

Aspect-based summarization involves generating focused summaries based on specific points of interest. WikiAsp(Hayashi et al., 2021), a large-scale dataset for multi-domain aspect-based summarizations, has been introduced. One study was conducted to provide insights into hotels that ratings might not fully capture by analyzing customer reviews from hotel booking websites. The topic modeling technique, Latent Dirichlet Allocation (LDA), was applied to uncover hidden information and aspects, followed by sentiment analysis on classified sentences and summarization(Akhtar et al., 2017). An interactive attention mechanism was proposed for aspect- and sentiment-aware abstractive review summarization(Yang et al., 2018). The model(Kunneman et al., 2018) incorporates representations of context, sentiment, and aspect words within reviews into the summary generation process. The authors developed three systems for generating pros and cons summaries of product reviews, which included a system based on syntactic phrases and two neural-network-based systems. These systems were evaluated in two ways: using held-out reviews with gold-standard pros and cons, and by soliciting human annotators to rate the systems' outputs in terms of relevance and completeness.

2.4 Peer Review Summarization

Peer-review summarization is a specific task that aims to automatically generate a summary of peer reviews for a particular research paper. Numerous studies have focused on this task, employing various techniques and models. Several works have built systems to generate meta-reviews from peer reviews by summarizing them.

The authors present MetaGen(Bhatia et al., 2020), a system that generates meta-reviews from peer reviews to aid the decision-making process in scientific papers and proposals. It utilizes an extractive and fine-tuned UniLM approach for crafting final abstractive meta-reviews and making acceptance/rejection decisions. A deep neural architecture was proposed for generating decision-aware meta-reviews from peer reviews(Bhatia et al., 2020). The model employs a multi-encoder transformer network for predicting the decision and generating the meta-review.

Previous studies have employed classification and regression techniques to evaluate the quality of scientific papers through analysis of peer reviews. Additionally, some research has focused on generating meta-reviews by summarizing the content of multiple reviews. To the best of our knowledge, our work is the first to summarize the argument based pros and cons of peer reviews.

3 Methodology

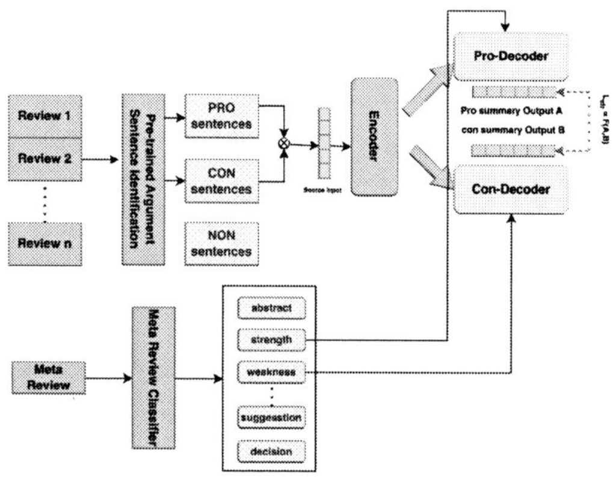

Figure 1: Our proposed architecture for generic Pros and Cons summarization

Figure 1 shows the architecture of our proposed model for generating pro and con summary.

3.1 Input Layer

Initially, we have a group or set of reviews $D = \{R_1, R_2, ..., R_n\}$, associated with a specific document or article. We merge all the reviews of a document into one comprehensive review S. Each $S = \{s_1, s_2, ..., s_m\}$, is a set of sentences, where $s_i \in S$ denotes a single sentence.

3.2 Argument Classification

Next, the set of sentences S are passed with a classifier to identify those review sentences which are argumentative. Following (Fromm et al., 2020) , we utlized a BERT large model with 340M parameters fine-tuned on the Argument Mining dataset (based on bert-large-cased) to classify the sentences into pro, con and non summary. We

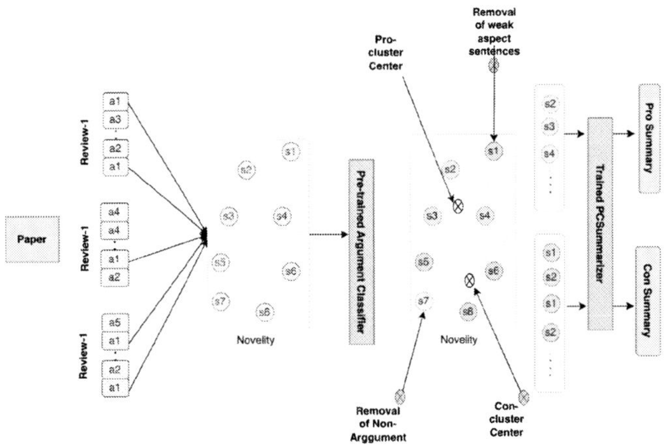

Figure 2: Our proposed aspect based pros and cons summarization architecture

reported a micro F1 score of 0.759%, which is almost the same as the original paper. For example :-

$$S_{pros} = \{s_1, s_3, ...s_{n-1}\}$$
$$S_{cons} = \{s_2, s_5, ...s_{n-3}\}$$
$$S_{nons} = \{s_4, s_6, ...s_n\}$$

Here, S_{pros} contains a set of sentences classified as pro, S_{cons} contains the sentences classified as con and S_{non} contains the sentences classified as $nons$. Non-argument sentences typically do not contain important information that is necessary for making a decision. Therefore, we discarded them.

3.3 Meta Review Classification

The reference summary of pros and cons summary is unavailable and the annotation of the summary is costly and need domain experienced experts. So we utilized the MReD dataset (Shen et al., 2022) which consists of 7,089 meta-reviews and all its 45k meta-review sentences. Each sentence in a meta-review is classified into one of the 9 pre-defined intent categories: abstract, strength, weakness, rating summary, area chair (AC) disagreement, rebuttal process, suggestion, decision, and miscellaneous(misc). We trained the RoBERTa-large + CRF with the same setting as mentioned in the paper. We hypothesize that a meta-reviewer will mention both the strengths and weaknesses of a product or research study in their summary, akin to a pro and con summary. So, we used the pre-trained model to extract the strength and weaknesses. Suppose, M is the set of review sentences in meta review. We utilize the set of sentences classified into strength $M_{strength} \in M$ and belonging to weakness $M_{weaknesses} \in M$ for training PCSummarizer, described in the next section.

3.4 PCSummarizer

Generative pre-trained models have exhibited outstanding results in the field of natural language generation, specifically in the area of text summarization (Dong et al., 2019; Lewis et al., 2020a). The adaptation of natural language processing models to specific domains, also known as domain adaptation, is a widely researched topic (Fu and Liu, 2022; III, 2009; Yu et al., 2021). Hua and Wang (2017) (Hua and Wang, 2017) were the pioneers in researching the adaptation of neural summarization models to specific domains, and it was found that these models possess the capability to select pertinent information even when trained on out-of-domain data.

In order to make the model capture the argumentative reviews (i.e. both pro and con sentences), the input text is formatted in the following way as source input for the Encoder.

Pro sentences [SEP] Con sentences

Here [SEP] is a special token.

The encoder first transforms the input into a sequence of hidden representations M.

$$h_t = ProsDecoder(M, y_{t-1}) \quad (1)$$

We initialized the ProsDecoder i.e. decoder for pros summary generation with the pre-trained Bart Large (Lewis et al., 2020a) decoder trained on CNN-daily mail. We implement the teacher forcing method on the ProsDecoder with the $M_{strength}$ to fine-tune the decoder.

$$P(y_t | y_{<t,C})^{(k)} = softmax(W_d h_t + b_d) \quad (2)$$

where h_t is the hidden representation of y_t (the t-th word in the target summary). k is the probability of generating the k-th token y_t given the previously generated $< t$ tokens and some context C.

We maximize the conditional log likelihood for a given N observation
$(C^{(i)}, Y^{(i)})_{i=1}^{N}$

$$L_{pros} = -\sum_{i=1}^{i=N}\sum_{t=1}^{t=T} logP(y_t^{(i)}|y_{<t}^{(i)}C^{(i)}) \quad (3)$$

Similarly, we define the ConDecoder :-

$$h_t = ConsDecoder(M, y_{t-1}) \quad (4)$$

The ConsDecoder (i.e. decoder for cons summary generation) is initialized with the pre-trained Bart Large decoder trained on CNN-daily mail. We implement the teacher forcing method on the ConsDecoder with the $M_{weakness}$ to train the decoder.

$$P(y_t|y_{<t,C})^{(k)} = softmax(W_d h_t + b_d) \quad (5)$$

We maximize the conditional log likelihood for a given N observation
$(C^{(i)}, Y^{(i)})_{i=1}^{N}$

$$L_{cons} = -\sum_{i=1}^{i=N}\sum_{t=1}^{t=T} logP(y_t^{(i)}|y_{<t}^{(i)}C^{(i)}) \quad (6)$$

We introduced an appropriate loss function as defined below to ensure that the similar summaries are not generated for pros and cons :-

$$L_{diss} = sim(S_{pros}, S_{cons}) \quad (7)$$

Here, sim is the similarity between the two summaries. We calculate the similarity between the two summaries by [CLS] pooling as in BERT(Devlin et al., 2019).

We employ the following loss function as our final training loss :-

$$L = L_{pros} + L_{cons} + L_{diss} \quad (8)$$

Here, we combine the MLE loss from the ProsDecoder and ConsDecoder and the dissimilarity loss while training the summarizer.

3.5 Aspect based pros and cons summarization

In this section, we describe our proposed architecture for aspect-based pros and cons summarization. Figure 2 shows the architecture of our aspect based pro and con summarization. Supervised training is not possible due to the unavailability of golden pros and cons summary for each aspect. So, we propose an unsupervised technique. Similar to the previously described input layer, the reviews are combined. The reviews are then passed to the aspect classifier. We use the already annotated dataset for our evaluation. Suppose the output after the aspect classification is S_a, where S is the set of sentences that belongs to aspect category a. The sentences belonging to each aspect S_a are passed to the argument classifier, which classifies the pre-trained argument classifier as described in Section 3.2. The output is S_a^{pros}, S_a^{cons}, S_a^{nons}. Similarly, as the non-arguments S_a^{nons} do not play much role in the decision, it is filtered out.

3.5.1 Clustering

To remove the review sentences that weakly belong to an aspect category, we produce a vector A_i for each aspect category by computing the average of sentence embeddings of the sentences belonging to that aspect. In particular, for each aspect category, we produce a vector that best represents the category, represented by the centroid. We create the sentence embedding by pre-trained BERT [CLS] pooling. We further control the selection of review sentences by filtering them based on their aspect category. In particular, we select the review sentences in S_a^{pros} and S_a^{cons}, given the aspect category a it belongs to. Our goal is to select the review sentences close to their aspect centroid. We iterate through every review sentence sen in S_a^{pros} and S_a^{cons}, we add it to the filter review set Sf_a^{pros} and Sf_a^{cons} if $cos(E_i, A_k) \leq \theta^3$. Where E_i is the embedding of the review sentence sen.

3.5.2 Summarization

Next, we create a abstract summary of the Sf_a^{pros} and the Sf_a^{cons}. We used the model PCSummarizer trained to create pros and cons summary of the review to create the final summary for each aspect as described in Section 3.4. If review text $Sf_a^{pros/cons}$ is less than 30 words, i.e. short reviews, they don't need further summarization as they are already con-

[3]We set the threshold θ as 0.5 empirically

Conference	Number of papers	Number of reviews	Acceptance rate	avg words
ICLR 2017	427	1,304	67%	399
ICLR 2018	907	3,499	35%	403
ICLR 2019	1,419	4,332	35%	403
ICLR 2020	2,213	6,722	27%	409

Table 3: Dataset statistics

cise. Using PCSummarizer may not add any value, so in that case, we don't further summarize from it.

4 Experiments

4.1 Dataset

We use the dataset collected from OpenReview[4] by the papers (Yuan et al., 2022; Fromm et al., 2020). The dataset contains the reviews from computer-science conferences. Table 3 shows the statistics of the dataset used. For training PCSummarizer we split the dataset into 0.7, 0.1, 0.2 for training, validation and test respectively. To evaluate our aspect-based summarization method, we recruited two expert NLP annotators with a strong command of the English language. They generated summaries for 150 papers from the dataset presented in (Wicherts, 2016), which contains peer reviews classified into different aspects. The definition of these aspects is provided in Appendix Table 8.

4.2 Implementation details

For PCSummarizer, we use the BART large model pre-trained on CNN/DailyMail dataset from the hugging face library [5]. We initialized the pre-trained weights to both the decoder and the encoder before fine-tuning them. We performed hyperparameter tuning on the validation set and reported the best-performing parameters. We use a dynamic learning rate, warm up 1000 iterations, and decay afterwards. We trained the model for 10 epochs with a batch size of 4. We train all the models on a single GPU (NVIDIA A100-PCIE 40GB).

4.3 Result and Analysis

Tables 4 and 5 present the results of a comparison between the various summarization methods, including extractive methods (LexRank, TextRank, SumBasic, Luhn) and abstractive methods (Pegasus and Bart) for summarization without aspects and with aspects, respectively. The results indicate that the abstractive methods performed better than the extractive methods in terms of the ROUGE score for both the summarization tasks. The pros and cons were separately input into the extractive systems, and we report the average. Similarly, for aspect-based pros and cons summarization, we calculated the score aspect-wise for each aspect and reported the average. BERTScore (Zhang et al., 2020b) computes a similarity score between each token of a candidate sentence and that of a reference sentence, relying on contextual embeddings to calculate token similarity, as opposed to exact matches. BERTScore is mainly used in abstractive summarization, so we also report BERTScore for the abstractive baselines Pegasus and BART. Similar to the extractive summarization, we trained the pros and cons encoder and decoder architecture separately and reported the average. We found that BART performed better compared to Pegasus with 1.63 F1 BERTScore and 2.12 Rouge-1 F1 score for full reviews pros and cons and BART with 1.96 BERTScore and 0.6 Rouge-1 F1 score for aspect-based summarization. Our proposed method APCS performed better than simple BART with 0.71 BERTScore and 1.21 Rouge-1 F1 score points for full reviews and 0.75 BERTScore and 1.68 Rouge-1 F1 score for aspect-based summarization. As we used the pre-trained model for argument classification and meta review classification, we don't report those results. However the result can be found in the original paper.

4.4 Ablation Study

We analyze the effectiveness of our proposed model (APCS) by conducting an ablation study, as shown in Table 7. By comparing the results of "APCS w/o diss" in Table 7 with an improvement of 0.93 and the original BART with a distinct encoder in Table 4, it is evident that inputting the pros and cons together improves the results compared to training them separately. This is likely due to the fact that sharing an encoder allows the model to learn general features that are useful for both summarization tasks.

When we ran the model (APCS without differentiation loss), we observed that the generated summaries for the cons sometimes included information that was more appropriate for the pros. This may be due to the fact that during the annotation

[4]https://openreview.net

[5]`https://huggingface.co/`

Model	BERTScore			Rouge		
	P	R	F1	R1	R2	RL
LexRank (Erkan and Radev, 2011)	–	–	–	24.30	5.90	25.18
TextRank (Mihalcea and Tarau, 2004)	–	–	–	24.32	5.89	25.12
LSA (Ozsoy et al., 2011)	–	–	–	25.88	6.20	25.72
Luhn (Luhn, 1958a)	–	–	–	26.26	6.18	25.81
KL-Sum (Haghighi and Vanderwende, 2009)	–	–	–	27.43	6.89	25.87
Pegasus (Zhang et al., 2020a)	50.17	49.55	49.98	28.42	7.05	26.32
BART (Lewis et al., 2020b)	50.73	52.65	51.61	30.40	8.76	27.14
APCS	**51.43**	**53.43**	**52.32**	**31.61**	**9.12**	**28.80**

Table 4: Experimental results on generic pros and cons summarization; ROUGE(F1), BERTScore. Here, P→Precision, R→Recall, R1→ROUGE with unigram, R2→ROUGE-2 for bigram overlap, RL→ROUGE-L for Longest Common Subsequence

Model	BERTScore			Rouge		
	P	R	F1	R1	R2	RL
LexRank (Erkan and Radev, 2011)	–	–	–	26.30	7.86	27.17
TextRank (Mihalcea and Tarau, 2004)	–	–	–	26.29	7.81	27.10
LSA (Ozsoy et al., 2011)	–	–	–	27.82	8.16	27.71
Luhn (Luhn, 1958a)	–	–	–	28.11	8.12	27.59
KL-Sum (Haghighi and Vanderwende, 2009)	–	–	–	29.39	8.78	27.86
Pegasus (Zhang et al., 2020a)	51.67	51.64	51.60	30.29	7.05	28.31
BART (Lewis et al., 2020b)	52.71	54.62	53.56	32.41	10.74	29.11
APCS	**53.41**	**55.42**	**54.31**	**32.62**	**11.09**	**30.79**

Table 5: Experimental results on aspect-based pros and cons summarization

Model	w/o Aspect				Aspect based			
	A-Coverage	Readability	Diversity	I	A-Coverage	Readability	Diversity	I
KL-Sum(Erkan and Radev, 2011)	3.0	**8.5**	3.0	3.0	5.0	8.0	3.5	3.5
Pegasus (Zhang et al., 2020a)	4.0	4.5	3.0	3.0	5.5	4.5	3.0	3.5
BART	4.25	5.0	4.5	4.0	4.5	**5.0**	4.5	6.0
APCS	**4.5**	5.0	**5.0**	**4.25**	**7.25**	**5.0**	**5.0**	**6.25**

Table 6: Human evaluation results. Here, A-Coverage denotes Aspect coverage; I → Informativeness ; Bold text is intended to highlight the best performance.

	R-1	R-2	R-L
APCS w/o diss	31.33	9.02	28.24
APCS(aspect based) w/o clustering filter	32.03	10.78	30.12

Table 7: Ablation study of our experiments

process, reviewers/editors often use polite language when discussing cons/weakness, such as "I like the paper but..." or "The paper is written well but there are a few technical...". As a result, the ConsDecoder may have learned to include some pros information in the summary as well during the training process. We observed a slight improvement in the results when the differentiation loss was included in the model, which resulted in a better separation of the pros and cons summaries.

For aspect-based unsupervised summarization, we also removed the aspect sentence filtering and observed a drop in the results by 0.59 Rouge-1 F1 score. This demonstrates the effectiveness of aspect-based cluster filtering in improving the overall performance of the model.

4.5 Human Evaluation

We conducted a human evaluation to assess the effectiveness of our model by providing a set of 150 randomly selected papers along with their ground-truth reviews and generated summaries to three domain experts in NLP with a minimum of 5 years of experience. Table 6 shows the results of the evaluation. We asked the responders to evaluate the summaries by rating them between 1 to 10 on Likert Scale (Taherdoost, 2019) based on the following :

- Q1 (Aspect-coverage): Assesses which summary effectively captures the opinions about the specified aspects.
- Q2 (Readability): Evaluates the readability of the summaries.
- Q3 (Diversity): Identifies which summary contains the least amount of repetitive information.
- Q4 (Informativeness): Assesses the usefulness of the summary by providing information about the original reviews.

Consistent with the automated evaluation results, summaries generated by "APCS without aspect" achieved the best scores for Aspect-Coverage, Informativeness, and Diversity compared to the baselines. However, the model may still generate redundant phrases in summaries, particularly in the pros and cons, resulting in a low diversity score. Additionally, the readability score for APCS (both) was lower than that of KL-Sum. The reason for this is that KL-Sum is extractive, meaning that the summaries are taken directly from human-written reviews, while APCS generates abstractive summaries. The readability of BART and APCS (both) is similar. In contrast, the abstractive summary generated by APCS (aspect) effectively captures ideas on aspects. The APCS aspect-based model achieved high Aspect-coverage as it focuses mainly on each aspect of the reviews. However, APCS (both) performed better than PEGASUS on every score, despite both being abstractive methods of summary generation. These results validate the quality of our generation method. We also observed that our model fails when argument is misclassified by the pre-trained model or the aspect classification model makes wrong prdecitions.

5 Conclusion and Future Work

We have proposed a novel architecture for generating both generic and aspect-based pros and cons summaries of peer reviews, utilizing both supervised and unsupervised methods. Our results demonstrate the effectiveness of our proposed architecture. As a future work, investigating the scalability of our proposed architecture for larger datasets and its performance on a diverse range of research domains would also be valuable.

ACKNOWLEDGEMENT

Sandeep Kumar acknowledges the Prime Minister Research Fellowship (PMRF) program of the Govt of India for its support.

References

Nadeem Akhtar, Nashez Zubair, Abhishek Kumar, and Tameem Ahmad. 2017. Aspect based sentiment oriented summarization of hotel reviews. *Procedia Computer Science*, 115:563–571. 7th International Conference on Advances in Computing Communications, ICACC-2017, 22-24 August 2017, Cochin, India.

Phyllis B. Baxendale. 1958. Machine-made index for technical literature - an experiment. *IBM J. Res. Dev.*, 2(4):354–361.

Chaitanya Bhatia, Tribikram Pradhan, and Sukomal Pal. 2020. Metagen: An academic meta-review generation system. In *Proceedings of the 43rd International ACM SIGIR Conference on Research and Development in Information Retrieval*, SIGIR '20, page 1653–1656, New York, NY, USA. Association for Computing Machinery.

Lutz Bornmann and Hans-Dieter Daniel. 2010. Reliability of reviewers' ratings when using public peer review: a case study. *Learn. Publ.*, 23(2):124–131.

Lutz Bornmann, Markus Wolf, and Hans-Dieter Daniel. 2012. Closed versus open reviewing of journal manuscripts: how far do comments differ in language use? *Scientometrics*, 91(3):843–856.

Jianpeng Cheng and Mirella Lapata. 2016. Neural summarization by extracting sentences and words. In *Proceedings of the 54th Annual Meeting of the Association for Computational Linguistics, ACL 2016, August 7-12, 2016, Berlin, Germany, Volume 1: Long Papers*. The Association for Computer Linguistics.

Ed Collins, Isabelle Augenstein, and Sebastian Riedel. 2017. A supervised approach to extractive summarisation of scientific papers. In *Proceedings of the 21st Conference on Computational Natural Language Learning (CoNLL 2017), Vancouver, Canada, August 3-4, 2017*, pages 195–205. Association for Computational Linguistics.

Jacob Devlin, Ming-Wei Chang, Kenton Lee, and Kristina Toutanova. 2019. BERT: pre-training of deep bidirectional transformers for language understanding. In *Proceedings of the 2019 Conference of the North American Chapter of the Association for Computational Linguistics: Human Language Technologies, NAACL-HLT 2019, Minneapolis, MN, USA, June 2-7, 2019, Volume 1 (Long and Short Papers)*, pages 4171–4186. Association for Computational Linguistics.

Li Dong, Nan Yang, Wenhui Wang, Furu Wei, Xiaodong Liu, Yu Wang, Jianfeng Gao, Ming Zhou, and Hsiao-Wuen Hon. 2019. Unified language model pre-training for natural language understanding and generation. In *Advances in Neural Information Processing Systems 32: Annual Conference on Neural Information Processing Systems 2019, NeurIPS 2019, December 8-14, 2019, Vancouver, BC, Canada*, pages 13042–13054.

Günes Erkan and Dragomir R. Radev. 2004. Lexrank: Graph-based lexical centrality as salience in text summarization. *J. Artif. Intell. Res.*, 22:457–479.

Günes Erkan and Dragomir R. Radev. 2011. Lexrank: Graph-based lexical centrality as salience in text summarization. *CoRR*, abs/1109.2128.

Michael Fromm, Evgeniy Faerman, Max Berrendorf, Siddhartha Bhargava, Ruoxia Qi, Yao Zhang, Lukas Dennert, Sophia Selle, Yang Mao, and Thomas Seidl. 2020. Argument mining driven analysis of peer-reviews. In *AAAI Conference on Artificial Intelligence*.

Yanping Fu and Yun Liu. 2022. Domain adaptation with a shrinkable discrepancy strategy for cross-domain sentiment classification. *Neurocomputing*, 494:56–66.

Mahak Gambhir and Vishal Gupta. 2017. Recent automatic text summarization techniques: a survey. *Artif. Intell. Rev.*, 47(1):1–66.

Shima Gerani, Giuseppe Carenini, and Raymond T. Ng. 2019. Modeling content and structure for abstractive review summarization. *Comput. Speech Lang.*, 53:302–331.

Shima Gerani, Yashar Mehdad, Giuseppe Carenini, Raymond T. Ng, and Bita Nejat. 2014. Abstractive summarization of product reviews using discourse structure. In *Proceedings of the 2014 Conference on Empirical Methods in Natural Language Processing, EMNLP 2014, October 25-29, 2014, Doha, Qatar, A meeting of SIGDAT, a Special Interest Group of the ACL*, pages 1602–1613. ACL.

Aria Haghighi and Lucy Vanderwende. 2009. Exploring content models for multi-document summarization. In *Proceedings of Human Language Technologies: The 2009 Annual Conference of the North American Chapter of the Association for Computational Linguistics*, pages 362–370, Boulder, Colorado. Association for Computational Linguistics.

Hiroaki Hayashi, Prashant Budania, Peng Wang, Chris Ackerson, Raj Neervannan, and Graham Neubig. 2021. WikiAsp: A Dataset for Multi-domain Aspect-based Summarization. *Transactions of the Association for Computational Linguistics*, 9:211–225.

Xinyu Hua and Lu Wang. 2017. A pilot study of domain adaptation effect for neural abstractive summarization. In *Proceedings of the Workshop on New Frontiers in Summarization, NFiS@EMNLP 2017, Copenhagen, Denmark, September 7, 2017*, pages 100–106. Association for Computational Linguistics.

Hal Daumé III. 2009. Frustratingly easy domain adaptation. *CoRR*, abs/0907.1815.

Dongyeop Kang, Waleed Ammar, Bhavana Dalvi, Madeleine van Zuylen, Sebastian Kohlmeier, Eduard H. Hovy, and Roy Schwartz. 2018. A dataset of peer reviews (peerread): Collection, insights and NLP applications. In *Proceedings of the 2018 Conference of the North American Chapter of the Association for Computational Linguistics: Human Language Technologies, NAACL-HLT 2018, New Orleans, Louisiana, USA, June 1-6, 2018, Volume 1 (Long Papers)*, pages 1647–1661. Association for Computational Linguistics.

Hayato Kobayashi, Masaki Noguchi, and Taichi Yatsuka. 2015. Summarization based on embedding distributions. In *Proceedings of the 2015 Conference on Empirical Methods in Natural Language Processing, EMNLP 2015, Lisbon, Portugal, September 17-21, 2015*, pages 1984–1989. The Association for Computational Linguistics.

Michail Kovanis, Raphaël Porcher, Philippe Ravaud, and Ludovic Trinquart. 2016. The global burden of journal peer review in the biomedical literature: Strong imbalance in the collective enterprise. *PLoS ONE*, 11.

Sandeep Kumar, Tirthankar Ghosal, Prabhat Kumar Bharti, and Asif Ekbal. 2021. Sharing is caring! joint multitask learning helps aspect-category extraction and sentiment detection in scientific peer reviews. In *2021 ACM/IEEE Joint Conference on Digital Libraries (JCDL)*, pages 270–273.

Florian Kunneman, Sander Wubben, Antal van den Bosch, and Emiel Krahmer. 2018. Aspect-based summarization of pros and cons in unstructured product reviews. In *Proceedings of the 27th International Conference on Computational Linguistics*, pages 2219–2229, Santa Fe, New Mexico, USA. Association for Computational Linguistics.

Julian Kupiec, Jan O. Pedersen, and Francine Chen. 1995. A trainable document summarizer. In *SIGIR'95, Proceedings of the 18th Annual International ACM SIGIR Conference on Research and Development in Information Retrieval. Seattle, Washington, USA, July 9-13, 1995 (Special Issue of the SIGIR Forum)*, pages 68–73. ACM Press.

John Langford and Mark Guzdial. 2015. The arbitrariness of reviews, and advice for school administrators. *Commun. ACM*, 58(4):12–13.

HyunSoo Lee, YunSeok Choi, and Jee-Hyong Lee. 2020. Attention history-based attention for abstractive text summarization. In *SAC '20: The 35th ACM/SIGAPP Symposium on Applied Computing, online event, [Brno, Czech Republic], March 30 - April 3, 2020*, pages 1075–1081. ACM.

Mike Lewis, Yinhan Liu, Naman Goyal, Marjan Ghazvininejad, Abdelrahman Mohamed, Omer Levy, Veselin Stoyanov, and Luke Zettlemoyer. 2020a. BART: denoising sequence-to-sequence pre-training for natural language generation, translation, and comprehension. In *Proceedings of the 58th Annual Meeting of the Association for Computational Linguistics, ACL 2020, Online, July 5-10, 2020*, pages 7871–7880. Association for Computational Linguistics.

Mike Lewis, Yinhan Liu, Naman Goyal, Marjan Ghazvininejad, Abdelrahman Mohamed, Omer Levy, Veselin Stoyanov, and Luke Zettlemoyer. 2020b. BART: Denoising sequence-to-sequence pre-training for natural language generation, translation, and comprehension. In *Proceedings of the 58th Annual Meeting of the Association for Computational Linguistics*, pages 7871–7880, Online. Association for Computational Linguistics.

Fangtao Li, Chao Han, Minlie Huang, Xiaoyan Zhu, Yingju Xia, Shu Zhang, and Hao Yu. 2010. Structure-aware review mining and summarization. In *COLING 2010, 23rd International Conference on Computational Linguistics, Proceedings of the Conference, 23-27 August 2010, Beijing, China*, pages 653–661. Tsinghua University Press.

H. P. Luhn. 1958a. The automatic creation of literature abstracts. *IBM Journal of Research and Development*, 2(2):159–165.

Hans Peter Luhn. 1958b. The automatic creation of literature abstracts. *IBM J. Res. Dev.*, 2(2):159–165.

Rebecca Mason, Benjamin Gaska, Benjamin Van Durme, Pallavi Choudhury, Ted Hart, Bill Dolan, Kristina Toutanova, and Margaret Mitchell. 2016. Microsummarization of online reviews: An experimental study. In *Proceedings of the Thirtieth AAAI Conference on Artificial Intelligence, February 12-17, 2016, Phoenix, Arizona, USA*, pages 3015–3021. AAAI Press.

Rada Mihalcea and Paul Tarau. 2004. TextRank: Bringing order into text. In *Proceedings of the 2004 Conference on Empirical Methods in Natural Language Processing*, pages 404–411, Barcelona, Spain. Association for Computational Linguistics.

Ani Nenkova, Lucy Vanderwende, and Kathleen R. McKeown. 2006. A compositional context sensitive multi-document summarizer: exploring the factors that influence summarization. In *SIGIR 2006: Proceedings of the 29th Annual International ACM SIGIR Conference on Research and Development in Information Retrieval, Seattle, Washington, USA, August 6-11, 2006*, pages 573–580. ACM.

Makbule Gulcin Ozsoy, Ferda Nur Alpaslan, and Ilyas Cicekli. 2011. Text summarization using latent semantic analysis. *J. Inf. Sci.*, 37(4):405–417.

Daraksha Parveen, Mohsen Mesgar, and Michael Strube. 2016. Generating coherent summaries of scientific articles using coherence patterns. In *Proceedings of the 2016 Conference on Empirical Methods in Natural Language Processing, EMNLP 2016, Austin, Texas, USA, November 1-4, 2016*, pages 772–783. The Association for Computational Linguistics.

Barbara Plank and Reinard van Dalen. 2019. Citetracked: A longitudinal dataset of peer reviews and citations. In *Proceedings of the 4th Joint Workshop on Bibliometric-enhanced Information Retrieval and Natural Language Processing for Digital Libraries (BIRNDL 2019) co-located with the 42nd International ACM SIGIR Conference on Research and Development in Information Retrieval (SIGIR 2019), Paris, France, July 25, 2019*, volume 2414 of *CEUR Workshop Proceedings*, pages 116–122. CEUR-WS.org.

Chenhui Shen, Liying Cheng, Ran Zhou, Lidong Bing, Yang You, and Luo Si. 2022. Mred: A meta-review dataset for structure-controllable text generation. In *Findings of the Association for Computational Linguistics: ACL 2022, Dublin, Ireland, May 22-27, 2022*, pages 2521–2535. Association for Computational Linguistics.

Christian Stab, Tristan Miller, and Iryna Gurevych. 2018. Cross-topic argument mining from heterogeneous sources using attention-based neural networks. *ArXiv*, abs/1802.05758.

Hamed Taherdoost. 2019. What is the best response scale for survey and questionnaire design; review of different lengths of rating scale / attitude scale / likert scale.

Andrew Tomkins, Min Zhang, and William D. Heavlin. 2017. Reviewer bias in single- versus double-blind peer review. *Proc. Natl. Acad. Sci. USA*, 114(48):12708–12713.

Jelte M. Wicherts. 2016. Peer review quality and transparency of the peer-review process in open access and subscription journals. *PLoS ONE*, 11.

Adhika Pramita Widyassari, Supriadi Rustad, Guruh Fajar Shidik, Edi Noersasongko, Abdul Syukur, Affandy Affandy, and De Rosal Ignatius Moses Setiadi. 2022. Review of automatic text summarization techniques methods. *Journal of King Saud University - Computer and Information Sciences*, 34(4):1029–1046.

Weiran Xu, Chenliang Li, Minghao Lee, and Chi Zhang. 2020. Multi-task learning for abstractive text summarization with key information guide network. *EURASIP J. Adv. Signal Process.*, 2020(1):16.

Min Yang, Qiang Qu, Ying Shen, Qiao Liu, Wei Zhao, and Jia Zhu. 2018. Aspect and sentiment aware abstractive review summarization. In *Proceedings of the 27th International Conference on Computational Linguistics*, pages 1110–1120, Santa Fe, New Mexico, USA. Association for Computational Linguistics.

Yinfei Yang, Forrest Sheng Bao, and Ani Nenkova. 2017. Detecting (un)important content for single-document news summarization. In *Proceedings of the 15th Conference of the European Chapter of the Association for Computational Linguistics, EACL 2017, Valencia, Spain, April 3-7, 2017, Volume 2: Short Papers*, pages 707–712. Association for Computational Linguistics.

Kaichun Yao, Libo Zhang, Dawei Du, Tiejian Luo, Lili Tao, and Yanjun Wu. 2020. Dual encoding for abstractive text summarization. *IEEE Trans. Cybern.*, 50(3):985–996.

Tiezheng Yu, Zihan Liu, and Pascale Fung. 2021. Adaptsum: Towards low-resource domain adaptation for abstractive summarization. In *Proceedings of the 2021 Conference of the North American Chapter of the Association for Computational Linguistics:*

Human Language Technologies, NAACL-HLT 2021, Online, June 6-11, 2021, pages 5892–5904. Association for Computational Linguistics.

Weizhe Yuan, Pengfei Liu, and Graham Neubig. 2021. Can we automate scientific reviewing? *CoRR*, abs/2102.00176.

Weizhe Yuan, Pengfei Liu, and Graham Neubig. 2022. Can we automate scientific reviewing? *J. Artif. Intell. Res.*, 75:171–212.

Jingqing Zhang, Yao Zhao, Mohammad Saleh, and Peter J. Liu. 2020a. PEGASUS: pre-training with extracted gap-sentences for abstractive summarization. In *Proceedings of the 37th International Conference on Machine Learning, ICML 2020, 13-18 July 2020, Virtual Event*, volume 119 of *Proceedings of Machine Learning Research*, pages 11328–11339. PMLR.

Tianyi Zhang, Varsha Kishore, Felix Wu, Kilian Q. Weinberger, and Yoav Artzi. 2020b. Bertscore: Evaluating text generation with BERT. In *8th International Conference on Learning Representations, ICLR 2020, Addis Ababa, Ethiopia, April 26-30, 2020*. OpenReview.net.

Aspect	Definition
Substance	Does the paper contains substantial experiments to demonstrate the effectiveness of proposed methods? Are there detailed result analysis? Does it contain meaningful ablation studies?
Motivation	Does the paper address an important problem? Are other people (practitioners or researchers) likely to use these ideas or build on them?
Clarity	For a reasonably well-prepared reader, is it clear what was done and why? Is the paper well-written and well-structured?
Meaningful Comparison	Are the comparisons to prior work sufficient given the space constraints? Are the comparisons fair?
Originality	Are there new research topic, technique, methodology, or insight?, etc
Soundness	Is the proposed approach sound? Are the claims in the paper convincingly supported?
Replicability	Is it easy to reproduce the results and verify the correctness of the results? Is the supporting dataset and/or software provided?

Table 8: Definition of aspects

On the Use of Language Models for Function Identification of Citations in Scholarly Papers

Tomoki Ikoma[1] and **Shigeki Matsubara**[1,2]
[1]Graduate School of Informatics, Nagoya University, Japan
[2]Information Technology Center, Nagoya University, Japan
ikoma.tomoki.d0@s.mail.nagoya-u.ac.jp

Abstract

Citation graphs represent the citation relations between papers, and they are commonly used by researchers to identify relevant papers. However, citation graphs do not always represent how papers are related to each other. To make more effective use of citation graphs to discover relevant papers, we can consider identifying the functions of citations and label each edge in the citation graphs with its function. This paper proposes a method to identify the functions of citations automatically. The proposed model utilizes language models, e.g., SciBERT, to identify the description of citation functions. However, the language models are limited in terms of the number of input tokens; thus, the entire citing paragraph cannot be processed at once. To overcome this problem, we analyzed the distribution of the descriptions of citation functions in the citing paragraphs and determined the focusing part in identifying the citation functions. Experiments conducted on scientific paper data demonstrated the effectiveness of the proposed method.

1 Introduction

Scientific papers cite publications for various reasons, and the connections between papers are established through citations. In addition, citation graphs[1] represent citations in a graph structure, and they are commonly used by researchers to identify relevant papers. However, the edges in citation graphs only represent the citations between papers; thus, citation graphs do not always represent how papers are related to each other. To make more effective use of citation graphs in order to discover relevant papers, we can consider identifying the functions of citations and label each edge in the citation graphs with its function[2].

Thus, in this paper, we propose a method to identify the functions of citations automatically based on the text of citing paragraphs. The proposed model utilizes language models, e.g., SciBERT (Beltagy et al., 2019), to identify the citation functions. However, the language models are limited in terms of the number of input tokens; thus, the entire citing paragraph cannot be processed at once. To overcome this problem, we analyzed the distribution of the descriptions of citation functions in the citing paragraphs and determined the focusing part in identifying citation functions. Experiments conducted on scientific paper data demonstrated the effectiveness of the proposed method.

2 Datasets for Citation Function Identification

A previous study (Teufel et al., 2006) published the first dataset for the citation function identification task. They manually annotated 548 citation instances extracted from 161 papers in the computational linguistics domain as one of the 12 classes of citation functions. However, their dataset suffered from several limitations, e.g., the small data size and the coverage of only one research domain. Despite these issues, no new datasets were created for years due to various difficulties, including the definition of labeling schema and the annotation of gold labels (Kunnath et al., 2022b).

Recently, several new datasets for the citation classification task, e.g., ACL-ARC (Jurgens et al., 2018) and SciCite (Cohan et al., 2019), have been created and made available to the public. The ACL-ARC dataset comprises approximately 2,000 citation instances extracted from papers in the ACL Anthology, where each instance is labeled as either one of the six classes of citation functions, i.e., `background`, `compares_contrasts`, `extension`, `future`, `motivation` and `uses`. The SciCite dataset contains approximately 11,000 citation instances sampled from papers in the computer science and medical domains with class labels of either `background`, `method`, or `result`.

[1]`https://citationgraph.org/`

[2]For citations via URLs, (Tsunokake and Matsubara, 2022) proposed a method to identify the function of citations.

Proceedings of the 2nd Workshop on Information Extraction from Scientific Publications, pages 130–135
Nov 1, 2023.

In addition, a large and diverse dataset has been created for the Citation Context Classification Shared Task (Kunnath et al., 2020, 2021). The shared task provided a dataset of 3,000 citation instances sampled from papers in various domains. Here, each citation instance was labeled by the authors of the citing papers under the same schema as ACL-ARC. However, the classification labels were annotated at each author's own discretion; thus, the consistency of the labels over the entire dataset was not guaranteed.

3 Task Definition and Data Analysis

3.1 Task Definition

We propose a method to automatically identify the citation functions based on the text containing citations. Specifically, from a given paragraph containing citations, we propose a method to extract the part that describes why the target paper was cited, and classify the described citation function into one of the eight categories[3]: `background`, `motivation`, `uses`, `extends`, `similarities`, `differences`, `compare/contrast`, and `future work`.

3.2 FOCAL Dataset

In this study, we used the dataset from the Function Of Citation in Astrophysics Literature (FOCAL) shared task (Grezes et al., 2023). The FOCAL dataset comprises of 2,421 training examples, 606 validation examples, and 821 test examples extracted from papers in the astrophysics domain, and each example contains the paragraph text and the single or multiple positional information of the target citation. Training examples also include the positional information and the class label of the descriptions of the citation functions for data analysis and model training. Note that some examples have multiple spans that describe the citation function, and the class label is annotated on each span in such cases.

3.3 Data Analysis

We analyzed the class label distribution of the citation functions and the positional relations between citation tags and citation function descriptions in the training set.

[3]A detailed explanation of each category is available at `https://ui.adsabs.harvard.edu/WIESP/2023/LabelDefinitions`.

Table 1: Number of examples with each class of citation function. Note that the sum of each row does not match the number of training examples, because some examples are labeled with more than one citation function class.

Function class	Number of examples	
Background	1,098	45.35%
Motivation	161	6.65%
Uses	605	24.99%
Extends	7	0.29%
Similarities	202	8.34%
Differences	87	3.59%
Compare/Contrast	400	16.52%
Future work	27	1.12%

Table 2: Percentage of sentences containing descriptions of citation functions. For preceding sentences, cases with no sentences before the citing sentence are excluded. For following sentences, cases with no sentences after the citing sentence are excluded.

	Inclusion percentage	
Preceding sentences	285/2,419	11.78%
Citing sentences	2,436/2,464	98.86%
Following sentences	258/2,419	10.66%

3.3.1 Distribution of Citation Function Label

Table 1 shows the number of examples labeled for each class of citation function. As can be seen, the most frequent class is background representing approximately 45% of the analyzed examples. In contrast, other classes, e.g., extends and future work, include low number of examples.

3.3.2 Positional Relation with Citation Tags

We analyzed the positional relations between the citation tags and the citation function descriptions. Here, we initially split each paragraph into sentences using the NLTK sentence tokenizer (Bird et al., 2009), and then we extracted the citing sentences and their preceding and following sentences. Next, we computed the percentage of sentences containing the descriptions of the citation functions for the citing, preceding and following sentences.

Table 2 shows the percentage of sentences containing the descriptions of the citation functions. As shown, the preceding and following sentences contained descriptions of citation functions approximately 10% of cases. In contrast, only 28 citing sentences without citation function descriptions were found. These results indicate that the citing sentences almost always contain descriptions of

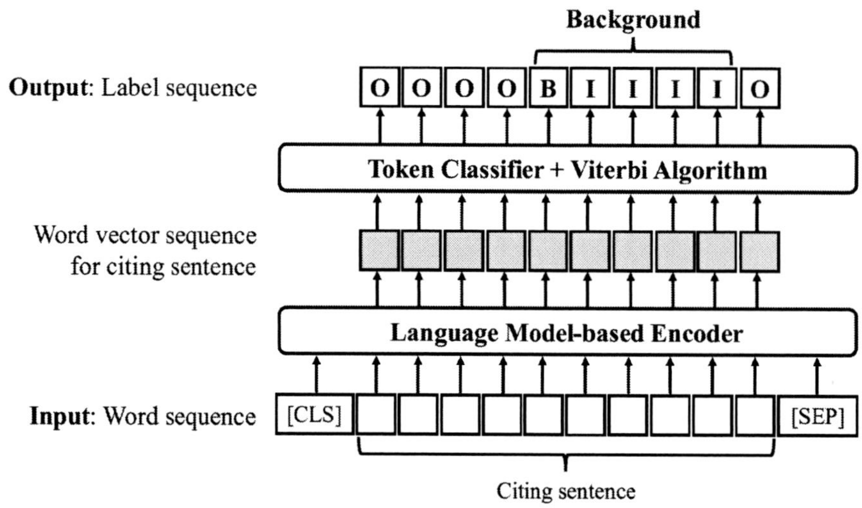

Figure 1: Structure of the proposed model

the citation functions; however, it is rare for such descriptions to extend to nearby sentences.

4 Method

4.1 Model Structure

The proposed method utilizes language models, e.g., SciBERT (Beltagy et al., 2019) to identify the citation functions as shown in Figure 1. The model comprises an encoder and a token classifier, and it identifies the citation functions as follows:

1. Convert the input text to a sequence of words and add [CLS] and [SEP] at the start and end of the sequence.

2. Transform the words in the citing sentence to feature vectors using the encoder.

3. Output a BIO tag sequence that indicates whether each word is the beginning, inside or outside of the span describing the citation function with the token classifier. Here, the Viterbi algorithm (Forney, 1973) is employed to avoid generating invalid sequences, e.g., sequences where I follows O.

4. Generate a class label of citation functions for each subsequence starting with B.

4.2 Range of Input Text

Note that the citing paragraph cannot be processed at once by language models, e.g., SciBERT, due to the limitation in the number of input tokens; thus, we must determine which part of a paragraph to focus on prior to inputting the text to the model. When training the model, the focusing part can be determined as the sentence containing the annotated span of the citation function descriptions and the m preceding and n following sentences. However, such annotations of the span of the citation function descriptions are not given at the time of prediction. Thus, based on the results of the analysis described in Section 3.3.2, we determine the focusing part for prediction as the citing sentence and the m preceding and n following sentences.

Table 3: Citation function identification performance of different language models

Model	Word accuracy	Exact match
SciBERT	**68.13**	34.14
RoBERTa	67.33	33.70
ALBERT-v2	67.01	32.06
DeBERTa-v3	67.76	**35.02**

5 Experiment

5.1 Selection of Language Models

We compared the performance of several language models on identifying the citation functions. Here, we trained the SciBERT (Beltagy et al., 2019), RoBERTa (Liu et al., 2019), ALBERT-v2 (Lan et al., 2019), and DeBERTa-v3 (He et al., 2023) models on 85% of the FOCAL training data as the training subset, and we evaluated each model on the remaining 15% of the data as the development subset. During the training process, we fine-tuned

Table 4: Citation function identification performance with different input text window sizes

Input text window		Evaluation metrics		
prev(m)	next(n)	Full	Generic	Labels
0	0	51.11	78.03	64.82
0	1	51.26	75.49	66.23
0	2	49.23	74.16	64.61
0	3	49.60	74.83	65.15
1	0	50.87	79.82	64.57
1	1	50.93	76.61	64.75
1	2	49.08	76.45	64.72
2	0	**51.97**	**79.99**	64.23
2	1	49.73	74.52	65.96
3	0	51.90	79.13	**67.10**

each language model on 2,677 sentences containing citation function descriptions in the training subset over 30 epochs. At the end of each epoch, we evaluated the trained models by the word-based labeling accuracy on 454 sentences in the development subset and saved the best model.

Table 3 shows the performance of each model evaluated by the word-based accuracy and sentence-based exact match rate on the development subset. As can be seen, the best word-based accuracy was achieved by the SciBERT, and the best sentence-based exact match rate was obtained by the DeBERTa-v3 model.

5.2 Selection of Input Text Window Size

We searched for the best setting for the focusing part in the citing paragraphs by training the SciBERT with different settings. Following the experimental setup presented in the literature (Kunnath et al., 2022a), we set the number of m preceding and n following sentences. Here, for each m and n value, we fine-tuned the SciBERT model on the sentence containing citation function descriptions, m preceding sentences, and n following sentences in the training subset. We then saved the best model over 30 epochs and evaluated this model on the development subset in terms of the following metrics.

Full F1 score that considers the predictions to be correct if both of the predicted placement and class labels are correct.

Generic F1 score that considers the predictions to be correct if the predicted placement is correct.

Table 5: Experimental result on validation data

	Full	Generic	Labels
Baseline	23.68	59.86	42.87
Proposed model	**54.08**	**79.92**	**65.94**

Labels F1 score that considers the predictions to be correct if the predicted class label is correct.

The evaluation results are shown in Table 4. As can be seen, model performance was improved by extending the focusing part to the preceding sentences; however, extending the focusing part to the following sentences did not contribute performance improvement.

5.3 Final Evaluaiton

Based on the results of the experiments discussed in Sections 5.1 and 5.2, we fine-tuned the SciBERT model over 30 epochs on the sentences containing the citation function descriptions and 3 preceding sentences in the training subset. At the end of each epoch, we evaluated the performance of the model according to the word-based accuracy on the development subset and saved the best model. Then, on the FOCAL validation and test data, we identified the citation functions using the trained model. On the validation data, we compared the performance to a baseline that always predicts the description of the citation function as the citing sentence and labels as background.

Table 5 shows the experimental results obtained on the validation data. As shown, the proposed model exhibited better results for all three evaluation metrics compared to the baseline, which indicates the effectiveness of the proposed model.

On the testing data, the proposed model achieved the scores of 51.97 Full, 73.00 Generic and 69.44 Labels.

6 Conclusion

This paper has proposed a method to identify the functions of citations automatically based on the text of citing paragraphs. The proposed method utilizes the SciBERT model to identify the citation function based on the citing sentences and nearby sentences under the assumption that citation functions are described near the citation. Experiments conducted on scientific paper data demonstrated the effectiveness of the proposed method.

Table 6: Performance of identifying sentences containing citation function descriptions

Citing sentences (365 examples)			
	Precision	Recall	F1 score
Baseline	99.18	100.00	99.59
SciBERT	99.39	90.06	94.49
Non-citing sentences (4,153 examples)			
	Precision	Recall	F1 score
Baseline	0.00	0.00	0.00
SciBERT	0.73	10.87	1.36
Overall (4,518 examples)			
	Precision	Recall	F1 score
Baseline	99.18	79.74	88.40
SciBERT	19.74	74.01	31.17

Limitations

The proposed method assumes that the function of the citation is always described in the citing sentence and its surrounding sentences, while sentences distant from the citing sentence do not contain descriptions of citation functions. Thus, the proposed method cannot extract descriptions of citation functions for cases where the citation function is described in text distant from the citing sentence. Although we uniformly determined the part of the citing paragraph to focus on experimentally, the part of the citing paragraph to focus on should be dynamically determined.

To decide the focusing part of the citing paragraph, we can consider using language models, e.g., SciBERT, to identify sentences that are likely to contain descriptions of the citation function. To evaluate the effectiveness of this strategy, we trained SciBERT to predict whether a given sentence is likely to contain description of the citation function and evaluated the performance of the trained model. Here, for training, we split the citing paragraphs in the training subset into sentences using the NLTK sentence tokenizer and used sentences containing descriptions of the citation functions as positive examples, and sentences without description of citation functions were used as negative examples. Then, the model was trained using all positive examples and 10% of randomly sampled negative examples and evaluated in terms of precision, recall and F1 score on the development subset. To better understand of the model's performance, we computed the evaluation metrics for citing and non-citing sentences separately, and we compared this model to a baseline that always predicts citing sentences to contain descriptions of the citation functions.

Table 6 shows evaluation results. As can be seen, the performance of the trained model for non-citing sentences was very poor. In addition, the overall performance was considerably worse than that of the baseline. These results indicate that the predictions are influenced greatly by whether each given sentence is a citing sentence; thus, classifying sentences with language models is not an effective method to identify the sentences containing the descriptions of citation functions.

Acknowledgments

This work was partially supported by the Grant-in-Aid for Challenging Research (Exploratory) (No. 23K18506) of JSPS and by JST SPRING, Grant Number JPMJSP2125. The computation was carried out on supercomputer "Flow" at Information Technology Center, Nagoya University.

References

Iz Beltagy, Kyle Lo, and Arman Cohan. 2019. SciBERT: A pretrained language model for scientific text. In *Proceedings of the 2019 Conference on Empirical Methods in Natural Language Processing and the 9th International Joint Conference on Natural Language Processing*, pages 3615–3620.

Steven Bird, Ewan Klein, and Edward Loper. 2009. *Natural Language Processing with Python*, 1st edition. O'Reilly Media, Inc.

Arman Cohan, Waleed Ammar, Madeleine van Zuylen, and Field Cady. 2019. Structural scaffolds for citation intent classification in scientific publications. In *Proceedings of the 2019 Conference of the North American Chapter of the Association for Computational Linguistics: Human Language Technologies, Volume 1 (Long and Short Papers)*, pages 3586–3596. Association for Computational Linguistics.

G.D. Forney. 1973. The Viterbi algorithm. *Proceedings of the IEEE*, 61(3):268–278.

Felix Grezes, Thomas Allen, Tirthankar Ghosal, and Sergi Blanco-Cuaresma. 2023. Function of citation in astrophysics literature (FOCAL): Findings of the shared task. In *Proceedings of the 2nd Workshop on Information Extraction from Scientific Publications*. Association for Computational Linguistics.

Pengcheng He, Jianfeng Gao, and Weizhu Chen. 2023. DeBERTaV3: Improving DeBERTa using ELECTRA-style pre-training with gradient-disentangled embedding sharing. In *The 11th International Conference on Learning Representations*.

David Jurgens, Srijan Kumar, Raine Hoover, Dan McFarland, and Dan Jurafsky. 2018. Measuring the evolution of a scientific field through citation frames. *Transactions of the Association for Computational Linguistics*, 6:391–406.

Suchetha Nambanoor Kunnath, David Pride, Bikash Gyawali, and Petr Knoth. 2020. Overview of the 2020 WOSP 3C citation context classification task. In *Proceedings of 8th International Workshop on Mining Scientific Publications*, pages 75–83. Association for Computational Linguistics.

Suchetha Nambanoor Kunnath, David Pride, Drahomira Herrmannova, and Petr Knoth. 2021. Overview of the 2021 SDP 3C citation context classification shared task. In *Proceedings of 2nd Workshop on Scholarly Document Processing*, pages 150–158. Association for Computational Linguistics.

Suchetha Nambanoor Kunnath, David Pride, and Petr Knoth. 2022a. Dynamic context extraction for citation classification. In *Proceedings of the 2nd Conference of the Asia-Pacific Chapter of the Association for Computational Linguistics and the 12th International Joint Conference on Natural Language Processing (Volume 1: Long Papers)*, pages 539–549. Association for Computational Linguistics.

Suchetha Nambanoor Kunnath, Valentin Stauber, Ronin Wu, David Pride, Viktor Botev, and Petr Knoth. 2022b. ACT2: A multi-disciplinary semi-structured dataset for importance and purpose classification of citations. In *Proceedings of the 13th Language Resources and Evaluation Conference*, pages 3398–3406. European Language Resources Association.

Zhenzhong Lan, Mingda Chen, Sebastian Goodman, Kevin Gimpel, Piyush Sharma, and Radu Soricut. 2019. ALBERT: A lite BERT for self-supervised learning of language representations. *arXiv:1909.11942[cs.CL]*.

Yinhan Liu, Myle Ott, Naman Goyal, Jingfei Du, Mandar Joshi, Danqi Chen, Omer Levy, Mike Lewis, Luke Zettlemoyer, and Veselin Stoyanov. 2019. Roberta: A robustly optimized BERT pretraining approach. *arXiv:1907.11692[cs.CL]*.

Simone Teufel, Advaith Siddharthan, and Dan Tidhar. 2006. Automatic classification of citation function. In *Proceedings of the 2006 Conference on Empirical Methods in Natural Language Processing*, pages 103–110. Association for Computational Linguistics.

Masaya Tsunokake and Shigeki Matsubara. 2022. Classification of URL citations in scholarly papers for promoting utilization of research artifacts. In *Proceedings of the 1st Workshop on Information Extraction from Scientific Publications*, pages 8–19. Association for Computational Linguistics.

Automated Citation Function Classification and Context Extraction in Astrophysics: Leveraging Paraphrasing and Question Answering

Hariram Veeramani
Department of Electrical and Computer Engineering, UCLA, USA
hariram@ucla.edu

Surendrabikram Thapa
Department of Computer Science, Virginia Tech
Blacksburg, USA
sbt@vt.edu

Usman Naseem
College of Science and Engineering, James Cook University, Australia
usman.naseem@jcu.edu.au

Abstract

Scientific research relies heavily on the exchange of knowledge through citations in academic literature. In the domain of astrophysics, the precise classification of citation functions and the extraction of contextual information are critical for understanding the vast universe of research papers. This paper presents the system description for the WIESP 2023 FOCAL shared task. We introduce an automated approach that leverages state-of-the-art language models, including ALBERT, RoBERTa, BERT, and DistillBERT, to classify citation functions and extract context within astrophysical paragraphs. Our system combines paraphrasing and question-answering techniques to achieve accurate results. Through comprehensive experiments, we demonstrate the robustness of our approach, with ALBERT consistently delivering strong performance.

1 Introduction

Scientific research is a dynamic process fueled by the exchange of knowledge and ideas among researchers (Goodman and Royall, 1988; Ghosal et al., 2022; Tsunokake and Matsubara, 2022). In the context of scientific research, citations also serve as evidence and reference to past studies (Garfield et al., 1964). In the realm of astrophysics, the citation of existing literature plays a pivotal role in advancing our understanding of the universe Researchers rely on citations to establish the foundation of their work, compare results, and build upon previous discoveries. However, not all citations serve the same purpose. Some citations provide essential background knowledge, while others are used for comparison, validation, or to support specific claims within a research paper (Lauscher et al., 2022).

The citation graph is a foundational concept in scientific research, including astrophysics, where it plays a pivotal role in knowledge dissemination and discovery (Jurgens et al., 2018; Guo and Dai, 2022). This intricate network of references connects research papers, providing a basis for understanding, validation, and navigation within the vast and dynamic field of astrophysics literature. Citations serve as the foundation of knowledge, allowing researchers to establish context, validate findings, and trace the intellectual lineage of ideas (Cohan et al., 2019a). They also facilitate collaboration, highlight emerging trends, and aid in the navigation of extensive literature. Understanding the functions of citations is crucial in harnessing the full potential of the citation graph, and the FOCAL challenge at IJCNLP-AACL 2023 (Grezes et al., 2023) seeks to automate this classification, contributing to the advancement of astrophysical research and knowledge dissemination. Furthermore, as part of this challenge, we aim to identify not only the functions of citations but also the associated span of text in the paragraph that justifies these functions, enhancing the depth of understanding within astrophysical literature.

Moreover, recent advancements in language models (LMs) have provided exciting opportunities to tackle this challenge more effectively. These models, which are at the forefront of natural language processing (NLP), stand as powerful tools at the intersection of artificial intelligence and linguistics (Min et al., 2023; Thapa and Adhikari, 2023). Their growing capabilities, marked by their ability to understand and generate human-like text, present an opportunity to automate the classification of citation functions and the extraction of associated contextual information within the scientific literature.

In this paper, we introduce a comprehensive approach that leverages recent advancements in language models. Our methodology harnesses the power of paraphrasing and question-answering techniques to classify citation functions and extract relevant contextual spans within astrophysical paragraphs. We emphasize the adaptability and ver-

Proceedings of the 2nd Workshop on Information Extraction from Scientific Publications, pages 136–142
Nov 1, 2023.

satility of this approach, showcasing its potential applicability to various state-of-the-art language models. Through our efforts, we aim to contribute to the automation of citation function classification, ultimately advancing the accessibility and utility of astrophysics literature for researchers.

2 Task Description

The FOCAL (Function Of Citation in Astrophysics Literature) challenge (Grezes et al., 2023) presents a unique opportunity to delve into the intricate interplay between scientific literature and automated natural language processing.

2.1 Objective

Given a paragraph of text from the astrophysics literature, the challenge aims to develop machine learning models that can accurately determine why a citation is made in a given paragraph of astrophysics literature and identify the precise span of text within that paragraph that justifies the citation's function.

2.2 Dataset

The dataset provided for the FOCAL shared task consists of full-text fragments extracted from the NASA Astrophysics Data System (ADS) and has been meticulously annotated by domain experts to include essential information for the task.

Each entry in the dataset[1] for FOCAL 2023 adheres to the JSON Lines format, comprising a JSON dictionary with the following key elements:

- "Identifier": A unique string serving as an identifier for the entry, ensuring traceability and organization.
- "Paragraph": A text string extracted from astrophysics papers, which forms the basis for the citation function classification task.
- "Citation Text": A list of strings representing the citation(s) within the paragraph. While in most cases, this is a single string, there are instances where the citation text may be divided into multiple strings.

In the training dataset, the following additional information is provided:

- "Citation Start End": A list of integer pairs indicating the starting and ending positions of the citation(s) within the "Paragraph" text. In cases where the citation text is divided, multiple pairs are provided in corresponding order.
- "Functions Text": A list of strings highlighting portions of the paragraph that elucidate the function(s) of the citation(s). These strings serve as contextual evidence for understanding why the citation(s) were made.
- "Functions Label": A list of strings containing labels for each text element in "Functions Text." These labels correspond to the classification of the citation(s)' function(s) within the paragraph.
- "Functions Start End": A list of integer pairs indicating the starting and ending positions of the elements in "Functions Text" within the "Paragraph" text. Similar to the "Citation Start End" information, multiple pairs may exist when the "Functions Text" is divided.

> In some cases, when the pulse broadening time is a significant fraction of the pulse period (30 per cent or more) one can see a relatively sharp pulse, but at the same time the extended scattering tail may obscure the real baseline level, which leads to an underestimation of the pulsar flux. For pulsars with DMs in 200–300 pc cm-3 range this usually happens between 300 and 600 MHz (Lewandowski et al. 2013, 2015a). This leads to a somewhat pseudo-correlation between high DM and GPS pulsars (Kijak et al. 2007, 2011b) where serious underestimation of the flux at lower frequencies for high DM pulsars may give rise to an inverted spectra. The interferometric imaging technique provide a more robust measurement of the pulsar flux owing to the baseline lying at zero level thereby reducing errors made during the baseline subtraction.

As shown in the above paragraph, for the citation "Kijak et al. 2007" with start position = 495 and end position = 511, the expected model output is as follows:

- Function Labels: [Uses, Uses]
- Functions Start End: [(418, 492), (521, 640)]

[1] https://huggingface.co/datasets/adsabs/FOCAL

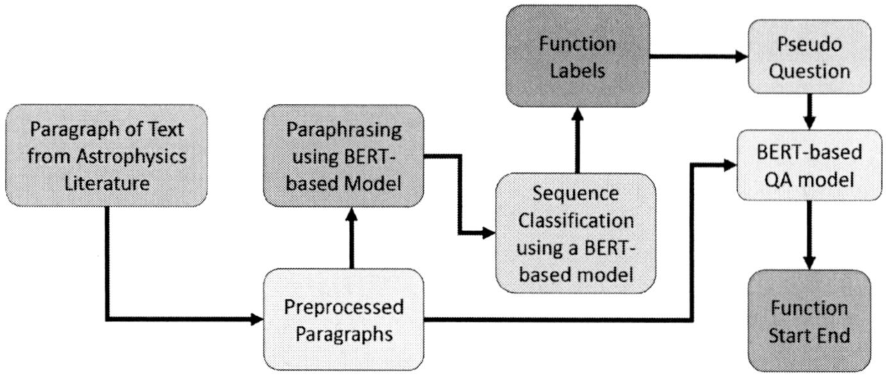

Figure 1: Our proposed approach for predicting citation function and associated span of text. We conduct tests with BERT, RoBERTa, DistillBERT, and ALBERT. A single language model (LM) is used for paraphrasing, sequence classification, and question-answering throughout the pipeline, resulting in four different configurations for the four models.

This output corresponds to the following textual evidence for the citation function:

Function Text:

- "This leads to a somewhat pseudo-correlation between high DM and GPS pulsars"
- "where serious underestimation of the flux at lower frequencies for high DM pulsars may give rise to an inverted spectra."

3 System Description

Our model leverages paraphrasing of the paragraphs and question answering for this task. Figure 1 shows the high-level overview of our model. We describe the system below:

3.1 Preprocessing of Paragraphs

We preprocess the text to input to our model. In the example paragraph shown above, we break them down into further parts based on the number of citations. For each citation, we take one fragment out of the paragraph. For each citation, we take the sentence in which the citation is up to the position where next citation starts. For Lewandowski et al. 2013, 2015a as shown above, we use the text as "*For pulsars with DMs in 200–300 pc cm-3 range this usually happens between 300 and 600 MHz (Lewandowski et al. 2013, 2015a). This leads to a somewhat pseudo-correlation between high DM and GPS pulsars*". Similarly, if the citation is the last one in the paragraph, we take the sentence in which a citation is in till the end of the paragraph. For Kijak et al. 2007, 2011b as shown above, we use the text as "*This leads to a somewhat pseudo-correlation between high DM and GPS pulsars (Kijak et al. 2007, 2011b) where serious underestimation of the flux at lower frequencies for high DM pulsars may give rise to an inverted spectra. The interferometric imaging technique provide a more robust measurement of the pulsar flux owing to the baseline lying at zero level thereby reducing errors made during the baseline subtraction.*" The preprocessed paragraphs are then fed into the paraphrasing model.

3.2 Language Models

Specifically, we use four BERT-based language models for paraphrasing, sequence classification, and QA model which are briefly described as follows.

BERT has achieved remarkable success in language understanding tasks by training on a massive amount of text data in a bidirectional manner, allowing it to understand the context and nuances of words and phrases (Devlin et al., 2019). This contextual understanding enables BERT to excel in a wide range of natural language understanding tasks, including text classification, question answering, and language translation (Papadopoulos et al., 2022; Zhou and Srikumar, 2022; Veeramani et al., 2023a,b,d,f). BERT's pre-trained embeddings have become a foundational resource in the world of natural language processing, serving as a starting point for various downstream tasks and research advancements (Adhikari et al., 2023).

RoBERTa is an acronym for "A Robustly Optimized BERT Pretraining Approach" (Liu et al.,

2019). It is a variant of the Bidirectional Encoder Representations from Transformers (BERT) (Devlin et al., 2019) model. RoBERTa builds upon the success of BERT by refining its pretraining methodology. It incorporates extensive training data, larger batch sizes, and longer training times, resulting in significantly improved performance on various natural language understanding tasks. RoBERTa is known for its robustness and exceptional performance on a wide range of text classification and language understanding tasks.

ALBERT is a model designed to reduce the computational and memory requirements of BERT while maintaining or even improving its performance (Lan et al., 2019). ALBERT achieves this by introducing parameter-sharing techniques, effectively reducing the model's size and training time. Despite its lighter architecture, ALBERT demonstrates remarkable efficiency and competitive performance across various natural language processing tasks (Kanagasabai et al., 2023). Its ability to handle large-scale text data with fewer computational resources makes it an appealing choice for resource-efficient applications.

DistillBERT is a distilled version of the original BERT model, emphasizing model compression and efficiency (Sanh et al., 2019). DistillBERT retains much of the performance of the larger BERT model while significantly reducing its size and computational requirements. This model distillation process involves training a smaller model (the "student") to mimic the behavior of a larger, more complex model (the "teacher"). DistillBERT is characterized by its compact size, making it suitable for deployment in resource-constrained environments without compromising accuracy.

3.3 Paraphrasing using BERT-based Model

In our approach, we leverage BERT-based models mentioned in section 3.2. BERT's contextual embeddings enable us to rephrase citation-related text effectively. We use paraphrasing in our pipeline in order to limit the input context to a length of 512.

3.4 Sequence Classification

Sequence classification serves as a fundamental component of our methodology (Cohan et al., 2019b; Veeramani et al., 2023c,e). We employ advanced language models mentioned in section 3.2 to classify the functions of citations within astrophysical paragraphs. This involves mapping citation-related segments to predefined categories, enabling us to clarify why each citation is made within the context of the research paper. The output is a multi-label output since a citation might be used for multiple purposes. The sequence classification component effectively outputs the "Functions Label".

3.5 Pseudo Question Generation

For each of the corresponding preprocessed text, we use their "Function Label" to form a pseudo question. This pseudo question serves as an input to the QA model. We form questions as *"What is the paragraph segment that corresponds to the function <FUNCTION LABEL>?"* For example, if we are looking for what part is background, our question is formed as *"What is the paragraph segment that corresponds to the function background?"*

3.6 BERT-based QA model

In our approach, we employ a BERT-based Question Answering (QA) model to further enhance the extraction of citation functions and their associated context. The QA model plays a pivotal role in our pipeline. The preprocessed text, as described in section 3.1, serves as one of the two inputs to our BERT-based QA model. This text contains the segmented paragraphs with citation-related information.

In our formulation, we formulate a pseudo question for each segment of the preprocessed text as the second input. This pseudo question is designed to encapsulate the essence of the citation function within the segment. It prompts the model to identify and extract the relevant information.

The output of our BERT-based QA model is a pair of integer values denoting the starting and ending positions of the citation function within the segment of text. These values pinpoint the exact location of the text that explains why the citation was made. We make the necessary adjustments for the offsets. By utilizing this QA model, we refine the precision and accuracy of our approach, providing explicit boundaries for the citation functions within the context of astrophysical paragraphs.

4 Results

The results presented in Table 1 demonstrate the performance of our approach utilizing various language models on the validation dataset for the FOCAL challenge. We evaluated our models using three key metrics: 'seqeval_full', 'seqeval_generic', and 'labels_only'. Table

Model	seqeval_full	seqeval_generic	labels_only
BERT	0.2222	0.4393	0.4100
DistillBERT	0.2215	0.4369	**0.4985**
RoBERTa	0.2369	0.4356	0.4166
ALBERT	**0.2380**	**0.4396**	0.4261

Table 1: Performance of our approach with different language models on validation dataset

4.1 Validation Results

In terms of the 'seqeval_full' metric, which assesses the overall ability to correctly classify the functions of citations while ensuring accurate function labels, ALBERT achieved the highest score of 0.2380, closely followed by RoBERTa with a score of 0.2369. BERT and DistillBERT also performed reasonably well but exhibited slightly lower scores.

The 'seqeval_generic' metric, which evaluates the model's proficiency in identifying the portions of the paragraph that explain the functions of citations, showed a similar trend. ALBERT outperformed the other models with a score of 0.4396, followed closely by BERT, DistillBERT, and RoBERTa.

In terms of 'labels_only', which focuses solely on the accuracy of predicted function labels, DistillBERT led the pack with an F1-score of 0.4261, followed by ALBERT, RoBERTa, and BERT.

4.2 Test Results

In Table 2, we present the F1-score results on the test dataset using our approach with three different language models: BERT, RoBERTa, and ALBERT. The F1-scores are reported for three different evaluation metrics: seqeval_full, seqeval_generic, and labels_only.

seqeval_full Metrics: These metrics evaluate the overall ability to correctly classify the functions of citations while considering function labels.

- Micro F1-score: BERT achieved a micro F1-score of 0.27, RoBERTa scored 0.27, and ALBERT outperformed both with a micro F1-score of 0.30. Among the three, ALBERT shows the highest performance in this aspect.
- Macro F1-score: BERT scored the highest macro F1-score of 0.13, followed by RoBERTa (0.12) and ALBERT (0.12). BERT exhibits the highest average F1 score across different classes.
- Weighted F1-score: ALBERT achieves the highest weighted F1-score of 0.28, followed by BERT (0.28) and RoBERTa (0.28).

seqeval_generic Metrics: These metrics assess the model's proficiency in identifying portions of the paragraph that explain citation functions, regardless of the correctness of predicted function labels.

- Micro F1-score: ALBERT performs the best with a micro F1-score of 0.48, followed by RoBERTa (0.48) and BERT (0.47).
- Macro F1-score: ALBERT also achieves the highest macro F1-score of 0.48, while BERT and RoBERTa score similarly at 0.47 and 0.48 respectively.
- Weighted F1-score: ALBERT leads with a weighted F1-score of 0.48, followed by BERT (0.47) and RoBERTa (0.48).

labels_only Metrics: These metrics focus solely on the accuracy of predicted function labels, excluding the assessment of identified spans in the text.

- Micro F1-score: ALBERT outperforms the other models with a micro F1-score of 0.58, while BERT scores 0.48 and RoBERTa scores 0.48.
- Macro F1-score: BERT and RoBERTa have similar macro F1-scores of 0.24 and 0.22, respectively, while ALBERT scores lower at 0.21.
- Weighted F1-score: BERT achieves the highest weighted F1-score of 0.54, followed by ALBERT (0.53) and RoBERTa (0.53).

Overall, these results suggest that ALBERT consistently performs well across all three evaluation metrics, indicating its effectiveness in classifying citation functions and extracting contextual information within astrophysical literature. However, it's important to note that all models demonstrated reasonable performance, underscoring the viability of our approach across different language models.

5 Conclusions

In this paper, we have presented a comprehensive approach for automated citation function classification and context extraction in the domain of

Model	seqeval_full			seqeval_generic			labels_only		
	micro	macro	weighted	micro	macro	weighted	micro	macro	weighted
BERT	0.27	**0.13**	0.28	0.47	0.47	0.47	0.48	**0.24**	**0.54**
RoBERTa	0.27	0.12	0.28	0.48	0.48	0.48	0.48	0.22	0.53
ALBERT	**0.30**	0.12	**0.28**	**0.48**	**0.48**	**0.48**	**0.58**	0.21	0.53

Table 2: F1-score on the test dataset using our approach.

astrophysics literature. Leveraging advanced language models, including BERT, RoBERTa, ALBERT, and DistillBERT, our system showcases a robust pipeline that combines paraphrasing and question-answering techniques to achieve accurate and insightful results. Our experiments demonstrate the robustness of our approach, with ALBERT consistently performing well in classifying citation functions and extracting contextual information. However, all models exhibit reasonable performance, showcasing the adaptability of our system. In the future, we aim to refine our approach further, potentially incorporating more advanced models and techniques to enhance citation function classification and context extraction for deeper insights in astrophysical research.

Limitations

The limitations of this work include the potential challenges associated with accurately classifying citation functions within the nuanced landscape of astrophysical literature. Despite the effectiveness of our approach, the inherent complexity and subjectivity of citation functions may result in instances of misclassification or incomplete understanding. Finally, while we strive for generalizability, the specificities of astrophysical language and citation practices may limit the applicability of our approach to other scientific domains.

Ethics Statement

Our study adheres to principles of academic integrity, transparency, and respect for intellectual property rights. We have meticulously cited and credited all sources and data used in our work, ensuring due recognition for prior research contributions.

References

Surabhi Adhikari, Surendrabikram Thapa, Usman Naseem, Hai Ya Lu, Gnana Bharathy, and Mukesh Prasad. 2023. Explainable hybrid word representations for sentiment analysis of financial news. *Neural Networks*, 164:115–123.

Arman Cohan, Waleed Ammar, Madeleine van Zuylen, and Field Cady. 2019a. Structural scaffolds for citation intent classification in scientific publications. In *Proceedings of NAACL-HLT*, pages 3586–3596.

Arman Cohan, Iz Beltagy, Daniel King, Bhavana Dalvi, and Dan Weld. 2019b. Pretrained language models for sequential sentence classification. In *Proceedings of the 2019 Conference on Empirical Methods in Natural Language Processing and the 9th International Joint Conference on Natural Language Processing (EMNLP-IJCNLP)*, pages 3693–3699, Hong Kong, China. Association for Computational Linguistics.

Jacob Devlin, Ming-Wei Chang, Kenton Lee, and Kristina Toutanova. 2019. BERT: Pre-training of deep bidirectional transformers for language understanding. In *Proceedings of the 2019 Conference of the North American Chapter of the Association for Computational Linguistics: Human Language Technologies, Volume 1 (Long and Short Papers)*, pages 4171–4186, Minneapolis, Minnesota. Association for Computational Linguistics.

Eugene Garfield, Irving H Sher, Richard J Torpie, et al. 1964. The use of citation data in writing the history of science.

Tirthankar Ghosal, Sergi Blanco-Cuaresma, Alberto Accomazzi, Robert M. Patton, Felix Grezes, and Thomas Allen, editors. 2022. *Proceedings of the first Workshop on Information Extraction from Scientific Publications*. Association for Computational Linguistics, Online.

Steven N Goodman and Richard Royall. 1988. Evidence and scientific research. *American Journal of Public Health*, 78(12):1568–1574.

Felix Grezes, Thomas Allen, Tirthankar Ghosal, and Sergi Blanco-Cuaresma. 2023. Function of citation in astrophysics literature (focal): Findings of the shared task. In *Proceedings of the 2nd Workshop on Information Extraction from Scientific Publications*, Online. Association for Computational Linguistics.

Lin Guo and Qun Dai. 2022. Graph clustering via variational graph embedding. *Pattern Recognition*, 122:108334.

David Jurgens, Srijan Kumar, Raine Hoover, Dan McFarland, and Dan Jurafsky. 2018. Measuring the evolution of a scientific field through citation frames. *Transactions of the Association for Computational Linguistics*, 6:391–406.

Rajaraman Kanagasabai, Saravanan Rajamanickam, Hariram Veeramani, Adam Westerski, and Kim Jung Jae. 2023. Semantists at ImageArg-2023: Exploring Cross-modal Contrastive and Ensemble Models for Multimodal Stance and Persuasiveness Classification. In *Proceedings of the 10th Workshop on Argument Mining*, Online and in Singapore. Association for Computational Linguistics.

Zhenzhong Lan, Mingda Chen, Sebastian Goodman, Kevin Gimpel, Piyush Sharma, and Radu Soricut. 2019. Albert: A lite bert for self-supervised learning of language representations. In *International Conference on Learning Representations*.

Anne Lauscher, Brandon Ko, Bailey Kuehl, Sophie Johnson, Arman Cohan, David Jurgens, and Kyle Lo. 2022. MultiCite: Modeling realistic citations requires moving beyond the single-sentence single-label setting. In *Proceedings of the 2022 Conference of the North American Chapter of the Association for Computational Linguistics: Human Language Technologies*, pages 1875–1889, Seattle, United States. Association for Computational Linguistics.

Yinhan Liu, Myle Ott, Naman Goyal, Jingfei Du, Mandar Joshi, Danqi Chen, Omer Levy, Mike Lewis, Luke Zettlemoyer, and Veselin Stoyanov. 2019. Roberta: A robustly optimized bert pretraining approach.

Bonan Min, Hayley Ross, Elior Sulem, Amir Pouran Ben Veyseh, Thien Huu Nguyen, Oscar Sainz, Eneko Agirre, Ilana Heintz, and Dan Roth. 2023. Recent advances in natural language processing via large pre-trained language models: A survey. *ACM Computing Surveys*, 56(2):1–40.

Christos Papadopoulos, Yannis Panagakis, Manolis Koubarakis, and Mihalis Nicolaou. 2022. Efficient learning of multiple NLP tasks via collective weight factorization on BERT. In *Findings of the Association for Computational Linguistics: NAACL 2022*, pages 882–890, Seattle, United States. Association for Computational Linguistics.

Victor Sanh, Lysandre Debut, Julien Chaumond, and Thomas Wolf. 2019. Distilbert, a distilled version of bert: smaller, faster, cheaper and lighter. *arXiv preprint arXiv:1910.01108*.

Surendrabikram Thapa and Surabhi Adhikari. 2023. Chatgpt, bard, and large language models for biomedical research: Opportunities and pitfalls. *Annals of Biomedical Engineering*, pages 1–5.

Masaya Tsunokake and Shigeki Matsubara. 2022. Classification of URL citations in scholarly papers for promoting utilization of research artifacts. In *Proceedings of the first Workshop on Information Extraction from Scientific Publications*, pages 8–19, Online. Association for Computational Linguistics.

Hariram Veeramani, Surendrabikram Thapa, and Usman Naseem. 2023a. DialectNLU at NADI 2023 Shared Task: Transformer Based MultiTask Approach Jointly Integrating Dialect and Machine Translation Tasks. In *Proceedings of The First Arabic Natural Language Processing Conference (ArabicNLP 2023)*, Singapore. Association for Computational Linguistics.

Hariram Veeramani, Surendrabikram Thapa, and Usman Naseem. 2023b. Enhancing ESG Impact Type Identification through Early Fusion and Multilingual Models. In *Proceedings of the Sixth Workshop on Financial Technology and Natural Language Processing (FinNLP)*. Association for Computational Linguistics.

Hariram Veeramani, Surendrabikram Thapa, and Usman Naseem. 2023c. KnowTellConvince at ArAIEval 2023: Disinformation and Persuasion Detection using Similar and Contrastive Representation Alignment. In *Proceedings of The First Arabic Natural Language Processing Conference (ArabicNLP 2023)*, Singapore. Association for Computational Linguistics.

Hariram Veeramani, Surendrabikram Thapa, and Usman Naseem. 2023d. LowResContextQA at Qur'an QA 2023 Shared Task: Temporal and Sequential Representation Augmented Question Answering Span Detection. In *Proceedings of The First Arabic Natural Language Processing Conference (ArabicNLP 2023)*, Singapore. Association for Computational Linguistics.

Hariram Veeramani, Surendrabikram Thapa, and Usman Naseem. 2023e. Lowresourcenlu at blp: Enhancing sentiment classification and violence incitement detection through aggregated language models. In *Proceedings of the 1st International Workshop on Bangla Language Processing (BLP-2023)*, Singapore. Association for Computational Linguistics.

Hariram Veeramani, Surendrabikram Thapa, and Usman Naseem. 2023f. Temporally Dynamic Session-Keyword Aware Sequential Recommendation system. In *2023 International Conference on Data Mining Workshops (ICDMW)*.

Yichu Zhou and Vivek Srikumar. 2022. A closer look at how fine-tuning changes BERT. In *Proceedings of the 60th Annual Meeting of the Association for Computational Linguistics (Volume 1: Long Papers)*, pages 1046–1061, Dublin, Ireland. Association for Computational Linguistics.

Function of Citation in Astrophysics Literature (FOCAL): Findings of the Shared Task

Felix Grezes[1], Thomas Allen[1], Tirthankar Ghosal[2], Sergi Blanco-Cuaresma[1 3]
[1]Center for Astrophysics, Harvard & Smithsonian, USA
[2]Oak Ridge National Laboratory, USA
[3]Laboratoire de Recherche en Neuroimagerie, University Hospital (CHUV) and University of Lausanne (UNIL), Lausanne, Switzerland
[1](felix.grezes, thomas.allen, sblancocuaresma)@cfa.harvard.edu
[2]ghosalt@ornl.gov

Abstract

In this article, we describe the overview of our shared task: Function of Citation in Astrophysics Literature (FOCAL). The FOCAL shared task was part of the Workshop on Information Extraction from Scientific Publications (WIESP)[1] in IJCNLP-AACL 2023. Information extraction from scientific publications is critical in several downstream tasks such as identification of critical entities, article summarization, citation classification, etc. In particular, the citation graph is an essential tool for helping researchers find relevant literature. To further empower discovery, the motivation of this shared task was to develop a community-wide effort to label the edges of the graph with the function of the citation: e.g. is the cited work necessary background knowledge, or is it used as a comparison, to the citing work? We propose a shared task of automatically labeling citations with a function based on the textual context of the citation, and analyze the systems, performances, and findings of FOCAL participants.

1 Introduction

In addition to its archival mission, the NASA Astrophysics Data System (Kurtz et al., 2000) aims to empower astrophysics researchers in their work. One powerful tool at their disposal is access to the citation graph, allowing them to find papers related to, and quantify the impact of, their research. By enriching the edges of the citation graph with labels that explain why a citation was made, and the relevant textual context to understand the citation, researchers can more rapidly assess the literature, and gain more granularity into impact metrics. For example a researcher who is already familiar with the *Background* of a topic may primarily be interested in citations that *Compare / Contrast* with other works. Further, by augmenting impact met-

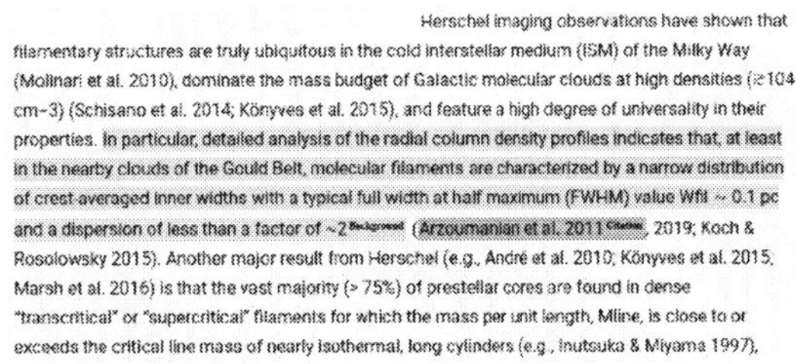
Herschel imaging observations have shown that filamentary structures are truly ubiquitous in the cold interstellar medium (ISM) of the Milky Way (Molinari et al. 2010), dominate the mass budget of Galactic molecular clouds at high densities (≳104 cm−3) (Schisano et al. 2014; Könyves et al. 2015), and feature a high degree of universality in their properties. In particular, detailed analysis of the radial column density profiles indicates that, at least in the nearby clouds of the Gould Belt, molecular filaments are characterized by a narrow distribution of crest-averaged inner widths with a typical full width at half maximum (FWHM) value Wfil ~ 0.1 pc and a dispersion of less than a factor of ~2 (Arzoumanian et al. 2011, 2019; Koch & Rosolowsky 2015). Another major result from Herschel (e.g., André et al. 2010; Könyves et al. 2015; Marsh et al. 2016) is that the vast majority (> 75%) of prestellar cores are found in dense "transcritical" or "supercritical" filaments for which the mass per unit length, Mline, is close to or exceeds the critical line mass of nearly isothermal, long cylinders (e.g., Inutsuka & Miyama 1997),

Figure 1: Sample annotation. The citation *Arzoumanian et al. 2011* is used as *Background* by the authors of this paragraph.

rics, such as citation counts, with metrics pertaining to citation function, researchers can gain finer grained insight into the impact of their work, e.g. if they provide the *Motivation* for the citing work or the *Background*. Large scale labeling of the citation graph requires automated methods. In our FOCAL@WIESP2023 shared task, we instigate a community initiative to design such methods.

2 Task

2.1 Definition

The shared task *Function of Citation in Astrophysics Literature (FOCAL)* (Grezes et al., 2023) consists of automatically labeling citations with a function based on the textual context of the citation.

More precisely, given a paragraph of text from the astrophysics literature, and the `start` and end position of a citation in the paragraph, the FOCAL participants are tasked with building a model that outputs why it was cited (the function) and the associated span of text in the paragraph (the context). Figure 1 shows a sample annotation.

2.2 Evaluation

For evaluation, submissions were first tokenized into words using the default spaCy tokenizer (Honnibal et al., 2020); references and predictions were converted into IOB2 style labels; and finally scored

[1]https://ui.adsabs.harvard.edu/WIESP/

Proceedings of the 2nd Workshop on Information Extraction from Scientific Publications, pages 143–147
Nov 1, 2023.

by three metrics derived from the CoNLL-2000 shared task seqeval (Nakayama, 2018):

- Full Seqeval: the full seqeval score and main evaluation metric. This metrics check that the functions of the citation were placed correctly in the paragraph along with the correct function labels.

- Generic Label Seqeval: a seqeval score with a generic label instead of functions. This metric checks that the parts of the paragraph that explain the functions of the citation were correctly found, without checking if the reason(s) a given citation was made (the function labels) were correctly predicted.

- Labels Only F1: an F1-score on the function labels only. This metric checks that the reason(s) a given citation was made were correctly predicted, without checking if the parts of the paragraph that explain the function of the citation were correctly found.

All reported scores use micro-averaging.

3 Dataset Description

3.1 Data Collection and Creation

The dataset consists of paragraph sized text fragments that were curated from over 25,000 astronomy articles, from the Astrophysical literature. The journals that the text fragments were obtained from are the Astrophysical Journal, Astronomy & Astrophysics, and the Monthly Notices of the Royal Astronomical Society. All text fragments are from recent publications, between the years of 2015 and 2023. From this set of articles, over 2 million citations and their context were harvested. Further, only citations with context sizes between 2,000 and 10,000 characters are selected. A domain area expert manually examined these text fragments to determine the citation function as well as label the relevant context.

We are considering a set of eight potential citation functions. These are:

- Background: The cited work provides background information needed to understand the citing work

- Motivation: The cited work is motivating the citing work

Function \ Split	Train	Val	Test
Background	1607	390	438
Uses	877	230	530
Compare/Contrast	615	178	140
Similarities	279	50	72
Motivation	233	70	56
Differences	125	24	40
Future Work	40	9	4
Extends	9	5	2
Totals	3785	956	1282

Table 1: Counts of function labels in the dataset. Note that totals are larger than dataset sizes because some samples have multiple function labels associated.

- Uses: The citing work used a result from the cited work

- Extends: The citing work extends a result from the cited work.

- Similarities: Results from the cited work are similar to results from the citing (or another) work.

- Differences: Results from the cited work are different to results from the citing (or another) work.

- Compare/Contrast: Results are being compared in a neutral manner between the cited and the citing (or another) work.

- Future Work: Citing work contains implications for future research that are beyond the scope of the citing work.

These citation functions were selected because of their similarity to the classification scheme used in Pride and Knoth (2020), see table 3 in the appendix for a full description with examples.

3.2 Data Segmentation for Shared Task

The FOCAL dataset consists of 3 components, the training dataset consisting of 2421 samples, the validation dataset consisting of 606 samples, and the testing dataset consisting of 821 samples. Table 1 shows the counting statistics of the function labels for each component.

4 Participant Systems

Ikoma and Matsubara (2023) proposed a SciBERT-based sequence labelling system that outputs IOB2

Model / Metric \ Split	Baseline val	Baseline test	(Ikoma and Matsubara, 2023) val	(Ikoma and Matsubara, 2023) test	Veeramani et al. (2023) val	Veeramani et al. (2023) test
Full Seqeval	23.68	20.94	54.08	**51.87**	23.79	30.17
Generic Label Seqeval	59.86	54.55	79.92	**73.00**	43.96	47.65
Labels Only F1	42.87	35.99	65.94	**69.44**	42.61	57.51

Table 2: Main FOCAL@WIESP 2023 shared task results. All scores computed using micro-averaging.

tags, and uses statistical insights on which sentences (preceding, citing, following) contain function labels to limit the range of the input text to what the language model can handle. The authors explore the performance of multiple BERT-based models.

Veeramani et al. (2023) proposed a system that leverages state-of-the-art BERT-based language models and combines paraphrasing and question-answering techniques. Paraphrasing is used in the pipeline to reduce the text input length to 512 tokens, allowing for sequence classification models to be applied, which provide the function label of the citation. To find the boundaries of the function, the authors apply BERT-based Question Answering techniques.

In addition to the above papers, two submissions were made to the Codalab platform hosting the shared task[2].

4.1 Baseline

Baseline scores from a simple model are provided as benchmark for the participants. This model is defined as follows:

- the function of the citation is the majority class (i.e. Background).
- the start and end of the function is the sentence that includes citation, as defined by pySBD (Sadvilkar and Neumann, 2020).

5 Results, Analysis, and Findings of FOCAL

We report the results of the participating teams in table 2. Both systems were able to outperform the baseline on the Full Seqeval and Labels-Only metric, but only Ikoma and Matsubara (2023) were able to improve on the Generic Label Seqeval. Upon further analysis, this is likely due to the method used by Veeramani et al. (2023) to label functions, which does not incorporate information specific to the citation given, versus any other that may appear in the paragraph. Indeed this difficulty is central to the task. Models cannot solely rely on the text of the paragraph to make function label predictions, since those will differ from citation to citation present in the text.

Both submissions make extensive use of BERT-based models, highlighting just how generically useful and practical those models have become, even as state-of-the-art architectures have grown much larger (ex: BLOOM, LLAMA2, etc ...).

6 Conclusion and Future Directions

The results of the FOCAL@WIESP2023 shared task show that the task of labelling the citation graph and locating the text relevant to the citation is far from solved. One aspect that future challenges can improve upon is the quantity of labeled data along with inter-annotator agreement statistics, to confirm that the task is sound and well understood. The advent of open-source Large Language Models also may be used as zero-shot systems that can form a more robust and challenging baseline.

[2]https://codalab.lisn.upsaclay.fr/competitions/15292

References

Felix Grezes, Thomas Allen, Tirthankar Ghosal, and Sergi Blanco-Cuaresma. 2023. Function of citation in astrophysics literature (focal): Findings of the shared task. In *Proceedings of the 2nd Workshop on Information Extraction from Scientific Publications*, Online. Association for Computational Linguistics.

Matthew Honnibal, Ines Montani, Sofie Van Landeghem, and Adriane Boyd. 2020. spaCy: Industrial-strength Natural Language Processing in Python.

Tomoki Ikoma and Shigeki Matsubara. 2023. On the use of language models for function identification of citations in scholarly papers. In *Proceedings of the 2nd Workshop on Information Extraction from Scientific Publications*, Online. Association for Computational Linguistics.

Michael J. Kurtz, Guenther Eichhorn, Alberto Accomazzi, Carolyn S. Grant, Stephen S. Murray, and

Joyce M. Watson. 2000. The NASA Astrophysics Data System: Overview. , 143:41–59.

Hiroki Nakayama. 2018. seqeval: A python framework for sequence labeling evaluation. Software available from https://github.com/chakki-works/seqeval.

David Pride and Petr Knoth. 2020. An authoritative approach to citation classification. In *ACM/IEEE Joint Conference on Digital Libraries in 2020 (JCDL 2020)*.

Nipun Sadvilkar and Mark Neumann. 2020. PySBD: Pragmatic sentence boundary disambiguation. In *Proceedings of Second Workshop for NLP Open Source Software (NLP-OSS)*, pages 110–114, Online. Association for Computational Linguistics.

Hariram Veeramani, Surendrabikram Thapa, and Usman Naseem. 2023. Automated citation function classification and context extraction in astrophysics: Leveraging paraphrasing and question answering. In *Proceedings of the 2nd Workshop on Information Extraction from Scientific Publications*, Online. Association for Computational Linguistics.

A Appendix

Label	Definition	Example
Background	Citation whose purpose is to provide background information so that the reader can understand the problem, or the object.	The AGN in these systems have been shown to deposit vast amounts of energy into the surrounding intracluster medium via heating and (mega-parsec scale) jets both observationally and by means of modelling (e.g. Binney 2004...
Motivation	Citation that is used to justify the current work or problem.	Unlike NGC 3894, for which no observations with Cherenkov telescopes have been performed, M 87 and 3C 84 are also detected at very high energy (VHE, E >100 GeV; Aharonian et al. 2006
Uses	Result or idea from cited work is used in the current work. Could be in the form of using data or an idea to build an argument.	Our data set consists of 4348 hr of data in both the nominal LPF configuration and the "Disturbance Reduction System" (DRS) configuration, in which a NASA-supplied controller and thruster system took over control of the spacecraft (Anderson et al. 2018).
Extends	Citing work is extending the results of the cited work.	In doing so we extend the analysis of Planck Collaboration Int. XXXVIII (2016) and Planck Collaboration Int. XLIV (2016) to sky areas in which the filaments have very little contrast with respect to the diffuse background emission.
Similarities	There are similarities, in results or observations, between the cited and citing works,	All of these galaxies are consistent with the relationship between X-ray luminosity and mid-IR luminosity for starburst galaxies (...; Sell et al. 2014).
Differences	There are differences, in results or observations, between the cited and citing works,	We also remark that the expression from Mishima et al. (1983) would give a penetration depth of 56 m at 2.2 cm, which is an order of magnitude larger than indicated by the laboratory measurements of Paillou et al. (2008)
Compare/Contrast	A neutral comparison between works or ideas	At these early epochs, this difference could be caused by the poor constraints on the GSMFs adopted by Duncan et al. (2019) which result in large uncertainties on their data, making it impossible to draw robust conclusions at z $\sim$5.
Future Work	Used when cited work provides a means to expand the scope of the citing work	The study presented here will also be further extended to explore the effects of different retention fractions of dark remnants (neutron stars and black holes; see, e.g., Giersz et al. 2019

Table 3: Definitions of the FOCAL labels.

Association for Computational Linguistics
209 N. Eighth Street
Stroudsburg, Pennsylvania 18360

ISBN 978-1-7138-9007-2

9 781713 890072

CURRAN ASSOCIATES INC.
proceedings.com